D0194571

B2B Digital Marketing

Michael Miller

800 East 96th Street,
Indianapolis, Indiana 46240 USA

B2B Digital Marketing

ISBN-13: 978-0-7897-4887-4
ISBN-10: 0-7897-4887-8

Library of Congress Cataloging-in-Publication data is on file.

First Printing: February 2012

Trademarks

Warning and Disclaimer

Bulk Sales

Que Publishing offers excellent discounts on this book when ordered in quantity for bulk purchases or special sales. For more information, please contact

U.S. Corporate and Government Sales
1-800-382-3419
corpsales@pearsontechgroup.com

For sales outside of the U.S., please contact

International Sales
international@pearsoned.com

Associate Publisher
Greg Wiegand

Acquisitions Editor
Rick Kughen

Development Editor
Rick Kughen

Technical Editor
John M. Coe

Managing Editor
Sandra Schroeder

Project Editor
Seth Kerney

Copy Editor
Mike Henry

Indexer
Tim Wright

Proofreader
Sarah Kearns

Publishing Coordinator
Cindy Teeters

Cover Designer
Anne Jones

Compositor
Mark Shirar

CONTENTS AT A GLANCE

TABLE OF CONTENTS

10   B2B Search Engine Marketing   123

17   B2B Mobile Marketing   275

III   MEASUREMENT AND REFOCUS

18   Quantifying Results   291

19   Qualifying Results   313

20   Looking Forward   321

Index   331

About the Author

Michael Miller has written more than 100 nonfiction how-to books over the past 20 years, including *The Ultimate Web Marketing Guide, YouTube for Business, Using Google AdWords and AdSense,* and *The Absolute Beginner's Guide to Computer Basics,* all for Que. His other best-selling online marketing books include *The Complete Idiot's Guide to Search Engine Optimization* (Alpha Books), *Sams Teach Yourself Google Analytics in 10 Minutes* (Sams), and *Online Marketing Heroes* (Wiley).

Mr. Miller has established a reputation for clearly explaining technical topics to nontechnical readers, and for offering useful real-world advice about complicated topics. More information can be found at the author's website, located at www. molehillgroup.com.

About the Technical Editor

John M. Coe is President and Founder of The Sales & Marketing Institute, a B2B consulting, training, and publishing firm specializing in the integration of direct and database marketing with field sales to produce greater sales and marketing productivity. John started at BF Goodrich Chemical as a Product Manager, and then joined the Quaker Oats Chemical Division as a Technical Sales Representative and rose to National Sales Manager in five years. Later, while at West Agro Chemical, he served as Director of Sales & Marketing and eventually was Vice President of Marketing at Samuel Bingham.

John is very well known in the B2B database and direct marketing world and has given more than 400 seminars and presentations at industry conferences all over the world, has been a lead seminar provider for the Direct Marketing Association, plus he writes numerous articles and white papers. His new book from McGraw-Hill titled *The Fundamentals of B2B Sales and Marketing* is now in bookstores.

Dedication

To all my grandkids: Alethia, Collin, Hayley, and Judah. You make life fun.

Acknowledgments

Thanks to all the usual suspects at Que who helped to turn my manuscript into a printed book, including but not limited to Rick Kughen, Seth Kerney, Mike Henry, and Greg Wiegand. Thanks also to John Coe, who provided valuable insights and ensured the accuracy of what you're reading.

We Want to Hear from You!

As the reader of this book, *you* are our most important critic and commentator. We value your opinion and want to know what we're doing right, what we could do better, what areas you'd like to see us publish in, and any other words of wisdom you're willing to pass our way.

As an Editor-in-Chief for Que Publishing, I welcome your comments. You can email or write me directly to let me know what you did or didn't like about this book—as well as what we can do to make our books better.

Please note that I cannot help you with technical problems related to the topic of this book. We do have a User Services group, however, where I will forward specific technical questions related to the book.

When you write, please be sure to include this book's title and author as well as your name, email address, and phone number. I will carefully review your comments and share them with the author and editors who worked on the book.

Email: feedback@quepublishing.com

Mail: Greg Wiegand
          Editor-in-Chief
          Que Publishing
          800 East 96th Street
          Indianapolis, IN 46240 USA

Reader Services

Visit our website and register this book at www.quepublishing.com/register for convenient access to any updates, downloads, or errata that might be available for this book.

Introduction

B2B marketing is different.

Of course, I don't need to tell you that. You deal with B2B-related issues every day. Reaching out to business customers requires a much different approach than reaching out to the average consumer; the sales cycle is much longer and more involved. (And often touches multiple decision makers in an organization!)

It goes without saying, then, that digital marketing in the B2B space is also different than B2C digital marketing. Oh, the tools are all the same, but how you use them is a much different deal.

That's assuming, of course, that you're using digital marketing in your business. I hope you are, but I can't assume so; for some reason, B2B companies have been slower to adopt new media than have B2C companies.

Which is why I wrote this book, I guess. That and the fact that in every interview or webinar I gave for my previous B2C-oriented marketing books, one or more people always asked—always—just how what I was talking about applied to B2B marketing. Ask me the same question enough times and I eventually realize there's a book topic there.

And there *is* a book topic there—or here, rather, as evidenced by the book you currently hold in your hands. (Or, if you're one of those early adopter types, are reading on your computer screen, smartphone, iPad, or e-book reader.) There's a lot to learn about using digital media in your B2B marketing, and that's what this book is all about.

What's in This Book

So, what can you expect to find in this book? Well, as the title implies, it's all about B2B digital marketing—that is, how to use various Internet-based marketing vehicles for B2B marketing.

More precisely, I try to cover everything you need to know about digital marketing for B2B companies. It doesn't matter how experienced or inexperienced you are with the various digital technologies and approaches, I'll get you up to speed—and help you figure out how best to use each technology for the various stages of your own marketing strategy.

I've organized much of this book around what some call the *B2B customer life cycle* (others call it the *B2B buying continuum*). That is, I talk about which digital media are best used to *reach* new potential customers, *acquire* prospective leads, *convert* those leads into sales, *retain* those customers going forward, and build customer *loyalty* that leads to referrals and recommendations to other potential prospects. As you might suspect, which media you use differs from stage to stage; it's kind of a jigsaw puzzle, trying to figure out what media to use when—and how. But that's why you bought this book, isn't it?

And here's the deal: Everything I talk about, I do so in plain English. No convoluted techno-speak here—nor, for that matter, are there many (if any) overused marketing clichés. I try to present things in a conversational manner that an average B2B marketer can understand. No insider technical knowledge necessary.

Who This Book Is For

This book is written for B2B marketers. I assume you have some knowledge of B2B marketing, and that you've probably been doing it for a while. That means you should be comfortable with terms such as *lead generation*, and *conversion*, and the like.

I do not, however, assume that you have much, if any, experience with digital marketing, or what some call online or web marketing. I don't assume you know search engine marketing from email marketing from social media marketing—although if you do, that's all the better.

How This Book Is Organized

B2B Digital Marketing is meant to be both a tutorial and reference, which means you can read it from front to back if you like (and that's certainly the way I wrote it), or put it on your shelf and reference individual chapters as necessary. Read it as a whole or out of order, whatever works best for you.

To make things a little easier to navigate, the book is organized into three main parts, each focused on a particular facet of B2B marketing:

- **Part I, "Planning,"** provides an introduction to B2B digital marketing, discusses how to segment your audience, shows how to plan activities for each stage of that B2B buying continuum, and walks you through creating your own B2B digital marketing plan.

- **Part II, "Execution,"** focuses on the various digital marketing vehicles and how to use them in your business. So, you'll find chapters devoted to each major digital marketing medium: website marketing; search engine marketing; online advertising; blog marketing; social media marketing (including Facebook and Twitter); audio, video, and interactive marketing (including webinars); online public relations; and mobile marketing.

- **Part III, "Measurement and Refocus,"** talks about how to analyze the performance of your B2B digital marketing—and then refocus your activities based on what you discover. It also talks about what to expect next in the ever-changing world of digital marketing, and how to cope with that change.

By the end of the book, you should have a basic understanding of all the different activities involved in B2B digital marketing and should be able to develop and implement your own digital marketing strategy.

Conventions Used in This Book

I hope that this book, is easy enough to figure out on its own without requiring its own instruction manual. As you read through the pages, however, it helps to know precisely how I've presented specific types of information.

As you read through this book you'll note several special elements, presented in what we in the publishing business call *margin notes*. These notes present additional information and advice beyond what you find in the regular text.

Note

This is a note that presents some interesting and useful information, even if it isn't wholly relevant to the discussion in the main text.

In addition to the main text and these little margin notes, I include in each chapter at least one sidebar observation. These sections aren't necessarily factual, as the rest of the text is supposed to be; they're more opinion, looking at B2B marketing from my personal viewpoint. Take 'em or leave 'em—that's up to you.

Prepare to Market—Online

Now that you know how to use this book, it's time to get busy doing just that. But when you're ready to take a break from marketing online, browse over to my personal website, located at www.molehillgroup.com. Here you'll find more information on this book and other books I've written—including any necessary corrections and clarifications, in the inevitable event that an error or two creeps into this text.

In addition, know that I love to hear from readers of my books. If you want to contact me, feel free to email me at b2b@molehillgroup.com. I can't promise that I'll answer every message, but I do promise that I'll read each one!

With these preliminaries out of the way, go ahead and turn the page—and start learning more about B2B digital marketing.

1

Understanding Digital Marketing

Evolution is part and parcel of marketing. Marketing as we know it today involves a number of different media and approaches that didn't even exist 20 years ago; who knows what marketing 20 years in the future will look like?

The most significant marketing development of the past decade or so has been the embrace of Internet-related media and the development of so-called digital marketing. It's not just about print ads and trade shows anymore; marketing today has to incorporate websites, search engines, email, blogs, and social networks. That makes for a lot more work than existed a decade prior, but also a lot more opportunities—especially for business-to-business (B2B) marketers.

What Is Digital Marketing?

Digital marketing. Online marketing. Internet marketing. Web marketing. Whatever you call it, it's all about marketing to current and potential customers online, via the Internet.

At its most basic, digital marketing is no different from traditional marketing; you're still trying to present customers with the information they need to make an informed purchase from you. What's different about digital marketing are the channels you use to relay these messages. Instead of using print and other traditional media, you're now using Internet-based media, such as websites, email, and social networks. The message is more or less the same; it's the medium that's changed.

Part of that change is the variety of channels available for presenting our marketing messages. We can reach customers and prospects via email. We can reach customers via websites. We can reach customers via podcasts and videos. We can reach customers via blogs and social networks. We can even, if we stretch the definition of the Web, reach customers via mobile phones that connect to the Internet. In short, there are a lot of ways to reach business customers online, and we have to consider them all.

We also have to consider what's different about these new marketing channels. Because, let's face it, placing a keyword-targeted pay-per-click (PPC) ad on a search engine results page is a bit different from placing a print ad in an industry trade publication, and managing the two-way conversations of today's hot social media is unlike anything you've experienced in the world of traditional one-way media. The new media force you to communicate differently than you did using the old media, and you need to both get used to that and figure out how to exploit the differences.

That said, digital marketing differs from traditional marketing mainly in the ways in which we do things. We still present our message to potential customers; we just do it using the various media and channels available online. That might require us to change some of the ways we do things—different media have their own personalities and quirks, after all. But it shouldn't change what we do. We still have to reach potential business buyers with messages about our products and services—we just do it online.

Why Digital Marketing Matters for B2B

If you've been in the B2B market for a while, you know how to reach potential customers. You know which publications work and which don't; you know how to run a successful direct mail campaign. Why, then, do you need to insert new digital media into the mix?

Digital Marketing Keeps You Competitive

I think there are two reasons to dive head-first into digital marketing. First, because your competitors are doing it. And second, because your customers expect it.

First reason first. If your competitors have figured out the digital marketing thing, that gives them a leg up. If a competitor has constructed a successful digital marketing program, he not only has realized a more effective way to contact existing customers, but also is out there in places you aren't trying to attract new customers. There's nothing worse than being second in line to reach a new customer base.

> "...there are two reasons to dive headfirst into digital marketing. First, because your competitors are doing it. And second, because your customers expect it."

In addition, more and more business buyers are going online to research new purchases; a recent Marketing Sherpa survey found that 71% of B2B purchases started with a web search.[1] Buyers appreciate the ease of finding information online, as well as the amount of information available. They're also adapting to the ease of ordering that comes when suppliers go online, and recognize the efficiency this presents. It's not just about saving a buck by using the Internet for more effective shopping; it's also about becoming better educated as to the options available and saving time by doing things quicker and easier online.

Bottom line, the business professionals you want to reach can be found online. That may not have always been the case, but it's certainly true today. According to Forrester Research,[2] 91% of business buyers read blogs, watch generated video, and participate in other social media. More than half (55%) of business decision makers participate in social networks, such as Facebook and LinkedIn. And 43% of these professionals actually create media online, such as making blog posts, uploading videos, writing articles, and so forth. In short, your target buyers are increasingly part of the online community; you can and should reach them online.

---

1. Marketing Sherpa, "2009-2010 B2B Marketing Benchmark Report," 2009

2. Forrester Research, "Social Technographics of Business Buyers," 2009

It might sound like one of those hollow business platitudes, but a successful company must grow and evolve to remain competitive. This is the same for B2B companies as it is for business to consumer (B2C) businesses; what B2C marketers discovered years ago is just as true for B2B companies today. You need to innovate just to stay in place, let alone to get ahead of the competitive curve.

> "You need to innovate just to stay in place, let alone to get ahead of the competitive curve."

Digital Marketing Is Becoming More Prevalent

I said before that you need to invest in digital marketing to remain competitive. How much, then, are other B2B companies spending on digital marketing?

There's no denying that B2B marketers have been slower to adopt digital marketing than their B2C cousins. Chalk that up to being cautious, having limited budgets, or maybe to some inherent Luddite tendencies; there might even be real market reasons for it. Whatever the case, the caution period appears to have ended, and previously-conservative B2B companies everywhere are embracing digital marketing strategies.

Back in 2005, Forrester Research found the beginnings of a switch from general business magazines, newspapers, and direct mail among B2B marketers.[3] At that time, 42% of B2B marketers were using digital marketing, and just 24% of budgets were spent online.

More recently Forrester Research issued a five-year forecast for B2B digital marketing spending.[4] This forecast indicates a quick changeover of spending priorities, with B2B digital marketing expenditures doubling over that period to $2.3 billion in 2014. If this happens, it will represent a major shift to digital media.

Indeed, MarketingSherpa finds that the majority of B2B organizations are increasing marketing budgets for digital marketing media that contribute to inbound marketing, including search engine marketing, PPC advertising, social media, and webinars and other virtual events.[5] Forrester also finds that B2B marketers are placing tools such as the company's website, search engine marketing, social networks, and webinars high on their list of spending plans.

---

3. Forrester Research, "The B2B Digital Marketing Shift," 2005

4. Forrester Research, "B2B U.S. Interactive Marketing Forecast, 2009 to 2014," 2010

5. MarketingSherpa, "2011 B2B Marketing Benchmark Report," 2010

In contrast, B2B marketers appear not to be increasing budgets for more traditional *outbound* marketing tools, such as print advertising, direct mail, and telemarketing. B2B marketers also don't appear to be *decreasing* budgets for these traditional marketing channels. Forrester found that in 2009, B2B organizations spent between 10% and 14% of their budgets on traditional tactics such as print advertising, direct mail, and public relations; another 20% went to trade shows and other physical events. That's even though many marketing executives readily admitted that these traditional tactics did not help increase awareness or generate demand as much as they would have liked.

I think this reluctance to abandon traditional marketing media might be a mistake—which you can exploit. If you can more fully embrace digital media, you can gain a foothold over slower-to-adapt competitors.

Digital Marketing Improves Customer Relationships

There's a reason that more and more B2B companies are embracing digital marketing: it works. Not only that, it works in a way that traditional media don't.

One of the chief benefits of digital marketing is the ability to establish a one-to-one connection with your customers and target new prospects. This direct connection is a two-way connection, which only makes it stronger; not only do you talk to them, but they have the unique opportunity to talk back to you, and on a regular basis.

This direct communication is particularly valuable to B2B companies, where your audience is typically smaller and more influential. It's enabled by digital marketing tools such as targeted PPC advertising, blog marketing, and (especially) social media marketing—and it's not something you can replicate with old school print or broadcast marketing media.

Digital Marketing: A 21st Century Imperative

What does all this mean to you? Simply put, now is the time to rethink your marketing mix. You need to shift your budget from traditional marketing channels to digital marketing channels, even if that means taking some risks and abandoning (or decreasing the importance of) channels that have worked well for you in the past. If you want to remain successful in the B2B space, you can't ignore the fundamental changes that are resulting from your customers embrace of the Internet. To keep pace, you have to adapt—and that means adopting digital media post haste.

Getting to Know the Components of Digital Marketing

Digital marketing is marketing via the Internet. But what exactly does that entail? There are many tools in the digital marketing arsenal, and it behooves you to become familiar with each—because it's likely they'll all play some part in your B2B digital marketing plan.

Website Marketing

The most important digital marketing tool is the one that virtually every B2B marketer will utilize: your website.

I suppose that not every B2B organization needs to have a website; you can get by, I suppose, with just a blog or a Facebook page, if you have to. It's also possible that your particular business is so old school that no web presence is required, although I'd like to see just which businesses fit the no-Web mold. But for the vast majority of B2B companies, a website is not just an important component of their digital marketing mix, it's the hub for all your online activities, marketing and otherwise. Everything else you do—your blog, your Facebook page, your Twitter feed, your YouTube videos—builds on what you do on your website. They are all subsidiary components to your website presence.

> "The most important digital marketing tool is the one that virtually every B2B marketer will utilize: your website."

Thinking of it this way, it's easy to see that your website is the most important thing you do online. Your website is the online face of your company, organization, brand, or products. It must reflect what you are, what you do, and how you do it; it is how current and potential customers view you and, in many cases, interface with you. A bad website will turn off potential customers, whereas an outstanding website will create new and more loyal customers. Everything else builds from your website—and leads back to it. You can't take it for granted.

Building an effective website for your business, then, is key. Both the content and design of your site should work toward establishing or supporting the products and services you offer to your customers. In addition, your site's content and design should fit in holistically with all your other marketing activities. Your customers should find a similar experience when they visit your site as they do when they view an ad in a trade magazine, read a direct mail piece, or receive an email newsletter. Everything should work in concert, while also exploiting the specific nature of each medium—an integrated marketing plan, if you will.

In addition, many B2B companies use their website to take orders from customers, so the entire process of ecommerce needs to be factored into the equation. Not only do you have to support your brand and products on your site, you also have to facilitate the sale of those products via ordering pages, a shopping cart, and checkout system. It's an added wrinkle, but an important one.

> ✉ *Note*
>
> Learn more about B2B websites in Chapter 9, "B2B Website Marketing."

Search Engine Marketing

In addition to being your company's online home base, your website also serves as a vehicle for attracting new customers—via search. That is, your site needs to rank high in the search results when business buyers search for topics related to your products and services. You'll find that most new visitors to your site—and thus most new potential customers—come directly from Google and other search engines.

Because of the search factor, the ability to rank highly in these search results is a critical component of your web marketing efforts. To gain a higher position on search results pages, then, you have to optimize your site for Google and other search engines. This is called *search engine optimization* (SEO) and is a major factor in website design and content creation. You have to design your site and create its content in ways that the search engines find attractive. The better optimized your site, the higher it will appear in those search results.

Why is it so important that Google's users see your site in the organic search results when they search for a related topic? It's simple: The higher your site is in the search results, the more it will be clicked. That's because most searchers, consumers and businesspeople alike, look at only the first few sites on a search results page. In fact, to get any clicks at all, your site needs to be on the first page of those search results, and it's even better to be near the top of that first page.

The nice thing about search engine marketing is that it's relatively free; you don't have to (and in fact can't) pay for placement on most search engines, search results pages. Your placement on a search results page is entire organic; the results you get are a direct result of how relevant your site's content is to the query being placed. The better your site matches the query, the higher it ranks in the search results—and the more visitors are sent to your site.

It's that simple—and that difficult. Because you can't buy your way to the top of the search results, you have to obtain your ranking via hard work, smarts, and skill.

That's good news for smaller B2B companies because all the money that a larger competitor might have is virtually useless against a site that does better SEO. A big company can spend big bucks on SEO services, of course, but a smaller company can get similar results by doing effective SEO in-house. This is one instance where a bigger budget doesn't necessarily guarantee better results.

"Because you can't buy your way to the top of the search results, you have to obtain your ranking via hard work, smarts, and skill."

Because most companies get so many visitors from the major search engines and because it's a relatively low-cost activity, search engine marketing is a major component of most B2B digital marketing plans. It's also an ongoing component; you have to constantly tinker with your site to maintain a high search ranking. That makes search engine marketing a bit time-consuming, but well worth the effort.

✉ *Note*

Learn more about search engine marketing and SEO in Chapter 10, "B2B Search Engine Marketing."

Online Advertising

There's another way to get your name in front of potential business buyers while they're searching, and that's by purchasing ad space on those very same search results pages. For this reason, most marketers consider search engine advertising to be part of search engine marketing. It's certainly an important component of most digital marketing plans.

To advertise with Google, Yahoo!, Bing, and other major search engines, you typically create a *pay-per-click* (PPC) advertisement. A PPC ad is so-named because you pay only when the ad is clicked by a customer; you don't pay for the placement itself. It's true results-oriented advertising, much more so than the typical ads you run in trade and industry publications.

PPC advertising is also different from traditional advertising in that you have to bid on those keywords that people are searching for. If you're a high bidder, your ad gets prominently displayed on the search results page for that particular keyword; if you're outbid, your ad gets displayed lower in the search results or not at all.

This sort of keyword bidding makes PPC advertising challenging for those used to traditional cost-per-thousand (CPM) advertising. Not only do you have to write compelling ad copy (but not a lot of it—PPC text ads are typically very short), you also have to figure out the right keywords and how much to bid on each one. It's tricky, but it's the way the advertising game is played on the Web—even for B2B companies.

Although targeted PPC advertising can be extremely effective for B2B marketers, it's not the only form of advertising available online. More traditional display advertising also exists, typically in the form of graphical banner ads found on the top or the sides of pages on some websites. These ads are typically paid for on a CPM impressions basis, although some banner ads are also sold as part of a PPC program. You can achieve good results by placing targeted display ads on those trade or industry websites your business buyers are most likely to frequent—essentially the online equivalent of placing print ads in trade and industry magazines.

✉ *Note*

Learn more about online advertising for B2B companies in Chapter 11, "B2B Online Advertising."

Email Marketing

B2B marketing is all about establishing and maintaining relationships. In the offline world, direct mail is a key factor in maintaining customer relationships; online, email marketing serves much the same function.

After you've established a relationship with a customer, you can use email to reach out to that customer on a regular basis. Maybe you send out weekly or monthly emails describing your current specials or new products; maybe you send out individual emails alerting customers when they need to reorder; maybe you produce a full-blown email newsletter that contains general industry or specific company information. However you use it, you use email to push your message via email directly to buyers' inboxes. It's a lot harder to ignore a targeted email message than it is a web page ad.

✉ *Note*

Don't confuse true email marketing with its bastard cousin, spam or junk email. Email marketing is *opt-in* marketing; that is, recipients have to actively agree to receive your email marketing messages. Spam, on the other hand, requires no prior approval and is in virtually all instances an unwanted intrusion. People ignore spam; many people, especially business buyers, actually look forward to opt-in email messages from their favorite companies.

The key to successful email marketing is to send out emails with information that directly benefits your customer base. If you provide something useful, you'll get a good return on your efforts.

> ✉ *Note*
>
> Learn more about email campaigns in Chapter 12, "B2B Email Marketing."

Blog Marketing

A website is just one kind of online presence. Many B2B companies also host their own blogs, which they use to announce new products, promotions, and the like to their business buyers. You can also use a blog to establish a more direct connection with your most loyal customers. In this instance, you use blog posts to take readers behind the scenes to see how your company works and to get to know your company's employees. It's a great way to put a human face on an otherwise faceless entity—and build that ever-important customer connection.

You can include a blog as part of your normal website or as a freestanding presence. The key is to update your blog regularly and frequently; customers have to have a reason to keep coming back, which they won't do if they keep seeing the same old posts over and over. That means spending the requisite amount of time to maintain and post to your blog—more work, I know, but necessary.

In addition, blogs—other company's and people's blogs, that is—also represent a new promotional channel for your company. There are lots of blogs out there that act as de facto authorities on a given topic or for a given region, and business buyers often look to these blogs when making related purchasing decisions. If you can gain the endorsement of these influential bloggers, new customers will follow.

This argues in favor of adding key bloggers to your online public relations mix. You should actively court the support of influential bloggers. In some instances, you can buy your way into their good graces by providing them with free products to review. Whether they actually review your goods or just mention them kindly in their blogs, it's welcome exposure.

> ✉ *Note*
>
> Learn more about blogs and bloggers in Chapter 13, "B2B Blog Marketing."

Social Media Marketing

The latest big thing in the B2C marketing world is social media marketing—that is, marketing conducting via Facebook, Twitter, Google+, and other social media. Social media marketing has been slower to catch on in the B2B world, but that's starting to change.

What exactly are social media? These are websites and services that let people and businesses of various types connect with each other to share what they're doing. Users create groups of "friends" or "followers" that they connect with; this connection is typically in the form of short messages that are sent to all of a user's or business's friends or followers.

The biggest social medium today is Facebook, which technically is a social networking site; it lets users and businesses network with each other via their own profile pages and status updates. It's de rigueur in the B2C world for a company or organization to create its own page on Facebook and sign up loyal customers as fans, who then receive updates on new products, promotions, and other activities. In the B2B world, companies are learning that many of their business customers are also Facebook fans, and concocting similar Facebook strategies to connect to these customers on a regular basis.

Google has its own social network, called Google+, which looks to be a major rival to Facebook. Google+ garnered 20 million users in its first few weeks of operation, and is attracting a lot of attention from the business community. Although similar in design to Facebook, it's a little easier to use and, because it comes from Google, might prove to be a little more marketing-friendly over time.

Twitter is also a big deal in the social media sphere, although it's technically more of a micro-blogging service than a social network. That is, you really don't have a company page, as you do on Facebook; all you do is post short (140-character) updates, or *tweets*, that are then received by those customers who choose to follow you. You use these tweets to keep your customers updated on what you're doing and what you have to offer.

Then there's LinkedIn, which is a social network specifically for business professionals. Where LinkedIn isn't that important for B2C companies, it has a higher profile in the B2B world because that's where more businesspeople tend to hang out for professional reasons. Many B2B companies are connecting with key buyers via LinkedIn, either on a first-contact or established relationship basis.

Note

There are also social media that let users share the things they like online, via bookmarks or references. These social bookmarking services, such as Digg and Delicious, are often used by B2C companies to encourage customers to spread the word across the Web; they're less useful in the B2B space.

The key with any type of B2B social marketing, whether on Facebook, Google+, Twitter, or LinkedIn, is participation. These sites are really nothing more than large online communities, and you need to be an active participant if you're going to make it work for you. You just can't put up a static page and expect that to do the job in terms of reaching your B2B customers; you have to continually post updates and other information of interest to community members. You also need to interact with members of the community by visiting and posting to their pages and discussions. People will follow you on these social networks, but only if you also follow them. It's a give and take sort of thing, just like life in a real-world community.

 Note

Learn more about social networking for B2B concerns in Chapter 14, "B2B Social Media Marketing."

Audio, Video, and Interactive Marketing

The Internet isn't all text, of course. Much web-based communication for B2B companies is done with sight and sound via digital videos and audios.

Audio marketing takes the form of *podcasts*, which are short audio broadcasts that can be streamed or downloaded from your website or from a third-party provider, such as Apple's iTunes Store. Think of a podcast as your own little radio show, which you can use to promote your company or products to existing or potential customers.

Video marketing takes the form of digital videos. You're familiar with YouTube, of course, which is the Internet's largest video-sharing community. Although YouTube is a haven for user-generated videos of all shapes and sizes, it's also a place where savvy businesses market themselves via videos that somehow promote their products and brands. Up until recently, YouTube has been used primarily by B2C businesses reaching out to consumers. But there is a place for YouTube in B2B marketing, if only because more and more business buyers are looking for information about products and services in video format. Videos are actually pretty good for presenting how-to information and keeping customers abreast on the latest industry news; if you can tap into this need for useful information presented in video format, you could have a one-up on your competition.

Finally, there's a more interactive form of audio/video marketing that many B2B companies are successfully exploring. I'm talking about *webinars*, web-based seminars that let you talk directly to groups of customers (and them to you) in real time. Whether you think of a webinar as a group web chat or a web-based sales conference (both comparisons are valid), it's a great use of emerging communications technology for B2B marketing purposes.

 Note

Learn more about multimedia marketing in Chapter 15, "B2B Audio, Video, and Interactive Marketing."

Public Relations

Most successful B2B companies employ public relations to get mentions in a variety of traditional media. It's all about making the right contacts (and sending out a few press releases) to get a favorable product placement.

Traditional PR methods, however, are migrating to the Internet; many of the old media people you deal with, even (and especially) for traditional publications, now prefer to be contacted online. Instead of sending out physical press releases via postal mail, you send out virtual press releases (and accompanying media) via email. It's a lot faster—and costs less, too.

Many B2B companies also find that supporting media of all types is made easier by putting key marketing materials in a press room on their websites. It's actually easier to put all your product images, press releases, management bios, or whatever on your website, where all media can access them, than it is to supply these materials via traditional methods. A well-stocked and easy-to-use online press room will actually get you more placements than you would have had otherwise.

For these reasons, you really need to think of online PR as a new activity in your B2B marketing bag. And unlike traditional PR, it's something you can measure; whereas you might never know what a mention in a traditional print magazine got you, it's easy enough to track those visitors to your website that resulted from an online press release or mention in a particular blog. Old-time PR people might not like this new accountability, but it puts the PR part of your program in the same league as your other measurable marketing activities.

Note

Learn more about online PR in Chapter 16, "B2B Public Relations."

Mobile Marketing

Up until recently, most business buyers accessed the Internet from their work computers. But that's not the only way businesspeople go online today; in fact, within a few short years, it might not even be the dominant way.

That's because more and people—businesspeople included—are accessing the Internet from their mobile devices. I'm talking about smartphones, like the Apple iPhone, Google Android, and Blackberry Torch, as well as tablets like the iPad, Samsung Galaxy, and Blackberry Playbook.

You might think that in the B2B world, because you're connecting with business buyers typically working from computers in their company's offices, mobile marketing wouldn't necessarily be a big thing. But things aren't always as they seem. More and more company buyers are getting comfortable with accessing information on their mobile devices; they don't necessarily limit themselves to computer screens during business hours. In other words, B2B purchasing is becoming more mobile, and you need to adapt to and exploit that shift.

When you think about connecting to the Web via a mobile device, especially a smartphone, you realize that lots of things are different. Not only do you need to rethink your web page design (to offer a version that looks good on and works well with mobile screens), but you also have to consider how you can connect with these mobile users.

In other words, mobile marketing is one more club you need in your B2B marketing bag. That bag keeps getting bigger as more opportunities arise online, and you need to keep developing new skills to keep up with the latest ways to connect with your business buyers.

 Note

Learn more about mobile marketing for B2B in Chapter 17, "B2B Mobile Marketing."

Migrating from Traditional Channels to Digital Channels

Here's a question: Do all these new digital marketing channels supplement your existing B2B marketing efforts, or do they replace some or all of what you're currently doing?

Because few if any B2B companies have unlimited marketing budgets (and, in fact, most have the expected budgetary constraints), it's likely that as you add digital marketing tools to your mix you'll need to conversely decrease your spending on some of your existing marketing activities. Think of it as a migration from traditional marketing channels to new digital marketing channels.

Which old school activities lead to which new school ones? It depends a lot on how many of your prospect and customers are online themselves, of course, but let's take a quick look at the possibilities.

✉ *Note*

Many B2B businesses have been slow to adopt digital media because their customer bases have been slow to move online. You don't want to get too far ahead of your customers; there's no point marketing online if your customers are still primarily wedded to traditional marketing methods. You need to follow your customers in this regard, not lead them—although you need to be right there when your customers and prospects do move online.

Migrating from Cold Calling to Search Engine Marketing

Drumming up new business is the bane of all B2B companies. In the old days, your salespeople had to reach out to potential customers by following a list of potential leads. Cold calling was the nature of the day.

With digital marketing, however, at least some potential new customers will seek you out—by clicking on your website in Google search results. Business customers are becoming more proactive, which means they're using technology (in the form of web search engines) to seek out information and possible suppliers. When they go searching, they'll find your company.

Having potential customers contact you is a heck of a lot more productive than having your sales force do a lot of cold calling. If you work your website (and the landing pages that lead from your search results listings) correctly, you can encourage or require visitors to provide their contact information. You, then, pass this contact information onto your sales force, and now they're calling better qualified buyers who've already expressed an interest in your company, products, and services. It's a lot better than cold calling.

Migrating from Literature to Websites

What do you provide when potential customers request more information? Yes, you want to get their contact info so that your salespeople can do their thing, but a lot of times buyers just want the information, not the contact.

In the old days, you probably mailed inquiring customers some sort of product literature—a brochure or two, maybe a fact sheet, maybe even a white paper. That's all good stuff, but they cost money to design and print, and even more money to mail. Plus, there's a time lag between when a prospect requests that information and when he or she receives it.

In the digital world, you can provide some if not all your current product information—and more—on your website. Fewer brochures to print, less information to mail, no more waiting for the customer to receive it all. Your customers get immediate gratification (and potentially more information than before) and you get lower costs. What's not to like?

Migrating from Trade Advertising to Web Advertising

Many B2B businesses spend a chunk of change on advertisements in a variety of trade and industry publications. Fine and dandy; these magazines and journals are highly targeted and often deliver good results.

You might be able, however, to generate similar results at a fraction of the cost by migrating some or all of your trade advertising to the Web. Instead of taking out an ad in an industry-specific magazine, you place a banner ad on an industry-specific website. In most instances, you're reaching the same or similar customers, and web ads typically cost less than print ads. In addition, you're likely to generate direct results (via click throughs) from your web advertising; results are much more difficult to track in print advertising.

Migrating from Direct Mail to Email

When it comes to keeping in regular contact with your customers, direct mail rules the roost. Whether it's a weekly list of specials, a monthly newsletter, or a quarterly catalog, most B2B companies have a robust direct mail operation.

Robust direct mail operations, unfortunately, are also costly direct mail operations. Again, it costs a lot of money to design, print, and mail everything you send out—even if they are effective at retaining customers and driving additional revenue.

You can reduce your direct mail costs by shifting your mailings to the Internet. Instead of sending all your flyers, newsletters, and catalogs via postal mail, you instead send them to your customer list via email. Sending an email message is essentially free; although you still have some design and management costs, you reduce your printing and mailing costs to near zero. Plus, your customers receive your mailings immediately, rather than waiting days or weeks for the post office to its thing. There's much benefit to this particular migration.

Migrating from Newsletters and Phone Calls to Social Media

How do you let your customers know when something new or important is happening? If you're like most B2B companies, you either send out a newsletter or similar mailing, or have your salespeople take to the phones.

Those approaches are old school in the extreme. Today, cutting-edge B2B companies are using social media, such as Twitter and Facebook, to notify customers of important events and happenings. Instead of sending out a barrage of calls or emails to announce a price reduction, for example, you simply tweet about it on Twitter and include the news in a post to your Facebook page. It's instant communication that often has more impact than more traditional methods.

Migrating from Trade Magazine PR to Blog PR

If you have a PR department, it's no doubt accustomed to sending out press releases and making calls to the most important trade magazines for your industry. That's good, but there are other places that your customers go for information online. You need to expand your PR efforts to include websites, online publications, and industry-related blogs. The effort is similar (but not identical), but the targets are all online.

Migrating from Live Events to Webinars

Finally, consider all the live events your company hosts or attends—conferences, seminars, trade shows, and the like. It costs real money to send a small army of personnel and equipment cross country for these events, and even though they're often effective in the whole, they might not be the most cost-effective marketing tools in your arsenal.

Forward-thinking B2B companies are migrating many of their live events online. Instead of hosting a seminar in a hotel or conference center, you instead host a web seminar (webinar) online. Your staff doesn't have to travel, and neither do your attendees—which both reduces costs and potentially increases the number of attendees. The whole thing takes place online, using web conferencing software and services. Your costs are dramatically reduced, as is the downtime for your staff.

How B2B Companies Can Use Digital Marketing

As you can see, there are a lot of current activities you can migrate online. But should you?

Here's where it pays to know your customers. If you understand where and how your existing and potential customers look for information, you'll know that they're increasingly turning to online sources. It's a simple maxim: Go where your customers are. When your customers go online, you need to follow them.

Precision, Scale, and Marketability

Moving your marketing online also has some very real benefits for your business. It's not just about lower costs (although there's probably some of that); you may see gains in both efficiency and effectiveness.

I like the way Jennifer Howard, head of Google's B2B Markets Group, put it:

"The value of digital marketing to a B2B marketer is about: Precision, Scale, and ultimate Measurability."

Looking at digital marketing in these terms, precision results from the use of search marketing, PPC advertising, and display advertising. These digital marketing tools result in more precise lead generation—better leads for less money.

Scale results from those digital marketing tools that have very little per-piece cost. This includes email marketing, social media marketing, and interactive marketing, in the form of webinars. It's kind of a publish-once (or create-once), distribute-many model, and lets you ramp up your business without increasing your costs correspondingly.

The measurability thing is inherent in almost all digital marketing vehicles. You can use various analytics tools to precisely track the number of leads you generate and what those leads end up doing. You can track visitors to your website, time spent there, conversions, you name it, all a lot easier and more accurately than you can track performance in traditional media.

Understanding the Digital Marketing Process Flow

So, how can your company use digital marketing? In most cases, you end up decreasing your existing marketing expenditures and shifting that spending to corresponding digital marketing vehicles; you don't have to increase your overall budget to go digital. You can then plan your activities according to the digital marketing process flow detailed in Figure 1.1, and described here:

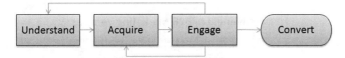

Figure 1.1   *The digital marketing process flow.*

1. **Understand**—Before you do anything else, you have to understand your B2B customers—who they are, where they are, what they're looking for, where they're looking for it, and so forth. You can do this via a variety of methods, including but not limited to online research.

2. **Acquire**—Next, you need to attract those customers into your orbit. With digital marketing, that means using various outbound marketing tools—search engine marketing, PPC advertising, display advertising, and public relations—to draw them to your website, or to provide their contact information.

3. **Engage**—Digital marketing offers various ways to engage potential customers. Your website is the primary vehicle, of course, but you can also use social media, audio and video, interactive media, and email—anything that keeps customers in your orbit and provides them with the content they require to make a purchasing decision.

4. **Convert**—This is the endpoint of the process, your ultimate goal—converting lookers into buyers. (Of course, a conversion can be something other than a sale; obtaining contact information for lead perusal can also be a conversion.) But if you can't convert them immediately, you can lead back to additional acquisition activity—or even leverage the process to better understand your customers' behavior.

Naturally, you can mix and match digital and traditional marketing activities at any point in the process. For example, trade shows can be an important component of the acquisition step, in addition to search engine marketing, et al. The point is to proceed step by step, acquiring and engaging potential customers until you can convert them into actual customers. Then, of course, you need to keep on engaging them to keep them in your customer base.

Choosing the Right Digital Marketing Tools

Which digital marketing tools can you use to further your goals? It will vary from business to business, of course, and evolve over time. But Figure 1.2 shows those activities that B2B marketers today find most effective. As you can see, website and search engine marketing are generally regarded as the most effective tools (much more effective than traditional marketing vehicles); social media brings up the rear, along with several more traditional media.

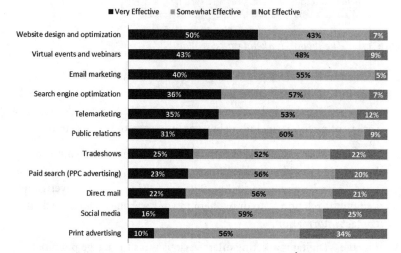

Effectiveness of B2B Marketing Vehicles

■ Very Effective   ■ Somewhat Effective   ■ Not Effective

	Very Effective	Somewhat Effective	Not Effective
Website design and optimization	50%	43%	7%
Virtual events and webinars	43%	48%	9%
Email marketing	40%	55%	5%
Search engine optimization	36%	57%	7%
Telemarketing	35%	53%	12%
Public relations	31%	60%	9%
Tradeshows	25%	52%	22%
Paid search (PPC advertising)	23%	56%	20%
Direct mail	22%	56%	21%
Social media	16%	59%	25%
Print advertising	10%	56%	34%

Figure 1.2   *Effectiveness of various B2B marketing vehicles.*[6]

Naturally, you need to make your own decisions—and monitor your ongoing effectiveness. Unlike traditional B2B marketing, which has remained virtually unchanged for decades, digital marketing is in a constant state of change. Consider, for example, that neither social networks nor online videos existed a half-dozen years ago, and they're both now established parts of the digital marketing mix. You have to stay on top of the trends, and be willing and able to adjust your plans to changes in technology and the marketplace. With digital marketing, it's survival of the fittest and the fastest; you have to evolve or get left behind.

The Bottom Line

Digital marketing consists of various activities to attract and engage potential and existing customers online. That typically means some combination of website marketing, search engine marketing, online advertising, email marketing, blog marketing, social media marketing, audio/video and interactive marketing, online public relations, and mobile marketing.

---

[6] MarketingSherpa, "B2B Marketing Benchmark Survey," 2010

Although the B2B industry in general has been slow to move to digital marketing, the migration from traditional marketing vehicles is starting to speed up. In most instances, you'll add digital marketing to your existing marketing mix; you'll probably shift expenditures from one to the other, rather than completely eliminate traditional marketing vehicles.

> "...digital marketing helps you establish a closer bond with your customers..."

There are many benefits from increasing the use of digital marketing in the B2B environment. In many instances, digital marketing costs less than similar traditional vehicles; many digital marketing channels scale effortlessly, letting you ramp up your efforts without correspondingly increasing your costs. In addition, digital marketing helps you establish a closer bond with your customers, and more precisely target your efforts to specific types of customers.

For all these reasons, savvy B2B marketers are making the shift from traditional marketing to digital marketing. How to do so is what we'll cover in the balance of this book.

HOW B2B MARKETING DIFFERS FROM B2C MARKETING—ESPECIALLY ONLINE

As you're no doubt aware, B2B marketing differs significantly from B2C marketing. This is especially apparent online; you can't use digital marketing tools the same way in a B2B environment as you can with B2C.

Of course, one of the key differences between B2B and B2C marketing is the length of the sales process. B2C is typically a short transaction with a quick response to an obvious appeal to a single decision maker. The B2B sales process, however, is longer and more complex; there is a more involved relationship-building process, with many stages in the journey and often multiple decision makers involved.

This also speaks to the difference in messaging between B2B and B2C marketing. B2C marketing is typically emotionally driven, sometimes accompanied by a low price or discount offer. B2B marketing is more fact-based; creativity takes a backseat to data dissemination and education, and price is less of a factor (at least in terms of immediate conversions—there's little to no impulse buying involved).

This messaging difference is most obviously seen in the design of B2B and B2C websites. B2C sites are typically glitzy with lots of pretty product images, Flash animations, and other state-of-the-art gewgaws; B2B sites, in contrast, are more staid and text-driven, with lots and lots of links to additional information and downloads.

B2C websites are also geared toward immediate and direct sales, complete with special offers, free shipping, and other enticements. Although some B2B sites are built to accept customer orders, most are more informational in design. And even those ecommerce-like B2B sites are more for the benefit of customers placing reorders on bulk merchandise; they're not designed to encourage impulse purchases.

The targeting aspect is another point of difference between B2B and B2C marketing. B2C companies typically cast a fairly wide net, even in the mass personalized world of social media; it still leans in the mass marketing direction. B2B marketing, of course, is much more targeted; a B2B website is not designed for viewing by the mass public, but rather by a focused group of industry-specific professionals.

It all boils down to using those digital marketing tools that best serve the needs of the B2B audience, and doing so in such a way that targets specific customer segments. For example, a B2B company will probably do less social networking than would a comparable B2C company, if only because companies are less likely to be monitoring Twitter and Facebook feeds than individuals might.

All this said, digital marketing is little different from traditional marketing for B2B professionals. You still need to focus on your target audience, build personal relationships with your customers, provide them with all the information they need to make informed decisions, and then build the credibility and confidence required to make your company a preferred vendor. Digital media are just tools you use in this quest.

2

Segmenting Your Audience

Before you begin devising your B2B digital marketing strategy, you need to better understand just who it is to which you are marketing. Key to this understanding is being able to identify the various segments of your customer base, and then determine how these different types of customers use digital media to make their purchasing decisions. Then, and only then, can you target specific digital media to these different customer segments.

Why Audience Segmentation Is Important

What is audience segmentation, and why is it important?

Audience segmentation, sometimes called *market* or *customer segmentation*, is simply the act of dividing your target audience into groups that share similar needs and demonstrate similar buyer behavior. This way you can target messages and even products and services to specific market segments, instead of sending the same general message and products/services to all potential customers.

 Note

Yoram Wind and Richard Cardozo, in a seminal 1974 paper, defined B2B market segmentation as the identification of "a group of present or potential customers with some common characteristic which is relevant in explaining (and predicting) their response to a supplier's marketing stimuli."

In this fashion, market segmentation is the polar opposite of mass marketing. A mass market has no (or few) segments; you send the same messages to all potential customers, and market the same products and services across the board. A segmented market, on the other hand, allows for more targeted or even personalized messages, and even the possibility of tailoring a unique product mix to each market segment.

This type of market segmentation is important for a number of reasons. It not only helps you focus on who you want to engage and shows you where the best market opportunities lie, but also lays the groundwork for better reception to your message. Customers who are talked to directly respond more positively than those who receive a generic message; the more relevant the message, the higher the customer engagement and response rates.

By identifying market segments and then fine-tuning your marketing message to each segment, you provide each customer with a more relevant message. Marketing that lacks this relevance, more often than not, ends up being a waste of everyone's time; in this age of mass personalization, nonpersonalized and nonrelevant messages are simply ignored.

> "Marketing that lacks this relevance, more often than not, ends up being a waste of everyone's time..."

It's easy to understand why irrelevant marketing messages can do more harm than good. Not only do you waste valuable marketing resources by sending the wrong messages to the wrong people, you might also end up offending your true customer base. When you send out mass-produced messages to people who couldn't care less about what you're saying, potential buyers may think (rightly) that your company is clueless and doesn't care about them.

On the other hand, when you correctly segment your customer base, you provide target customers with information relevant and useful to their purchasing decisions. Done properly, market segmentation can produce significant increases in response rates and customer engagement—and ultimately conversion.

Key to this successful audience segmentation is not only identifying like customers, but knowing what kinds of information they prefer to receive, and how. You end up sending targeted messages to specific groups of customers, using the media that best suit their buying behavior.

For example, if one customer segment likes to receive detailed information via email, that's what you provide—informative email missives. If another customer segment prefers to view video walkthroughs, you reach them via videos on YouTube or your own website. If another customer segment likes to ask a lot of questions and is active in social networks, you reach them via your Facebook page or other dynamic web forum.

What you don't do, however, is try to force specific media, digital or otherwise, onto unreceptive customer segments. There's no point in sending emails to potential customers who never check their inboxes, for example; there's also no point in producing fancy videos for customers in companies who have blocked YouTube and similar sites during work hours.

Successful market segmentation, then, results in the following quantifiable benefits:

- **Higher response rates** by providing relevant messages to each targeted segment.
- **Higher conversion rates** by targeting the right products to the right customers.
- **Lower immediate marketing expenditures** by using only those media that best reach targeted segments; you don't waste money by going outside the "sweet spot" for each segment.
- **Lower long-term costs** by not having to follow up on lower-potential leads.
- **Lower risk of negative feedback**, on social networks and elsewhere, by not sending unwanted messages to those uninterested in what you offer.

LEVERAGING SCARCE RESOURCES

Market segmentation is also a necessary strategy for dealing with a finite budget. By dividing a mass market into smaller, more manageable segments, you can identify those segments with more potential and allocate your marketing activities accordingly.

Because you can't produce all possible products for all the people, all the time, or afford to market to all possible customers, no matter how small, market segmentation is a way to leverage scarce resources. You focus on specific customer needs, in the most efficient and effective way possible.

You use audience segmentation to identify and rank groups of customers by their sales potential. You can then allocate your marketing budget accordingly, and thus get the most bang for your B2B marketing buck.

How to Segment Your Audience

There are many ways to segment your company's customer base. We'll examine some of the most common methods here.

Breakdown and Build-Up Segmentation

This first approach to market segmentation focuses on similarities and differences.

Breakdown segmentation starts with the worldview that any given market consists of customers that are essentially the same. You then identify groups within the whole that share specific differences; these differences form your market segments.

The mirror image of the breakdown approach is called *build-up segmentation*. With the build-up approach, you start with the worldview that a market consists of individual customers who are all inherently different. The task, then, is to find similarities between customers, and form market segments accordingly.

Both breakdown and build-up segmentation are bottom-up approaches, and each have their benefits. The breakdown method is perhaps the best-recognized and most established approach to market segmentation, especially in B2C marketing. If taken to the extreme, you end up with each individual customer being its own market segment—or the ultimate endpoint of mass personalization.

The build-up approach, by moving from the individual level (where all customers are different) to the general, is perhaps more customer oriented because it seeks to determine common customer needs. It's a more enveloping approach because it seeks to define audience homogeneity. And, in the eyes of many marketers, it's better suited to B2B marketing.

✉ *Note*

The build-up approach is championed by noted marketing professor Philip Kotler.

The nice thing about both breakdown and build-up segmentation is that they organically define the qualities of each market segment. Other approaches seek to define segments by applying predetermined characteristics—which sometimes results in fitting round pegs into square holes.

A Priori and Post Hoc Segmentation

With *a priori segmentation*, you determine the market segments in advance, and then fit each customer into the nearest segment. You start by defining the qualities that make up each segment, such as demographics, customer size, industry, and the like. You then collect appropriate data about all existing and potential customers, and then use that data to sort your customers into each of the predefined categories.

With *post hoc segmentation*, you start out by collecting data about your customers, and then slice and dice that data to determine the appropriate market segments. That is, you deduce your segments from the data, rather than determining the segments beforehand.

Both these approaches lend you more control over the results; you define segments on your own terms, based on those qualities that are important to your business. For example, you might find it easiest to segment by geographic location, or company size (revenues, employees, or number of locations), or adoption of specific technology. Unlike the breakdown or build-up methods, you control what your segments will look like.

Of course, the downside of both the a priori and post hoc approaches is that the qualities you define might not be the qualities that best define or matter to your customers. You might discover, sometime down the road, that all the businesses you lumped into a predefined category really have little in common, especially regarding their acceptance of digital marketing.

"You might start out with the best of intentions but end up creating segments that just don't fit the way your customers work."

For that reason, you need to constantly evaluate the segments you create. You might start out with the best of intentions but end up creating segments that just don't fit the way your customers work. If that is the case, you'll need to redefine your segments—not only which customers fit into which segments, but also the defining qualities of each segment on the top level.

 Note

> It's always better to define segments by customer behavior rather than customer description—if you can. That is, it's less important how big a company is than how it does a particular thing, which is better gauged from personal interaction than rote reading of SIC codes.

Common B2B Market Segments

If you use the breakdown or build-up methods to create your customer segments, you'll end up with your own unique customer definitions. That's great.

If, however, you adopt the a priori or post hoc approaches, you have to start somewhere in defining your segment characteristics. To that end, let's look at some of the more common segments used by other B2B companies.

Hierarchy of Characteristics

In their text *Segmenting the Industrial Market* (1984, Lexington Books), marketing experts Thomas Bonoma and Benson Shapiro defined the following five characteristics that can be used to defined B2B market segments:

- **Demographics**—These include factors such as the customer's industry, company size, location, age, and where the company stands in its life-cycle.
- **Operating variables**—These include elements such as the company's embrace of specific technologies, use of various products or brands, and other important capabilities. For the purposes of digital marketing, this should also include the customer's use of various digital media.
- **Purchasing approaches**—This should take into account the purchasing function within the company, the company's internal power structure, buyer-seller relationships, purchasing policies and criteria, and the like. For that matter, a company's purchasing unit may have specific requirements that influence purchasing decisions; there might be internal policies, purchasing strategies, and the like that you need to take into account.

- **Situational factors**—These are both immediate and changing, including the urgency of a specific order, the size of an order, product application, and the like.

- **Buyer's personal characteristics**—This is the most granular of the segmentation characteristics, based on the characteristics of specific individuals—that person's character, approach to purchasing, likes and dislikes, and so forth.

Bonoma and Shapiro suggest applying these characteristics in a nested hierarchy. That is, start by defining the customer's demographics, then the operating variables, then the purchasing approaches used, then the situational factors, and then the personal characteristics.

Organizational Characteristics

These hierarchical characteristics can be divided into organizational and buyer-related characteristics. Organizational characteristics are macro in nature; buyer characteristics are more micro.

Organization characteristics define the type of company to which you're selling, in terms of size, location, and the like. These characteristics include the following:

- **Company size**—This can be a rough indicator of the potential business that a company might represent, in the long term. In general terms, you're likely to get more and larger orders from a larger company than from a smaller one.

- **Location**—This can be used not only to assign sales staff, but also to determine how best to approach a given company; where a company is located, geographically, can tell a lot about that company's culture and communication requirements. For example, you'd want to adopt a different marketing strategy for an Asian company than a company in Europe. In addition, you can define customer segments by geographic range—whether a company is local, national, multinational, or the like.

- **SIC code**—Specific industries have their own unique needs, based on technology usage, standard practices, and the like. You can fine-tune your marketing strategy for specific industries.

✉ *Note*

The SIC (Standard Industry Classification) code defines specific industries. It's gradually being replaced by the similar-but-improved NAICS (National Industry Classification System); use whichever is most appropriate for your industry.

- **Type of institution**—It's important to note the culture and nature of a given company. For example, if you're selling office furniture, you should know that banks like designer furniture whereas government agencies require more functional fixtures.

- **Business model**—Businesses of the same type and size might still have differences in the way they purchase; the business model assumed by a company affects how and where it buys. For example, a company pursuing a cost leadership strategy is more committed to high-volume, low-cost purchasing, where a business that adopts a strategy of differentiation is more likely to purchase unique products at higher prices.

- **Benefit segmentation**—This refers to the product's economic value to the customer. This recognizes that different customers buy the same products but for different reasons. How a company uses your products will determine the specific marketing message you use when communicating with that company.

- **Decision-making stage**—When courting new customers, this refers to where the company is in the purchasing process. Obviously, you need to supply different information (and use different techniques) for each stage in the decision-making process.

- **Ongoing business potential**—For existing customers, you can then segment by the ongoing revenue potential, assuming supply can be guaranteed. You might want to segment by major accounts (your largest customers who require constant management attention), key accounts (medium-sized customers who are more regular in their purchases), and direct accounts (smaller companies who can be counted on to place orders without constant handholding on your part).

Purchasing Characteristics

Segmenting by purchasing characteristics involves understanding and catering to the individual components of the decision-making process. It's a more subjective approach, one based as much on personalities as on hard facts; it also creates numerous specific segments, as opposed to the fewer, broader segments of organizational segmentation.

When determining segments based on buyer characteristics, you should consider the following:

- **Buying decision criteria**—These are the factors a buyer uses to evaluate suppliers, including price, product quality, delivery time and accuracy, supply continuity, technical support, and the like.

- **Purchasing strategy**—Some companies prefer to use a selection of familiar suppliers, and place their orders with the first supplier that meets the buying criteria. Other companies like to consider a larger number of both familiar and new suppliers, solicit bids, and then place the order with the firm that makes the best offer.

- **Structure of the decision-making unit**—You need to know how the decision-making process works for each of the companies you sell to. This helps you develop an appropriate relationship with the person or people who have the real decision-making power in the organization— and not waste too much time selling to people who don't actually make the decision.

- **Perceived importance**—You also need to know how important your product or service is to the company to which you're selling. The more important your product is (or is perceived to be), the more personal interaction you're likely to have with key decision makers.

- **Attitudes toward suppliers**—Likewise, you need to know just how your potential customers feel about your company and your products. Getting on the good side of a buyer can make all the difference when otherwise similar suppliers are vying for a company's business.

How Different Segments Use Digital Media

Now we come to the intersection of market segmentation and digital marketing strategy: Just how do different market segments use digital media?

Digital Media by Organizational Characteristics

The type and location of a company will determine that company's use of digital media in the purchasing process. Although every situation is different, there are a few major issues to keep in mind.

First, a larger company is more likely to embrace newer technologies than a smaller one—to a point. It's mainly a budget thing; larger companies have larger budgets and larger IT departments that let them adopt new technologies faster than smaller companies can or can afford to do. That said, large IT departments often suffer from a form of technological inertia and are less likely to embrace any change to the status quo. (Just look at how many large companies are still using Windows XP and Office 2000; after they get something that works, they don't want to risk change.)

To that end, some smaller companies are faster to adapt to changes, including technological changes, and thus may embrace new technologies before their more entrenched larger competitors. Certainly, technology can be an equalizing factor, especially with costs coming down; new technology can help a smaller company look bigger to prospective customers.

You also need to be aware that many larger companies (and some smaller ones, too) block some websites and web-based technologies that they deem to be harmful to employee productivity. It's common, actually, to find companies blocking access to Facebook and Twitter, along with many consumer online shopping sites; I've also encountered a large number of companies that block access to YouTube and other video-sharing sites. If you're embracing these somewhat cutting-edge digital media, make sure your potential customers can actually access the media at work.

Location also plays a role in which technologies and sites are accessible. Companies based in some emerging regions might not have the same access to broadband Internet as we do here in the U.S. And some totalitarian companies might block access to websites that are thought dangerous to the current regime; China is a case in point here, blocking access to Google and other open-search sites. Again, make sure that the media you want to use are in fact accessible in the regions to which you market.

You also need to take the type of industry to which you're marketing into account. Some types of companies are just more old school than others. For example, a traditional manufacturing company might be more behind the curve than a cutting-edge advertising agency; don't necessarily expect a buyer of industrial supplies to be accessing Twitter on his iPhone. You'll need to adjust your digital media strategy to the ways your target industries actually use the technology.

Digital Media by Purchasing Characteristics

Beyond these company-based characteristics, you also need to determine how individual companies and buyers use technology in the decision-making and purchasing processes. This is going to vary from company to company, from department to department, and from individual to individual.

For example, some companies might be completely comfortable letting employees order supplies from suppliers' websites; other companies of the same size and type might frown on this, and instead dictate old-school purchasing processes involving printed purchase orders and the like. There's no point in building out your online ordering capabilities if your customers aren't allowed to order online.

There's more than just ordering to consider, however; you can also use the Internet to deliver important pre-purchase information. Again, how you deliver this information depends on the embrace of various digital media by specific companies and individuals.

Take mobile marketing, for example. Although it's unlikely that buyers are going to be placing orders from their mobile phones (although that might differ in certain types of companies), more and more decision makers are using their phones to peruse information about the products and services they buy. Maybe buyers are doing their purchasing homework at home, maybe while they're on the road, but mobile phones (or, for that matter, iPads and other tablets) are increasingly replacing desktop and notebook PCs as Internet access devices. For this reason, developing a mobile version of your website (and new ways to push content formatted for mobile devices) might be a critical part of your digital marketing strategy.

Social marketing is another interesting vehicle to consider. Although this is probably not a great medium for garnering new leads, it can be a terrific way to strengthen relationships and encourage communication with existing customers—assuming those customers are allowed to access Facebook et al from work. You might find that you can reduce your sales burden by transferring much of that interaction to social networks, blogs, and web-based message forums.

That said, individuals at different levels of an organization are likely to embrace digital media in different ways. It's a bit of a generalization, but the higher up an individual is in the management hierarchy, the less likely he or she is to use or even be aware of emerging digital technologies. It's stereotypical but not uncommon to find upper management types who don't (or can't!) access their own email; yes, some administrative assistants still print out email messages for their bosses to read. If a higher-up can't be relied on to hit his own email inbox, you definitely won't be able to reach him via Twitter or podcast.

Conversely, lower-echelon (and younger) staff are more likely to be familiar with new digital media. That assistant buyer just out of college is going to be more on top of technology (especially social media and mobile technology) than even you are, which means she'll be a willing recipient of all your new media marketing. In fact, if you don't embrace new technology in your marketing, you're likely to lose that individual as a customer.

It all comes down to knowing who you're selling to—being able to *think like the customer*, which is one of my long-time mantras. Just make sure to define your customer as not only the company but also the individual, and then determine just how they use which technologies.

> "It all comes down to knowing who you're selling to— being able to *think like the customer*, which is one of my long-time mantras."

The Bottom Line

Audience segmentation is important in order to deliver the most targeted message in the most appropriate fashion. There are many ways to segment your customer base; you can define your segment characteristics ahead of time, or let your customers naturally fall into appropriate segments. When defining your segments, you should consider both organizational and purchasing characteristics.

After you define your customer segments, you then need to determine which digital media are most appropriate to each segment. Different types of companies, and different types of buyers, all use technology differently. Make sure that your target customers have access to and actually use a given medium before you add it to your digital marketing mix.

3

Planning for Reach

Most B2B companies experience a similar customer life cycle. It all starts with making a potential customer aware of your company or products, moves through acquisition of that prospect and conversion into a paying customer, and ends up with efforts to retain that customer and build on his loyalty to attract additional customers.

There are specific marketing activities that drive the success (or failure) of each stage in this life cycle, starting with the first stage: reach. Digital media can play a significant role in making prospects aware of what you have to offer—or, at least, some digital media can. Different media are differently suited for the five parts of the customer life cycle, and you need to know which digital media can help you reach out to new customers.

Understanding the B2B Buying Continuum

I like the way that marketing experts Jim Sterne and Matt Cutler describe the B2B customer life cycle—or, as they call it, the buying continuum (see Figure 3.1). I particularly like the concept of a continuum, in that the final stage circles around and leads back into the first stage again for a new group of customers. It's a circle of life kind of thing.

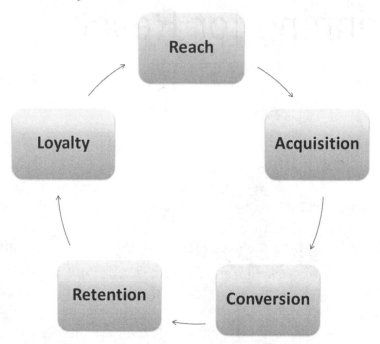

Figure 3.1   *The five stages of the B2B buying continuum.*

Sterne and Cutler define a five-step buying continuum, as follows:

- **Reach**—The life cycle begins by you reaching out to capture the attention of a prospective customer—to let him know about your company, products, and services.
- **Acquisition**—After you make yourself known to a prospect, you then bring that person or company into your sphere of influence—you provide the information necessary for that prospect's decision-making process.
- **Conversion**—If you do your work well, you then turn that potential customer into a paying customer—that is, the prospect makes a purchase.
- **Retention**—After the first purchase, you do whatever it takes to keep that person or company as a customer.

- **Loyalty**—Over time, the existing customer turns into a company advocate who reaches out to other people or companies with your company's message—and thus begins a new life cycle for another new customer.

> ✉ *Note*
>
> The five steps in the B2B buying continuum are not always clear cut; there's a bit of fuzziness between them. Where, for example, does reach end and acquisition begin? Is there really a hard line between retention and loyalty? The point isn't to obsess over the lines between the steps, but merely to recognize the continuum itself, and focus on the marketing strategies that best lead to success across the entire customer life cycle.

Of course, not all potential customers flow through the entire continuum; some aren't interested in your message, some don't convert into paying customers, and some paying customers become ex-customers over time, for whatever reason. Ideally, however, you can lead a prospect through all the steps in the life cycle and keep him satisfied enough to retain him as a repeating customer and turn him into a goodwill ambassador for your company.

As you might expect, different marketing activities are better suited for different steps in the buying continuum. Outbound marketing activities work best for reach and acquisition; conversion happens closer to home; and activities that inspire involvement and two-way communication are best for the retention and loyalty phases of the game. And it's the same whether you're using traditional or digital media; you need to choose the right marketing activities for what you're trying to accomplish at each stage of the buying continuum.

Reaching Out to New Customers

New customers are the lifeblood of any B2B company. Although you certainly need to maintain your existing customer base, you need new customers to grow—which is where reach comes in.

How Do You Reach New Customers?

Reach is the first part of the B2B buying continuum; everything starts from here (see Figure 3.2). Before you can make a sale, you have to acquire a new customer, and before that happens you have to make that potential customer aware of you and your offerings. That's what reach is all about.

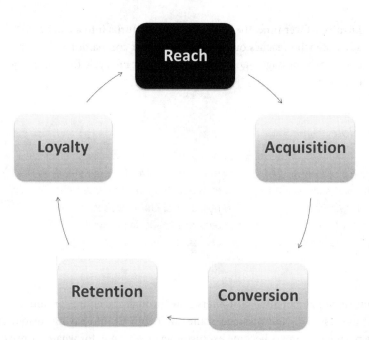

Figure 3.2 *The B2B customer life cycle starts with reach.*

Reach is all about spreading your message, hopefully in places where prospective customers will see or hear it. In traditional B2B marketing, reach is accomplished when your message is seen—or presumed to be seen. For example, reach can be accomplished by placing an ad in an industry periodical or getting an editorial mention from one of your press releases.

It's important to note that reach does not imply awareness—only potential awareness. That is, reach does not require proof that your message was actually read, studied, or paid attention to. It does, however, assume that such attention was possible, if not likely.

> "Reach is all about spreading your message, hopefully in places where prospective customers will see or hear it."

With digital marketing, you can quantify reach with more precision, if merely because you can track clicks online. (You can't track views of print or broadcast ads, as you're well aware.) Every time you get a click on a pay-per-click (PPC) ad, blog link, or similar item, you've achieved reach. What happens next, then, determines whether you actually acquire that customer.

Marketing for Reach

It goes without saying that marketing is the key factor in the reach process. Traditionally, reach has involved a variety of marketing activities designed to generate sales leads; your salespeople then follow up on these leads in the hope of acquiring a new customer.

These traditional reach-based marketing activities include the following:

- Advertising (typically in industry and trade publications)
- Public relations
- Trade shows and conferences
- Telemarketing
- Direct mail

In addition, many companies buy leads that then feed either into direct mail programs or are used for cold calling. Customer referrals also factor into the process.

Using Digital Media to Reach New Customers

Here's the good news: Digital marketing can enhance or even replace these traditional reach-based activities, often at a lower cost. When you're talking web-based marketing, you're looking at more and different ways to get the attention of potential customers.

Which digital media are best for reaching new B2B customers? See Figure 3.3. It's the outbound media that are key at the stage of the life cycle.

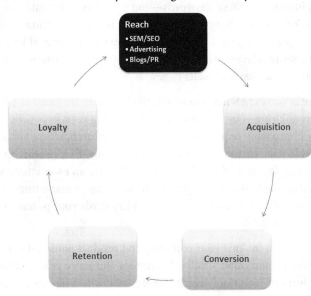

Figure 3.3   *Digital marketing activities used to achieve reach.*

Search Engine Marketing

When it comes to getting the attention of potential new customers, nothing beats Google. That is, more new customers are going to come to your website from Google and other search engines than from anyplace else online.

The importance of search engine marketing for B2B companies rivals that of their B2C cousins. It's a simple fact: More people, in the business world and out of it, find what they're looking for by searching for it.

This doesn't diminish the importance of other digital marketing vehicles; advertising and PR and all those things still matter and still need to be part of your marketing mix. It's just that search engines drive a considerable amount of traffic to your website, and that traffic can turn into valid acquisitions—and conversions.

As you're probably aware, the process of working to improve your search engine rankings is called *search engine marketing*, and it revolves around a process called *search engine optimization*. That is, you need to optimize your website for search so that your site shows up high in the rankings when someone searches for what you're selling.

Search engine optimization starts with the content of your website. Your site has to offer content that is of interest to and valuable for potential B2B customers.

You then have to identify what topics potential customers are likely to be searching for. This drives your selection of keywords, which are used to describe your site—both to customers and to the search engines.

Finally, you have to use those keywords—and design your website—in ways that help Google, Yahoo!, and Bing recognize what it is you're offering, and match your site up with appropriate searchers. The better you let Google et al know what you offer, and the more relevant what you offer is to potential customers, the higher your site will rank on search results pages.

The key here is knowing what potential B2B customers are likely to be searching for, and then tailoring your site content and choosing your keywords appropriately. This will probably require a bit of keyword research, where you or a research firm gets inside your customers' heads to find out how they're searching, what they're searching for, and where they're doing it. This isn't something you can guess at; a surprisingly significant portion of your digital marketing activities are driven by keywords, so you better know what keywords your potential customers are likely to be using.

These keywords can include your company and product names, the name of the industry you're in, and other similar descriptors. But more powerful keywords exist, in the form of "solution" words that describe what your customers hope to achieve from using your products or services. Again, I must stress how important it is to think of SEO from the external viewpoint of your existing and potential customers, not from the internal perspective of your middle or senior management.

✉ *Note*

Learn more about using search engine marketing for reach in Chapter 10, "B2B Search Engine Marketing."

PPC Advertising

You can't beat search engine marketing for putting your company in front of prospective new customers. But there are other digital media that are also effective, including (but not limited to) PPC advertising.

Pay-per-click (PPC) advertising puts your message, in the form of a small text ad, in front of people searching for the same keywords used in your search engine marketing. It's not an organic listing, and thus has a lower response rate than organic search results, but it still gets your name and message in front of interesting potential purchasers.

In essence, a PPC ad can double your presence on a search results page. Someone searching for "HVAC systems," for example, might see your web result in Google's normal search listings, but also see your paid ad on the same page. The appearance of both organic and paid listings reinforce each other; having two shots on the same page alone should increase your response rate.

That's the upside of PPC advertising, along with the fact that you don't pay for an ad until an interested party clicks on it. The downside is that most searchers, especially business professionals, recognize PPC ads for what they are, and are likely to dismiss them accordingly. Your response rate for a PPC ad is going to be much less than for an organic listing in Google's search results.

Another downside of PPC advertising, unique to the B2B community, is the ability (or lack of) to limit exposure of a PPC strictly to business searchers, and even to those in your particular industry niche. Delivering a B2B ad to an audience that consists of general consumer searchers is a waste of exposure; you can only hope that consumers seeing the ad don't feel compelled to click it and thus force you to pay for that click. Which means, of course, that you need to work hard on fine-tuning the list of keywords you bid on for your ad; any way you can filter the potential results to B2B customers will result in a more efficient ad buy.

With PPC advertising, you can't filter by demographics or even business type, only by keyword. This can result in too many consumers receiving your B2B message, which is wasteful on many counts. You don't want to waste scarce resources on unqualified leads such as those typically generated by PPC advertising—which is why some B2B marketers are minimizing or eliminating the use of PPC advertising in their campaigns, in favor of more demographically targeted vehicles.

✉ *Note*

Learn more about using PPC and display advertising for reach in Chapter 11, "B2B Online Advertising."

Display Advertising

To that end, online display advertising might be more efficient than PPC advertising for B2B campaigns. Instead of targeting ad visibility by keyword, you can instead purchase space on specific websites, based on any number of qualities you specify—including demographics.

This means you can target display advertising to specific industry websites and blogs. You pick where the ad appears, rather than relying on Google's AdWords PPC advertising program to do the picking for you. You end up with more control over your advertising, and ideally displaying your ad on a smaller but more appropriate list of sites.

In many ways, online display advertising is the digital equivalent of traditional trade advertising—that is, ads placed in trade periodicals. You reach much the same audience, only online instead of in print.

Of course, you then have the challenge of capturing those customers who view your ads; that's what the customer acquisition process is all about, as we'll discuss in the next chapter. This acquisition is made easier because of the ability to track every single click and view online—something you can't do with traditional print advertising.

Blog Marketing

Another effective way to get your name in front of prospective B2B customers is to get talked about on blogs that cater to those customers. Every industry has them; I'm talking about industry-specific blogs, run either by commercial entities or by individuals who know the business. A mention or recommendation from a respected blogger is the best word-of-mouth promotion any B2B company can receive, and can result in a large number of highly targeted leads.

Naturally, you want to be able to track the traffic you drive from these blogs, which is easy enough to do, so that you can determine which blogs are more effective than others. You also want to make it easy for potential customers who visit your website or call your toll-free number after reading a sympathetic blog post to leave their contact information, download additional information, or even place an order, if they're ready for that.

 Note

Learn more about using blogs for reach in Chapter 13, "B2B Blog Marketing."

Online PR

This type of marketing through third-party bloggers should be part of your online public relations program. That is, bloggers are just as important as trade journal editors and the like when it comes to helping to spread the word about what you offer. They just happen to publish their work online rather than off.

In fact, your entire public relations program changes when you move into the digital realm. Online PR needs to target any individual, online or off, who can reach and influence your potential customers. There's probably less real-world wining and dining and schmoozing involved with online PR; you're more likely to make contact via email or instant message than via press releases and phone calls.

It's not just bloggers you need to promote to. You'll want to target anyone who writes about your products or industry, figuring that even magazine writers today are likely to be connected and desire information and materials be sent to them online. The point here is to use web-based tools to make contact with influencers in any media.

 Note

Learn more about using PR for reach in Chapter 16, "B2B Public Relations."

Mobile Marketing

Mobile marketing is not a huge component of your reach marketing, but it is a factor, if only because the people you need to reach are increasingly accessing the Internet via mobile devices instead of PCs. To that end, you want to make sure that all your outbound marketing activities are optimized not just for viewing on computer monitors, but also for viewing on mobile screens. You'll also want to optimize your website for mobile search, and perhaps consider placing mobile PPC and display ads.

 Note

Learn more about using mobile marketing in Chapter 17, "B2B Mobile Marketing."

Which Digital Media Are Less Suited for Reach?

Those digital media that are best suited for reach are those focused on delivering an outbound message in a relatively targeted fashion. Other digital media are less well suited for reaching new customers—and should be held in reserve for the later stages of the B2B marketing continuum.

Email Marketing

Email marketing is an important weapon in the B2B digital marketing arsenal, every bit as important as direct mail is in traditional B2B marketing. But it's best used to maintain contact with your existing customer base, not to reach new customers.

Here's why.

If you use email to reach out to new customers, that email is by nature unsolicited. That is, the businesses to which you send these introductory emails did not explicitly agree in advance to receive such emails. This means you're sending out unsolicited commercial email (UCE), the very definition of *spam*. And nobody, especially those in the corporate environment, likes to be spammed.

That's right, unless you get explicit permission from a person or company to send them email, anything you email them is considered spam. Now, spam exists because some percentage of recipients actually do read, click, and purchase from the spam messages. This percentage, however, is low—and especially so in the corporate environment, where automated spam filters work amazingly well. The bulk of spam messages, then, are either caught by spam filters or end up as unwanted junk in recipients' inboxes, which does not endear senders to those recipients.

So, here's what happens if you send out unsolicited "get to know us" emails. One, most of them don't actually get read; that's spam filtering at work. Two, most of those that do get through the spam filters get summarily deleted by the recipients, without even being read. Three, those few messages that get through the spam filters and do get read register in a negative fashion with recipients; that is, a buyer reads your message, registers it as junk, and decides never, ever to do business with your company in the future.

Oh, and maybe one or two people who receive the email will actually contact you for more information. Is that small positive response worth the potential negative response?

Are there any exceptions to the no-email rule for reaching new customers? You might think so, but not really.

What about those names you rent or purchase from list brokers or related companies? Assuming you're dealing with legitimate companies, it's likely these names consist of individuals or companies who have checked an option on another site that their names can be shared with other companies. That's consent, I suppose, but typically not well considered. It's likely that any email you send to these names will still be considered spam, even though permission was implicitly (not explicitly) granted.

Then there are those names you acquire on your own, from your website, at trade shows, and so forth. Can you send introductory emails to these folks?

The answer here is, probably yes—assuming that you made clear that in return for providing their names, you'd be contacting them in some fashion. That's kind of an implicit agreement, in any case; you should probably make it explicit when collecting the names.

I would recommend, however, that even in this instance you avoid general cattle call emails. You'll get a better response if you personalize the emails you send, rather than sending out a generic "here's what we offer" message to all.

In any case, you'll get a much better response from emails you send to existing customers who've explicitly signed up for your email mailing lists. Email is a great way to keep in touch with your customer base—but a horribly ineffective and inefficient way to reach new customers.

Multimedia Marketing

When you think multimedia marketing, start by thinking about YouTube and other forms of video marketing. With tens of millions of videos being viewed every day, you'd think that YouTube would be a great way to reach prospective new customers.

Unfortunately, you'd be wrong—at least in the B2B field.

Although it's true that many B2C customers successfully use YouTube to attract new customers, it just doesn't cut the mustard when it comes to B2B. That's because YouTube is a community for the general public, not for businesses. It's a fun site, not one where you get a lot of work done. Because of that, YouTube just isn't a good place to find prospective new business customers; unlike regular consumers, key company employees don't spend their days surfing YouTube looking for fun videos to watch. The people you want to reach simply aren't there—at least not in a work-related mode.

That doesn't mean that YouTube shouldn't be part of your marketing mix, just that it isn't well suited to the reach stage of the customer life cycle. Yes, you can use YouTube to deliver all sorts of important product information in video format, but it isn't the place to make that first contact.

Nor, for that matter, are podcasts and webcasts great for reaching new customers. Again, podcasts and webcasts are great for delivering information necessary in other parts of the buying continuum, but just putting some podcasts out on the Internet and launching some interesting webinars aren't going to attract a lot of potential customers.

Social Media Marketing

Social media marketing is the hottest thing going today. And although Facebook, Google+, Twitter, and the like are powerful tools for building strong relationships with both B2C and B2B customers, they are not great media for making initial contact.

Social networks afford a distinctive two-way relationship between companies and their customers. This is true for both B2C and B2B companies, although it's taking off a little slower in the B2B world. You send out a communication via Facebook or Twitter or whatever, and your customers not only read that communication, they respond to it. It's that active and near-real-time talkback that makes social media marketing unique.

However, for someone or some company to both find you on Facebook or Twitter and commit to following you, they have to know about you, trust you, and have a vested interest in you. It is unlikely that someone who is not yet a customer will follow you on a social network—why should they?

No, most of the friends and fans and followers you get online will be existing customers—and not casual ones, either. Your social media followers will likely be your more loyal and vocal customers, those with a vested interest in your company, products, and services. That's great for solidifying that existing customer relationship, but not so great when it comes to attracting new customers.

Bottom line, it's unlikely that you'll attract a lot of new customers on Facebook, Twitter, and the like. It's not unheard of, but probably not a good focus for this particular digital marketing activity. Focus your social media marketing on your existing customer base, and turn to other digital media for reaching new customers.

Website Marketing

Reach is all about outbound marketing. Your website, however, isn't outbound at all; it just sits there waiting for people to visit it. You have to do a lot of outbound marketing to attract visitors to your site.

As such, your website is probably not a key component of your reach marketing. It's important for other stages of the buying continuum—acquisition and conversion, especially—but it doesn't reach out and touch anyone by itself.

> "Reach is all about outbound marketing. Your website, however, isn't outbound at all; it just sits there waiting for people to visit it."

CAN DIGITAL MEDIA REPLACE TRADITIONAL REACH ACTIVITIES?

Digital media can significantly expand your customer acquisition efforts, often at lower cost than traditional means. Does this mean that you should abandon traditional customer acquisition activities in favor of digital ones?

Not necessarily. In many cases, you reach *different* customers online than you do in print, at trade shows, or via telemarketing. Some companies are not yet comfortable moving their purchasing decisions online, which means they'll never see your online efforts. Other companies might have moved some parts of the process online, but still send buyers to trade shows and the like. In these instances, you'll still need to reach these prospects the old school way.

In other instances, you have industry biases to consider. That is, some industries are just slow in embracing new technology. If the industry is overly traditional, to the point of being Luddite-ish, you're stuck with reaching them via print ads and phone calls; you'll never get a response from PPC ads and emails.

That said, your budget for digital marketing activities will not appear out of thin air. Rare is the B2B company that doubles its budget so that it can do both traditional and digital marketing. It's likely that you'll have to fund digital marketing activities from your existing budget, which means reducing the funds you use for traditional activities. Not totally eliminating those activities, mind you, but scaling them back while you shift funds to the digital side.

When it comes to traditional versus digital B2B marketing, it doesn't have to and shouldn't be one or the other. The two can co-exist—if you manage your budget intelligently.

The Bottom Line

When it comes to reaching new customers, digital media can significantly supplement traditional marketing activities—and, perhaps, reach customers not accessible via traditional media. In particular, search engine marketing, PPC and display advertising, blog marketing, and online PR are good for reaching potential new customers, all at relatively low cost.

4

Planning for Customer Acquisition

After you reach out to get the attention of a potential customer, you need to bring that person or company into the fold. This is the customer acquisition process.

How do you acquire new customers? The process is part marketing-driven, part sales-driven—which means there's a significant role for digital media.

Understanding the Customer Acquisition Process

Customer acquisition typically involves capturing a prospect's name and contact information, and getting their okay to actually contact them about your products and services. That enters you into their purchasing decision-making process; it gets you into the game, which hopefully leads to a sale at some point in the future.

In the B2B buying continuum, customer acquisition follows from reach and leads into conversion (see Figure 4.1). It includes the following activities:

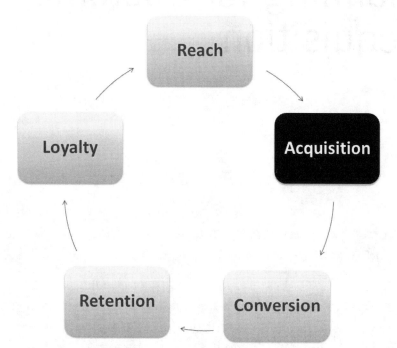

Figure 4.1 *Acquisition is the second stage of the B2B customer life cycle.*

- Generating customer inquiries
- Following up on customer inquiries
- Providing the customer with information to inform the decision-making process
- Leading the customer into the purchase itself

In other words, the acquisition process moves beyond initially getting the customer's attention to entice them into further inquiries, and providing all necessary information they need to make a purchasing decision—and move to the next stage of the customer life cycle, conversion.

Traditional Marketing for Customer Acquisition

Naturally, marketing plays a big part in the customer acquisition process. It's all about giving prospects enough information to enter into the decision-making process in an informed and intelligent fashion—and then generating solid leads that can lead to sales.

These activities typically include the following:

- Advertising (typically in industry and trade publications)
- Public relations
- Trade shows and conferences
- Direct mail

In addition, many companies buy or rent lists of names that then feed either into direct mail programs or are used for cold calling. Customer referrals also factor into the process—and, in fact, convert to sales at a much higher rate than any other source.

And, of course, the marketing department is responsible for generating all manner of sales collateral that provide vital information about your company and products for potential customers. We're talking brochures, handouts, white papers, catalogs, you name it.

Using Digital Media to Acquire New Customers

Here's the good news: Digital marketing can enhance or even replace these traditional customer acquisition activities, often at a lower cost. When you're talking web-based marketing, you're looking at more and different ways to inform potential customers and generate leads.

The reach process revolved around outbound digital media—search engine marketing, pay-per-click (PPC) and display advertising, blog marketing and PR. Customer acquisition builds on these media in ways that provide a more in-depth customer experience—primarily via use of your company website (see Figure 4.2).

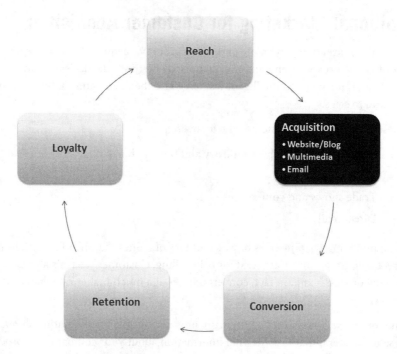

Figure 4.2 *Digital marketing activities used for customer acquisition.*

Website Marketing

Whichever digital media you use to get the attention of prospective customers, the actual acquisition process can still involve human beings—your sales force, meeting with potential clients either online or via the phone. With digital media, however, you can actually acquire new customers online as well—by directing all interested parties to your company's website.

Your website is the hub of all your online marketing activities. Everything you do leads customers to your website: people searching for what you offer click to your site from Google and other search engines; PPC and display ads, when clicked, lead customers to your site; even mentions in industry blogs, when clicked, drop readers on your site.

"Your website is the hub of all your online marketing activities. Everything you do leads customers to your website..."

To that end, you have to design your site with three distinct goals in mind:

- Provide the necessary information, in whatever format, for prospective customers to make a purchasing decision—or at least to inform their company's decision-making process.

- Provide the mechanism to collect prospect's contact information. After you have that contact info, you have a lead that your sales force can follow up on.

- Provide the mechanism to register a new account and accept customer orders. (Assuming you'll be selling online, that is; you might want to keep conversion a more traditional process.) This could involve collecting enough information to do a credit check, set up delayed billing or invoicing, and the like.

Let's stop and look at that first bullet in more depth because there's a lot that's involved there. Virtually every piece of collateral material you produce traditionally—catalogs, brochures, handouts, white papers, you name it—needs to be converted to digital format and made available on your website. In addition, you can place even *more* informative material online; consider creating digital versions of company presentations, product videos, and the like.

In short, you need to place as much information as possible online—because potential customers will be looking for it. The more information you place in the hands of prospective customers, the more comfortable they're going to be with your company—and the more likely they'll convert to paying customers. Don't skimp on what you make available; this is one area where you want to go whole hog.

And the good thing about placing marketing material online is that it's relatively cheap to do so. You don't actually have to print any of those expensive four-color brochures; just write them and design them and put them online in PDF format. Potential customers can do the downloading and printing, or just read them online. This makes your production costs minimal, while maximizing the available information.

✉ *Note*

You have to make sure that your marketing materials are easily found wherever potential customers happen to be on your website, and then easily viewed or downloaded from there. That might mean providing multiple means of access to a given piece, depending on where customers are coming from.

Just remember, your website is where prospects become customers, and perhaps even where interest is converted to sales. Provide whatever it takes to create a successful conversion.

✉ *Note*

Learn more about using your website for customer acquisition in Chapter 9, "B2B Website Marketing."

"Just remember, your website is where prospects become customers, and perhaps even where interest is converted to sales."

WHAT FORMAT IS BEST?

When it comes to providing brochures and such online, what is the best format for these items? There is a bit of debate on the subject.

Some companies see nothing wrong with making collateral materials available in Microsoft Office formats—brochures in Word format, presentations in PowerPoint format, and so forth. It might be safe to assume that corporate buyers will be using Microsoft Office and thus be able to read these file formats, but it misses the bigger issues of controlled display and security.

Security first. If you make a brochure available in Word format, for example, then a visitor to your site can download and view your document in Microsoft Word. That also means they'll be able to *edit* your document in Word—and you might not want them to do that. Do you really want someone else to have control over your message, even if it's just for the seemingly innocuous purpose of deleting those sections not of interest to some people in the customer's company? Any change to your official corporate message is unwelcome, and can have catastrophic results.

You also have the problem of accuracy of display. You go to a lot of trouble to design and lay out your brochures and such in a particular fashion. If you let someone view them in Word or PowerPoint on their own PCs, they might not have the same fonts installed or the same settings configured; the end result can look a lot different than you intended. Again, not ideal.

For this reason, I recommend you save and upload your collateral material in Adobe PDF format wherever possible. PDF files are designed to retain the integrity of the source document, which means they'll look like you want them to look, no matter what computer is used to view them. And, unless you change the default security settings, viewers can't edit or otherwise alter the document's contents. It's a win-win situation for marketers.

Blog Marketing

Perhaps the most important component of acquisition marketing is providing enough information for prospects to want to become customers. Any way you can provide that information should be pursued.

To that end, creating a company blog is a great way to impart all sorts of useful information to prospective and current customers. You can blog about new products and services; you can blog about industry trends; you can blog about the people behind the scenes at your company. It's all good, and it all provides useful background for any company thinking of doing business with you.

Of course, you don't want your blog to be purely self-serving and promotional. Your company blog has to offer information and advice of use to your customer base and those interested in joining the team. But providing that information serves a valuable role in the customer acquisition process; just make sure your blog is easily found by potential customers looking for more information.

 Note

Learn more about using your blog for customer acquisition in Chapter 13, "B2B Blog Marketing."

Multimedia Marketing

As you remember from the previous chapter, multimedia marketing—in particular video and audio marketing—isn't that well suited for attracting the attention of potential customers; search engine marketing, advertising, and PR are much better at getting the word out. But audios and videos are great for providing information useful to the decision-making process of potential customers researching and evaluating future purchases.

What's important here is the fact that different types of people—including and especially different types of business buyers—like to receive information in different ways. Some people like to pour over all the fine details in a product brochure or white sheet, whereas others prefer to find out what they need to know in visual fashion.

Does your product involve some sort of set up or configuration process? Then demonstrate that process in a YouTube video. Would some potential customers feel more comfortable if they could tour your factory first? Then give them a virtual factory tour, via video. Can't send a salesperson to personally demonstrate your product to every prospect on your list? Then put together a product tour video and let YouTube do the selling for you.

You get the idea; there's a lot of supplemental information you can disseminate via online videos and podcasts. This information can help prospective customers make informed purchasing decisions, and in a more cost-effective way (especially for smaller and mid-size customers) than traditional methods.

For that matter, you might be able to reduce your trade show or conference presence by hosting a regular series of webcasts or webinars instead. It's a lot cheaper to put together a web-based conference for potential customers around the country than it is to fly them all in to a central physical conference. Plus, you're likely to get better attendance, especially when prospects can schedule these webinars at their own convenience, instead of having to drop everything to travel on your schedule. It's a great way to get one-on-one interaction without having both parties to travel to the same room. You can also archive them for future use.

> ✉ *Note*
>
> Learn more about using multimedia for customer acquisition in Chapter 15, "B2B Audio, Video, and Interactive Marketing."

Email Marketing

Although you shouldn't blindly send out unsolicited emails to prospects (that's spam), you can send out emails in response to customer inquiries. Does a potential customer need more information to make a purchase decision? Naturally, you can send that information (or links to it posted elsewhere) via email.

It's a safe assumption that the businesspeople you communicate with will all have corporate email accounts. (That might no longer be true for the general population; consumers, especially younger ones, are instead trending away from email and using social media for communication.) If you can score an email address—or just have someone sign up on your website or at a trade show to receive more information—then you're in the clear.

Know, of course, that there's a limit to what and how much you can include in or attach to an email message. Some spam filters and corporate filters will block messages with large attachments, or with any attachments at all—even if the customer has opted into the mailing. Unless you're well acquainted with a given individual and what works and doesn't for him, it's probably safer to include links to where given materials can be found on your website or elsewhere.

> ✉ *Note*
>
> Learn more about using email for customer acquisition in Chapter 12, "B2B Email Marketing."

Mobile Marketing

What role does mobile marketing play in the customer acquisition process? When you note that business users of all stripes—including purchasing staff and senior management—are increasingly accessing the Internet via smart phones, tablets, and other mobile devices, you realize that mobile marketing affects every other acquisition-based digital marketing activity.

That is, everything you do online to acquire new customers has to be accessible both on traditional desktop and notebook PCs and on the smaller screens of smart phones and other mobile devices. That starts with creating a mobile-friendly version of your website, and leads to optimizing your site for mobile search, placing mobile PPC and display ads, optimizing your videos for mobile viewing, and the like.

Equally important, all your online collateral materials—brochures, white papers, presentations, and the like—have to be formatted to be properly viewed on mobile devices. Even if prospective customers use traditional PCs to access the Internet while in the office, they might be using their iPhones and BlackBerrys to do their pre-purchase research while they're out of the office. You have to be prepared for that, and embrace mobile marketing accordingly.

> ✉ *Note*
>
> Learn more about using mobile media for customer acquisition in Chapter 17, "B2B Mobile Marketing."

Which Digital Media Are Less Suited for Acquisition?

In the world of digital marketing, the customer acquisition process revolves around your company's website and the information you make available there. That makes other digital media less important to and effective in customer acquisition.

Search Engine Marketing

Potential customers use search engines to find you; that's part of the reach process. After they've found you, they don't need to search for you anymore. Which means that search engine marketing, as crucial as it is for initial reach, becomes increasingly irrelevant the further one progresses through the B2B customer life cycle.

PPC and Display Advertising

It's the same thing with online advertising. You use online ads to reach potential customers, not to provide in-depth information. It's simply not an important part of acquisition marketing.

Online PR

Public relations is great for getting in front of potential customers. It's not so great for delivering in-depth information. That's just the way it is.

Social Media Marketing

Facebook, Twitter, and Google+ are great ways to connect with existing customers—but not with not-yet-acquired customers. Acquire the customer first, and then maintain the relationship via social networking.

The Bottom Line

When it comes to acquiring new customers, digital media can significantly supplement traditional marketing activities. In this part of the B2B buying continuum, it's your website that's most important, supplemented by your company blog, multimedia activities, and email. Equally important, you should make all your collateral material available online—and formatted for mobile devices as well as traditional computers.

5

Planning for Sales Conversion

Arguably the most important part of the B2B buying continuum is the part where the customer actually buys something. This is the conversion process, where serious leads convert to become actual customers.

Traditionally, conversion was the responsibility of your company's sales force; all your marketing activities led to this point, and then the marketing department handed off to the sales department to close the deal. Although that is still the way it happens in many cases, you can also use digital media to convert leads into customers. It's all a matter of trusting technology as much as you trust your flesh-and-blood sales experts.

Understanding Conversion

Conversion lies in the middle of the B2B customer life cycle, and it's what the entire cycle revolves around (see Figure 5.1). You reach out to attract potential customers, acquire them as serious leads, and then convert them to paying customers. After conversion, you work to retain them in your customer base, and use their loyalty to reach more potential customers.

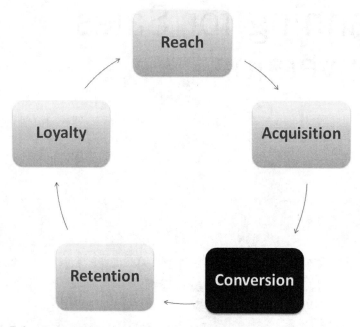

Figure 5.1   *Conversion is the focal point of the B2B buying continuum.*

As I said, it all revolves around conversion. The sole reason to reach and acquire customers is to convert them. And conversion leads to retention and loyalty-based recommendations. It's the center of the B2B buying continuum.

How, exactly, do you convert a lead to a customer? The exact details might differ from industry to industry and company to company, but in general you get the customer to sign on the bottom line. The customer either places an order or generates a purchase order; it's a revenue-generating activity, however it's done.

> "The sole reason to reach and acquire customers is to convert them. And conversion leads to retention and loyalty-based recommendations."

Note that the B2B conversion process is often a lengthy one (see Figure 5.2). When dealing with corporate buyers, it can take a significant amount of time to convert a potential customer into an actual one. It is seldom an immediate or impulse-based process; according to research from MarketingSherpa, 21% of all B2B leads take 12 months or more to convert.[1]

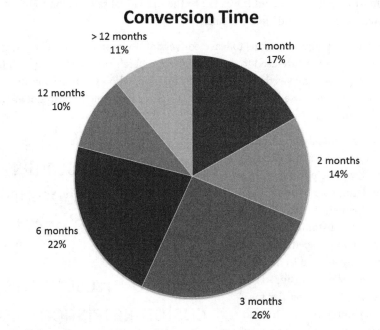

Figure 5.2 *The conversion process is often a lengthy one.*

This explains why reach and acquisition are such important steps in the buying continuum. You have to do your job right in the previous steps in order for the conversion process to occur.

 Note

Don't confuse B2B customer conversion with the type of conversion referenced in website analytics. When it comes to measuring web analytics, conversion refers to the completion of *any* activity on a website. This type of conversion might be a sale, but could also be garnering customer contact information, signing a visitor up for a newsletter, having a customer download a file, or whatever. In contrast, B2B conversion is strictly sales-based; you convert a customer when he or she places the first order.

---

1. MarketingSherpa, "2009-2010 B2B Marketing Benchmark Report," 2009

Converting Customers, the Traditional Way

Up until recently, conversion was the province of the sales department. (It could be the company's sales department, of that of a distributor, VAR, or other business partner.) Marketing might have generated the leads and helped to inform the decision-making process, but it was left to the individual salesperson to make a personal connection and close the sale.

There are several good reasons to leave conversion to your sales force. First, it's the way most customers are used to doing business. There's nothing wrong with tradition; if that's what makes the customer comfortable, who's to argue? Because the ultimate goal is to close the sale, it shouldn't matter how you do it; might as well do it the time-proven way.

Second, and equally important, when you get your sales force involved, you help to forge a personal relationship between your two companies. A one-time sale is fine, but a customer becomes truly profitable over the long term; this means you need to invest in the customer relationship. There's no denying that it's harder for a customer to reject a live human being than it is to ignore a purchase request on a website.

> "A one-time sale is fine, but a customer becomes truly profitable over the long term; this means you need to invest in the customer relationship."

Using Digital Media to Convert Customers

That said, using salespeople to convert *all* potential customers can be both ineffective and inefficient; it costs a lot to personally service each customers, and you might not have enough salespeople to service every prospect you encounter.

This is why many B2B companies are supplementing their traditional conversion operations with online-based conversion. It might be a better and less-costly way to convert smaller customers, or those who aren't serviced with a sales rep close enough to make an in-person call. It's also a good way to help you reach customers you didn't have time or personnel for before.

How do you use digital media in the conversion process? Of all the digital media available, there are only two you can effectively use: your website and your email (see Figure 5.3).

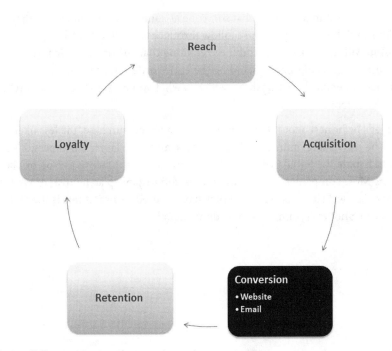

Figure 5.3   *Use your website and email to convert new customers.*

Converting from Your Website

When it comes to enticing the initial order from a would-be customer, your web-site is the tool of choice. You set up your site for secure e-commerce, provide all the necessary ordering information, display a web-based order form, and let the customer have at it.

Or, perhaps, you simply use your website to collect key information from your cus-tomer in preparation of a purchase. That might mean using a web form to gather the information necessary for a credit check, or for recurring billing, or whatever. Again, make sure you provide sufficient instructions for what you need from the purchaser; never leave a customer guessing when it comes to order.

Naturally, you'll need to use SSL security on your site, for secure encrypted trans-actions—even if you're just gathering customer information. You'll also want to make sure that all orders or submissions are handled immediately; you don't want orders sitting around for a few days before you get to them. And always, *always* make sure a human being is around to handle any questions or issues that might arise.

You'll also want to make sure that someone at some point follows up from the customer's initial order. If you don't follow through, you risk establishing a solid relationship with that customer, and thus retaining that customer in the future. You can automate lots of things, including the entire ordering process, but you can't automate a personal relationship—which is what you need to keep that purchaser as a loyal client.

And let's be honest about this. The larger the average purchase, the less likely that you'll be converting online. For larger orders, and even larger customers, it's still best to handle the initial order the old-fashioned way—either in person or via phone. Most companies are not going to be comfortable placing five- or six-figure orders via a website, especially one they haven't used before. If this is the case, that's okay; not everything has to be done digitally.

✉ Note

Learn more about building a website for B2B ecommerce in Chapter 9, "B2B Website Marketing."

IMPROVING CONVERSION ON YOUR WEBSITE

Yes, you can use your website for the all-important conversion process. But how do you ensure that potential customers make that first purchase online? Here are some tips to consider:

- **Build trust**—Do everything you can to establish trust with your potential customer. That means establishing your brand identity and credentials, including strong "about us" content, linking to privacy and returns policies, clearly stating your ordering procedure, and the like.

- **Make it easy**—However you're using your website for conversion, make sure that customers have clear instructions. If you need initial contact or payment information, make that clear. If you have an online shopping cart or order form, post clear instructions on how to place an order. Don't make customers guess; tell them exactly what they need to do.

- **Make it simple**—Along the same lines, don't make the customer work too hard. Simplify your registration or order forms so that they include the minimum number of steps necessary; eliminate any fields that really aren't necessary. And it doesn't hurt to test your forms occasionally to make sure they're really as easy to use as you think they are.

- **Answer their questions**—Some customers might not be completely comfortable ordering online; others might simply have questions about your process or products. To this end, provide appropriate mechanisms for customers to ask their questions, whether that be "live" chat or instant messaging, email, or (better yet) your toll-free phone number.

- **Provide a live alternative**—To the previous point, you should always provide a way for prospects to contact a live person, ideally via an inbound call center. Even if online customers never take advantage of the offline resource, it's good for peace of mind. (And, besides, some prospects will want or need to have that human contact, at some point in the process.)

- **Make it secure**—Naturally, all information that customers submit must be securely encrypted. You don't want your customers to hand any important information to hackers.

- **Make it compelling**—If you want customers to order from your website, tell them that, via a strong call to action. Don't assume that customers will just sit down and order; let prospects know what you want them to do, and strongly encourage them to do it.

Bottom line, you need to make the ordering process as quick and easy as possible. The more you ask of potential customers, the less likely they are to convert. Keeping it simple is paramount.

Converting via Email

> "The more you ask of potential customers, the less likely they are to convert. Keeping it simple is paramount."

Your customers can also send purchase information via email. Instead of slapping a stamp on an envelope and relying on snail mail to wind its way to your office, it's often a lot faster and easier to attach purchase orders to email messages. The order is placed immediately and fulfilled almost as.

Don't get me wrong here. You should never encourage customers to send sensitive payment data via email because it's not secure enough; you need an SSL-encrypted website for that. What you can do, however, is use email to close the sales process and confirm the sale. That is, customers can send purchase information (but not payment information) in the body of an email message, or as a purchase order in another file format attached to an email message. You can then send confirmation information back via email, as well.

What you can't do is let your customers send payment information—bank account or credit card info—via email. It's one thing to send a purchase order saying the customer wants to buy 100 widgets; it's quite another to send payment info via such a nonsecure medium. The last thing you want is some hacker intercepting your customer's email and then draining their credit card or bank accounts.

In addition, as with website ordering, you want to make sure someone in your organization personally follows up on the initial order, especially for larger customers. Yes, you can (and should) send an email confirmation that the order has been received and will be shipped, but it's the personal touch that creates repeat business.

Which Digital Media Are Less Suited for Conversion?

Customer conversion is an extremely important step in the B2B marketing continuum—so important that it's best handled close to home. It's an inbound activity, not an outbound one, and thus less well suited for most digital marketing vehicles.

Here's why:

- **Search engine marketing (SEM)**—Although it's search engine marketing that helps most prospects find out about your company and products, SEM has no role to play in the actual purchasing process; the search is long over by the time the initial purchase is made.

- **Online advertising**—Same thing with pay-per-click (PPC) and display advertising; advertising is how you reach new prospects and has nothing to do with closing the sale.

- **Blog marketing**—Blogs are great for getting the word out and disseminating important information, but they simply aren't a part of the conversion process—short of linking to your website, where orders can then be placed.

- **Social media marketing**—Although you can have your own profile or fan page on Facebook and other social networks, you really can't accept orders from this page. You still need to direct prospects to your real website for the conversion process.

- **Multimedia marketing**—You can't take an order from a YouTube video. 'Nuff said.

- **Online public relations**—PR people are great, but they're not closers. Use your PR department to get the word out, but leave the actual conversion to your salespeople (or your website).

Notice that I haven't yet mentioned mobile marketing as part of the conversion process. That's because mobile's role in this part of the buying continuum is still evolving. Although mobile ecommerce solutions certainly exist, I'm not sure that mobile purchasing is widely accepted in the B2B community—at least for initial orders. While you definitely want to develop a mobile version of your website, including the ability to let customers place orders from their mobile devices, it's likely that this will be used for repeat orders, not for initial ones.

(Of course, I could be wrong on this one; mobile is a rapidly evolving situation. It probably makes sense, then, to provide for new customers on your mobile ecommerce site, but don't be disappointed if that facility is not widely used.)

The Bottom Line

Although many B2B companies still prefer to use their salespeople for conversion (and many customers prefer the human touch, as well), others are moving some or all conversion activities online. You might be able to use your website to sign up more customers than your sales force can currently get to; it's an especially good way to handle smaller customers who might not warrant the hands-on approach. In any case, it makes sense to develop your website for signing up new customers and taking initial orders; you should also be prepared to receive some orders via email.

6

Planning for Customer Retention

After you've converted a prospect into a customer, you now have to work hard—really hard—to retain that customers. Repeat customers are the most profitable, especially for B2B customers; you don't want to waste all the time and money you spend on gaining the customer by losing him to a competitor.

The retention process is where digital media really shine. Retention is all about establishing and maintaining a strong relationship with your customer base, and digital media can do this better than anything available in the world of traditional B2B marketing.

Understanding Customer Retention

Customer retention is what happens—or what you hope happens—after you convert a prospect to a paying customer (see Figure 6.1). A retained customer is one that places a *second* order from you—and a third, and a fourth, and a fifth. It's a customer that's a loyal customer, one who doesn't drop off the radar screen, one that keeps giving and giving.

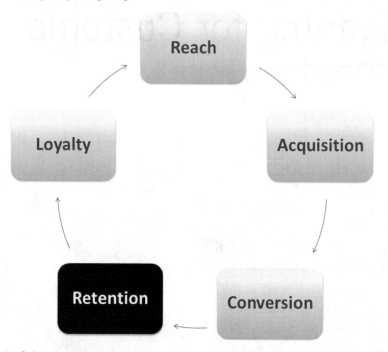

Figure 6.1 *Customer retention is what happens after the conversion process.*

By definition, a retained customer is one who has not defected to competitors. That doesn't always mean that the customer has reordered; some products and services have a very long life cycle, and thus a customer might be in the middle of the process without having yet reordered, and still be retained. It's probably more important to look at intent to reorder, especially on large-ticket products and services, and say a customer is retained when he has that intent.

For B2B customers, customer retention is critical. Given the length and expense of the conversion process, losing a customer means wasting a considerable amount of time and resources; you don't want to spend all that time acquiring a customer and then lose him to a competitor. Indeed, business customers tend to be fewer and more valuable, which means you can't afford to lose even one of them.

What happens if you *don't* retain a customer? Worst case, he's gone forever; you've wasted the initial acquisition resources and will receive no further revenues. You could attempt to re-acquire a lost customer, but that means beginning the acquisition process all over again, pretty much, and incurring additional expense to do so.

In short, it's cheaper to retain an existing customer than it is to acquire a new one. The impact on your bottom line can be substantial; marketing consultant Frederick Reichheld famously estimated that a 5% reduction in defections can increase per-customer profit by anywhere from 35% to 95%.[1] That's right, you can almost double your profit per customer by making sure that customer stays in the fold.

It's unfortunate, then, that the average B2B business loses 50% of its customers every five years. (Or so Reichheld states.) What can you do to improve your retention rate—and your profitability?

Retaining Customers, the Old-Fashioned Way

A client becomes an active part of your customer base when he's happy. Which means, of course, that retention marketing is all about making happy customers. It's that simple—and that complex.

 Note

Retention marketing is one facet of customer relationship management, also known as *CRM*.

Traditional retention marketing revolved around personal relationships. You retained a customer because he liked you. That's the job of your sales force, of course, and nothing could (and still can) beat forging a close, hands-on relationship with your key customers.

Of course, a good sales force needs collateral material for support, especially when massaging new sales out of old customers. That typically means things such as catalogs, newsletters, mailings about sales and specials and new products, and the like. Supporting the sales force could also involve onsite or offsite conferences for key accounts, local or regional get-togethers, and other excuses for meeting face to face. And don't forget all the hand-holding necessary in the name of customer and technical support. As some might say, it takes a village to retain a customer.

---

1. *The Loyalty Effect: The Hidden Force Behind Growth, Profits, and Lasting Value,* Frederick F. Richheld, Harvard Business School Press, 1996 (revised 2001)

Using Digital Media to Retain Your Customers

As you can see, customer retention is resource intensive; a lot of people spend a lot of time making sure that your best customers don't leave the fold. The digital realm, however, can change the equation—at least in regards to certain aspects of customer retention.

Providing Ongoing Customer Service and Support

One of the most important things you can do to keep existing customers happy is to support them if and when they have problems or questions. As you're well aware, providing good customer support is a costly endeavor; it's necessary but expensive. Fortunately, taking customer support digital can save your company big bucks, while providing similar (if not better) support for your customer base.

For example, one of the biggest reasons customers call your support line is to ask for instruction manuals, quickstart guides, and the like—items they should have been (and probably were) supplied with initially but have, like many good things, gone missing. By putting all your documentation and manuals online, you only make it easier for customers to get what they need, reduce your own printing costs, and reduce the number of calls to your support line regarding these materials. That's a nice little hat trick, and all it takes is creating a section of your website devoted to customer support materials.

I also recommend creating a frequently asked questions (FAQ) section on your website, where you address the most common customer questions or problems. I also like using online videos to demonstrate tricky setup or configuration issues, or just show customers how to use what you've just sold them; you'd be surprised how much a good how-to video can reduce the incidence of customer support calls.

You can also encourage customers to submit their customer support questions via email or instant messaging or online chat or even on your company's Facebook page. Going digital with support requests lets you answer more questions on your own timetable, thus improving the efficiency of your support staff.

> ✉ *Note*
>
> It's imperative that you answer online questions *promptly*. Studies have found that if you don't respond to an online question in four hours or less, it negatively affects your brand image.

Finally, consider letting other customers answer your support questions for you. This is one of the joys of social media, being able to "crowd source" questions and answers. All you need to do is creating a message forum on your website or Facebook page, and encourage customers to post their questions there. You'll be amazed how many loyal customers step up to answer tricky questions from other customers—saving you from having to do so.

> ✉ *Note*
>
> By the way, I'm not recommending you fire all your telephone support staff and start answering email questions only. I am suggesting, however, that if you put a lot of support information online, it can reduce the need for phone-based support.

Encouraging Repeat Orders

It might seem a little obvious, but one of the keys to exploiting your existing customer base is simply encouraging repeat orders. Digital media is good for this, even if it's just asking a customer whether he wants to order more of what he did the first time around.

There are many ways to encourage reordering online, but the most common is to send a regularly scheduled email reminding the customer that his supplies are probably running low and now is the time to reorder. Include a link in the email to a personalized page on your website with the suggested order items and quantities already filled in (but editable, of course).

It also helps to design your website so that once an existing customer logs in, the site knows what the customer has previously ordered. That way you can suggest ordering more of what was purchased previously, or suggest similar items or add-on merchandise or services. Definitely work on a "click to reorder" button that takes the customer to a prefilled order page.

Bottom line, make it easy for existing customers to reorder, and don't be shy about suggesting it.

Announcing New Products and Services

Along the same lines, existing customers are prime candidates for any new products and services you launch. You'll want to make sure that you use digital media to make sure your existing customer base is among the first to know about new items they can purchase—especially if these new items supplant or supplement existing products they've been using.

Reinforcing the Customer Relationship

Salespeople work hard to build and then maintain personal relationships with their key customers. You can use various online media to supplement this effort.

Start by making your website as welcoming to existing customers as it is to new ones. Create a section of your site just for current customers, accessible when they sign in with their assigned username and password. Fill this section with information about new products and services, popular add-ons and add-ins, specials and discounts just for old customers, as well as links to available support services.

You should also create a company blog that caters to your existing customer base. Write about your company, your products, and (especially) your people. Consider profiling key customers in the blog, or letting selected customers contribute to the blog from time to time. Do it in such a way that customers will feel like they're part of your family.

You can also use videos to keep in touch with existing customers. Post a regular "message from the president" (or some other important personage), where you keep your customers informed of what's happening in your company and your industry. Make it personal, and focus on items of interest to your customer base.

As to keeping in touch, consider creating a series of web-based seminars, or *webinars*, to replace or supplement your current conference schedule. It's a lot easier for all concerned to get together for a few hours online than it is to schedule a multi-day meeting in some common location. There are lots of tools available for this, and you get the benefit of face-to-face interaction without having actually to be in the same city.

And don't forget email. For many businesses, regular email notices and newsletters can replace existing direct mail efforts, at much lower cost. Set up a periodic email newsletter for your customers, and supplement it with targeted email messages about sales, events, new products, and the like. Use email in this fashion to stay in constant contact with your customers, big and small.

Finally, there's social networking. You can forge a strong customer relationship via the two-way communications encouraged by Facebook, Google+, and other social networks. This is a great way to stay connected with your most loyal customers—and keep them loyal. If you can make customers feel like they're a valued part of your team, they're much less likely to leave you.

CAN DIGITAL MARKETING REPLACE YOUR SALES FORCE?

Although I'm obviously excited about the many ways that digital media can enhance customer retention, I'm not at all suggesting that digital media can replace the people on your sales force. I believe that, in most cases, digital media can supplement the efforts of your human sales force, rather than replace it.

Let's face it; nothing can forge a more resilient tie than a strong personal relationship. If your customer thinks he's dealing with friends (or, even better, with family), he's yours for life. And the only way to forge a personal relationship is personally.

As powerful as today's digital media are, they can't replace the human factor. That said, you can use digital media to support these personal relationships, and to build ties to smaller accounts where frequent personal interaction simply isn't cost effective. But don't even think about canning your star salesman in favor of your Facebook page; today's technology, including social media, are still somewhat impersonal.

Choosing the Right Digital Media for Customer Retention

Given the many ways that digital media can support your customer retention efforts, which digital should you focus on? There are really quite a few, as you can see in Figure 6.2.

"As powerful as today's digital media are, they can't replace the human factor."

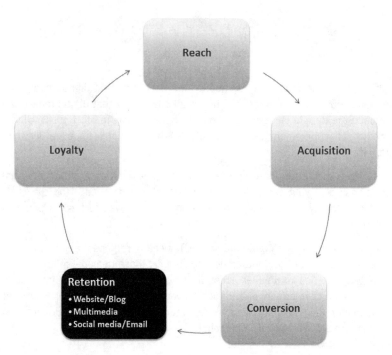

Figure 6.2 *Choose the best media for retaining existing customers.*

Website Marketing

Customer retention, like conversion, is centered on your website—and particularly focused on the ordering function. That is, you need to make it easy for existing customers to place new orders. You should have their ordering and payment information already on hand, so logging in and ordering more stuff needs to be a piece of cake.

In addition, you need to design a customer-only part of your site that houses all the support material you have. Make it easy for customers to read or download instruction manuals and other material that help them use your products and services.

For that matter, consider hosting (or co-hosting) instructional videos on your site. Some customers learn better by watching than by reading, so if you have something that's particularly difficult to do, create a series of how-to videos to show them how to do it.

Finally, make your website the go-to point for all customer support activities. In addition to the downloadable support materials, create a FAQ page, post answers to the most commonly asked questions, offer a web form to post new questions, and include email links to your support staff. If you're into it, consider offering live chat-based support. And don't forget the customer message forum, where all your customers can support each other online.

 Note

Learn more about using your website for customer retention in Chapter 9, "B2B Website Marketing."

Blog Marketing

A company blog is a great form of indirect marketing. That is, don't expect direct results in the form of immediate reorders. Instead, position your blog as a means to solidify existing relationships, to create a family feeling between your company and your customer base. Write about issues of interest to your customers, encourage comments on your posts, and even consider letting selected customers post to your blog. It might seem like a warm fuzzy, but it's a good warm fuzzy that will help to keep customers interested, informed, and in the fold.

 Note

Learn more about using your company blog for customer retention in Chapter 13, "B2B Blog Marketing."

Email Marketing

You can't beat email for putting your message in front of your customer base. You can create all manner of email messages that you send out either en masse or in targeted fashion to selected customers. You can send out sales notices, periodic company or product newsletters, new product announcements, you name it—and the good thing is, your cost per mailing is next to nothing.

Remember, though, that you need to get your customer's permission before you send out any of these emails. Email marketing, even to existing customers, is permission marketing. If it's not, it's spam—and that can annoy existing customers every bit as much as it does anonymous prospects. Make sure your

> "You can't beat email for putting your message in front of your customer base."

customers explicitly sign up to receive your mailings (or voice their approval to a sales rep), then once they do, exploit the medium as much as you can.

✉ *Note*

Learn more about using email for customer retention in Chapter 12, "B2B Email Marketing."

Multimedia Marketing

Multimedia marketing is made for customer retention. Here's what I mean:

- Videos are great for showing customers how to install, configure, and use what you sell. You can also create informative "talking head" videos that talk about company and industry issues; you can even do video tours of your facilities or key customer installations. You can post your videos on YouTube, and then cross-post to your own website. (This lets YouTube absorb the hosting and traffic costs.) Video is a great way to put a personal face on an otherwise impersonal company or product.

- Audio podcasts are another way to keep your customer base informed of company and industry goings on. Record new podcasts on a regular schedule and then encourage your customers to listen in.

- Interactive webinars are a terrific way to get face-to-face interaction without anyone having to travel. Create a series of small webinars for your key accounts, or do big everybody's invited sales presentations online. Either way, it's a hip way to be personal in a new age of curtailed corporate travel.

✉ *Note*

Learn more about using multimedia resources for customer retention in Chapter 15, "B2B Audio, Video, and Interactive Marketing."

Social Media Marketing

When you want to establish a two-way communication online, social networking is the way to go. Create a Facebook page, build a Google+ profile, establish a Twitter feed—do whatever it takes to start the online conversation with your most interested customers.

Social media is unique in its ability to forge direct relationships between your company and your customers. It's not just about making a new post every day or two; it requires constant attention to respond to all the comments and responses that your customers will make. In this regard, social media marketing demands a large time investment (not so much of a monetary investment) on your part. But it's worth it; there's no other medium, online or off, that builds this type of strong connection to your most loyal customers.

 Note

Learn more about using social networks for customer retention in Chapter 14, "B2B Social Media Marketing."

Mobile Marketing

Finally, don't forget mobile. Whether it's placing a reorder, looking for customer support, watching a how-to video, or checking your Twitter feed, it's more and more likely that your customers will be doing it via their mobile phones or iPads instead of their computers. That's just the way it is, and you need to be aware of and prepare for it. Everything you do has to be made mobile-friendly—and you need to consider new activities specifically designed for your more mobile customers.

 Note

Learn more about using mobile marketing for customer retention in Chapter 17, "B2B Mobile Marketing."

Which Digital Media Are Less Likely for Customer Retention?

That's a lot of different ways to reach your customer base online. Are there any digital media that are less effective in retention marketing?

You bet there are. In particular, these media aren't that suited for customer retention:

- **Search engine marketing**—Search results are meaningless after a customer has already found you. Leave search engine marketing for the reach and acquisition phases of the B2B buying continuum.

> ✉ *Note*
>
> Search *within* your website can be important to existing customers, however. Consider adding cross-site search functionality to help customers more quickly find the information and resources they're looking for.

- **Online advertising**—Same thing here. You don't need to advertise to them once you've got them—unless you're a big believer in image advertising to alleviate buyer's remorse.
- **Online public relations**—There might be some value of using PR for retention, although it's minimal. Obviously, you'll task your PR department with publicizing new products and services you introduce, and some of these efforts might reach your existing customer base. But it's really an add-on effect rather than a campaign directed specifically at existing customers. It's more accurate to say that there are few if any PR activities that are exclusive to the retention process.

> "Search results are meaningless after a customer has already found you. Leave search engine marketing for the reach and acquisition phases of the B2B buying continuum."

And there you have it. Aside from these few outbound marketing activities, digital marketing can have a big impact on customer retention.

The Bottom Line

After you've converted a prospect into a customer, you then need to retain that customer as part of your existing and (hopefully) active customer base. Although customer retention is traditionally a hands-on activity designed to build a strong personal relationship, you can enhance the retention process by using a variety of digital media, including your website, your blog, email, audio and video, interactive webinars, and social networks. You should also make sure that all your online retention activities are optimized for mobile users.

7

Planning for
Customer Loyalty

The final stage of the B2B buying continuum or customer life cycle is called loyalty. In this context, a loyal customer isn't just one who has been retained, it's one who recommends your product or services to other potential customers. It brings the life cycle full circle.

How can you build this type of customer loyalty? It's all about making the customer a part of your team—which is something you can use digital media for.

Understanding Customer Loyalty

In the B2B buying continuum, loyalty is all about referrals. That is, the loyalty phase goes beyond simple customer retention into building such a loyal customer that he or she readily recommends you to other potential customers (see Figure 7.1). This starts the life cycle over from scratch for this new prospect, as a new potential customer is reached and hopefully acquired.

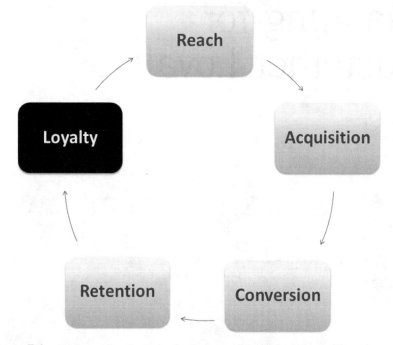

Figure 7.1   *Customer loyalty is the final phase of the B2B customer life cycle.*

> **Note**
>
> Loyal customers are also more directly profitable than regular customers, in that they buy most or all of their requirements from those suppliers they're most loyal to.

Loyalty is built upon a strong long-term relationship between you and the client. It's like planting a seed: When the seed grows into a new plant, your relationship with the first customer has spawned a new relationship with a different potential customer.

The goal, then, is not just to convert a prospect into a customer, or even to retain that customer over the long term; it's to use that customer as a goodwill ambassador to create additional business for your company. One good customer begets another; it's the ultimate expression of word of mouth advertising.

Encouraging Customer Loyalty, the Old School Way

How do you encourage the sort of customer loyalty that leads to new customer referrals? It's a matter of building a strong relationship with the initial customer—and, sometimes, rewarding the customer for spreading the word.

> "The goal, then, is not just to convert a prospect into a customer, or even to retain that customer over the long term; it's to use that customer as a goodwill ambassador to create additional business for your company."

Let's start with the relationship part. This starts, of course, in the retention phase of the B2B buying continuum. As we discussed in the previous chapter, it's a matter of establishing a personal relationship—often literally one-on-one between your salesperson and a contact in the client company. The stronger the relationship, the more likely that the customer will speak highly of you to others.

Of course, there's nothing to say you can't nudge the loyalty process a little. Which is what many B2B companies do, by offering some sort of reward or "finder's fee" for attracting new business. That's right, you can buy loyalty. (And don't be so surprised about that; no one's that naïve!)

This old school approach is surprisingly effective, especially for companies offering lower-cost products and services, or those that tend to be more price sensitive. You offer a bounty of sorts for new customers, either a cash payment or rebate, or some sort of discount on future orders. When a new customer cites an existing customer as a reference, you pay that customer his or her reward.

Using Digital Media to Encourage Customer Loyalty

Customer loyalty takes a giant step forward when wedded to the Internet. That's because certain digital media—social media, specifically—are particularly suited for building strong, interactive relationships between companies and their clients.

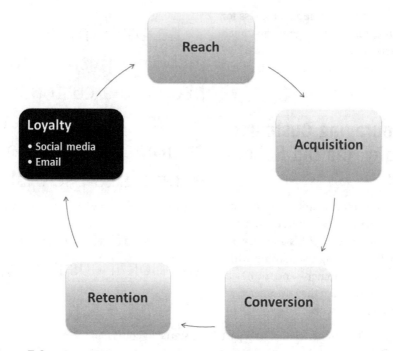

Figure 7.2 *Use social media and email to enhance customer loyalty.*

Social Media Marketing

Social networking is arguably the best way to ensure customer loyalty and encourage referrals and recommendations. Not only do social networks help you forge a tight bond with your best customers, they're also great places for these same customers to spread the word about your company and products.

Think about it. Social networks, such as Facebook and Google+, are all about friends and "liking" things. The opportunity certainly exists for your customers to become your friends (or fans), and for them to express their like of what you do to their other online friends. It's all about building a big online community—and then exploiting the relationships within that community for your own needs.

Key here is establishing a Facebook page, Google+ profile, and Twitter feed for your company or key products. You should promote these presences wherever possible; this includes putting Facebook "like," Google +1, and Twitter "tweet" buttons on your website, blog, and other pages online.

You then encourage your customers to sign up for or "like" your social networking presences, and start posting and tweeting. Remember, though, that social networking is a two-way street, so be prepared for (and actively encourage) comments from your customers on these pages and feeds. That's where the community and the relationship-building start.

From here, you want to encourage these loyal customers to share their like of you with their other social networking friends. (You can do this covertly or overtly; bribery via bounty works just as well online as it does in the real world.) The more people that your online friends bring into the fold, the more potential customers you have.

> ✉ *Note*
>
> Learn more about using social networks for customer loyalty in Chapter 14, "B2B Social Media Marketing."

Email Marketing

You can also use email, to some extent, to encourage referrals and recommendations. This plays along with the traditional approach of rewarding existing customers for recommending new ones. In the digital media world, you simply communicate the rewards via targeted emails.

That's right, you create your reward offer and put it into an email message that you send to some or all of your existing customer base. Maybe this is part of a regular communication, maybe it's a one-off email; in any case, you let your customers know that a reward of some sort is to be had when they bring a new customer into the fold. You can't overuse this particular vehicle, but it is a good way to get the word out.

"You can work Facebook and Twitter all day and all night and not generate a single new lead..."

> ✉ *Note*
>
> Learn more about using email for customer loyalty in Chapter 12, "B2B Email Marketing."

THE #1 WAY TO ENCOURAGE CUSTOMER LOYALTY AND REFERRALS

As effective as social networking is as a means to encourage customer recommendations and referrals, it's no guarantee. You can work Facebook and Twitter all day and all night and not generate a single new lead—unless you do the one most important thing necessary for customer loyalty.

What is this number-one approach to loyalty? It's simple: You need to offer something that customers actually want to recommend. That means creating the best product or service possible, backing it up with superb support, building solid personal relationships with your customers, and rewarding those customers for their support and loyalty. It's that simple, and that difficult.

If you have something worth recommending, your customers will. If whatever you offer is lacking, all the encouragement and rewards in the world won't make weary customers risk their own reputations by recommending it to others.

What Digital Media Are Less Likely for Loyalty Referrals?

As good as social networks are for the loyalty process, other digital media come up lacking; they just don't have the community-building features you find in Facebook and Google+. Let's face it, a passive website doesn't do much to build relationships or encourage referrals (short of promoting any referral program you might devise). Nor do outbound marketing vehicles designed primarily for customer acquisition, such as search engine marketing and online advertising, have any effect at all on building relationships with existing customers. It's just the way it is; when you're focusing on generating recommendations and referrals, everything else pales when compared to social media.

The Bottom Line

The final stage of the B2B buying continuum is the loyalty phase, where your existing customer base advocates for and recommends you to other potential customers. Social networking is ideal for encouraging these recommendations and referrals; email is also useful, especially in communicating bounty or rewards-type offers.

8

Creating a B2B Digital Marketing Plan

After you've decided how you want to include digital marketing in your overall marketing strategy, it's time to produce a formal plan—a B2B digital marketing plan. Such a plan is an important roadmap for your digital marketing activities, and a way to measure the success of these activities.

For many B2B companies, digital marketing is a new thing. You don't want to blindly enter into these new marketing activities; you need to know what you're doing and why, and what your goals are. That's why a digital marketing plan is the essential first step in implementing your B2B marketing strategy.

Why You Need a Digital Marketing Plan

I'm going to assume that, as a B2B marketing professional, you know all about marketing plans—why they're important, how to create one, and how to make best use of the plan in your day-to-day activities. Well, a digital marketing plan is much like a traditional marketing plan, just tweaked for digital media; the focus is on those online activities that contribute to your overall business goals.

An effective digital marketing plan is a roadmap to success. It forces marketing personnel (and your company's senior management) to embrace a set of common goals, strategies, and tactics; it keeps staff from going rogue, or from undertaking irrelevant or unwanted activities. It also encourages staff to think in terms of both internal and external goals, and to utilize the appropriate marketing vehicles to accomplish those goals.

A digital marketing plan is also necessary to achieve internal support for your online marketing activities. You know as well as anyone how difficult it can be to get some management comfortable with shifting from traditional media to digital media; some of the old guard is naturally adverse to change. To that end, a digital marketing plan is something you can put in front of senior management to let them know what you hope to accomplish, and to negotiate for the resources to accomplish those goals.

Finally, a digital marketing plan is a tool you can use to measure your accomplishments. A good marketing plan includes quantifiable goals, whether financial (revenues or profits) or market-oriented (market share, website traffic, and so on). How close you come to meeting or exceeding those goals determines how successful your marketing activities have been.

ONE PLAN OR TWO?

In this chapter, we're understandably focusing on digital marketing plans—a plan for your digital marketing activities. But do you want a digital marketing plan separate from your normal marketing plan, or should one all-encompassing marketing plan include both traditional and digital marketing activities?

I can go either way on this one. On one hand, having a separate digital marketing plan focuses attention on those activities that are probably newer and more difficult for many B2B companies. Viewing digital as something separate helps to provide the focus you might need to jump-start your online activities.

On the other hand, your digital marketing activities should not be wholly separate from traditional marketing activities. Everything you do should be related and closely coordinated; what you do in one medium affects what you do in another. (That's called *integrated marketing*, and it's key to success.) Your customers ultimately view you as a combination of what you project in all your marketing activities; digital should not be approached as something different from your other forms of marketing.

Perhaps the best approach, then, is to include a separate digital marketing section in your larger overall marketing plan. This enables you to plan holistically, while still focusing attention on your digital activities. It gives you the best of both worlds, planning-wise.

Understanding the Elements of a Digital Marketing Plan

A digital marketing plan contains the same elements as a traditional marketing plan. These elements include the following:

- Executive Summary
- Mission
- Situational Analysis
- Goals and Objectives
- Marketing Strategy
- Action Plan
- Budget

The plan itself should cover a defined time frame, typically one year. That is, you plan all your activities one year in advance—and your goal is what you hope to accomplish in the coming twelve months.

Let's look at each section of the plan in more detail.

Executive Summary

The Executive Summary is a one-page overview of the major points in your plan—from your mission all the way through your action plan and budget. Even though the Executive Summary is the first section of your plan, it's the part you write last, after you've come up with all the details in the other sections.

If the Executive Summary sounds redundant, it probably is—but in a good way. If your audience reads nothing but this one page (which is all some will read), they'll absorb the salient points of what you intend to accomplish with your marketing activities.

Mission

The meat of your digital marketing plan begins with the Mission section. This section provides the general rationale for your marketing activities; it explains why you want to do what you want to do.

You can express your mission in the form of a short mission statement, or with a longer explanation of why you're producing this plan. This section can be as short as a single sentence, but no longer than a paragraph.

The ideal Mission section should meet these criteria:

- It must define a clear direction for your marketing activities.
- It must define specific parameters for your marketing activities.
- It must be achievable.
- It must be measurable, in general terms—you either achieve your mission or you don't.

Naturally, the mission portion of a digital marketing plan should specifically address the Internet as a marketing medium.

Situational Analysis

The Situational Analysis section of your plan presents a snapshot of where things stand as the plan is conceived. It sets a baseline against which future action is both dictated and measured.

What sorts of things are we talking about? You should include subsections covering the following situations, tweaked to feature web-related issues:

- **Environment**—The big-picture trends (economic, demographic, social, and technological) that affect your company and its marketing activities. In a digital marketing plan, the chief environmental issue is almost always technological—more and more businesses are the web to research and make buying decisions.
- **Market**—The current size and growth trends for the B2B market in which you compete—including key segments of that market.
- **Competition**—A description of your major competitors, including their size, market share, key product lines, and (particularly) online activities.
- **Customer base**—A description of your current or target customer base, including an analysis of customer wants and needs and how they utilize new technology.

- **Products**—A description of your company's current products and services, including unit and dollar sales, pricing, and contribution margin, either by individual product or by major product line.

This section should be a mix of hard data and qualitative analysis and comment. You put together the Situational Analysis using internal data (for the internal items) and external market research (for the external items).

Opportunities and Issues

This section of your marketing plan analyzes the following opportunities and threats:

- **External opportunities**—These are market opportunities that your company is poised to take advantage of. Naturally, you should focus on online opportunities.

- **External issues**—These are market factors that present a threat to your company. Special attention should be given to Internet-related issues.

- **Internal strengths**—These are things that you do well, when compared to the competition, that can help you achieve the external opportunities you identify.

- **Internal issues**—These are inside-the-company issues that challenge the success of your marketing opportunities. (If you're not yet fully exploiting the Internet, that's an issue; you should examine why this is the case.)

After stating these individual opportunities and issues, you should then identify the *key issues* that need to be addressed by your company. These key issues will help you determine the strategies and tactics you pursue.

Goals and Objectives

This section builds from the key issues identified in the previous section. Here is where you set quantifiable goals you wish to achieve with your marketing activities.

These goals can be internal (a certain level of sales; a specific number of website visitors or referrals) or external (a particular market share; a defined search ranking on Google). What's important is that they be numeric and pegged to a specific time frame so that you can objectively state whether or not they've been achieve.

For example, if you state as a goal that you want to have "the best website in our industry," well, that's not very quantifiable, is it? What exactly do you mean by "best website?" There's no way to measure success.

On the other hand, if you set as a goal that you want to reach $100,000 in monthly website sales by July 1st, it will be easy to see whether you've achieved that goal. When July 1st rolls around, either you've hit that $100,000 mark or you haven't.

In other words, your goals and objectives are those things you aspire to, and can thus measure your success against. This is the section of the plan you'll return to in six or twelve months to see whether you've accomplished what you set out to do.

This section can contain a single goal or multiple goals. When talking about a website, for example, you might set goals for number of visitors, number of page views, average time on site, and search ranking. (Heck, you can even set a goal of when you want your site—or its redesign—to go live.) Product goals can include unit sales, dollar sales, profit margin, and the like. You get the picture.

 Note

Your goals and objectives should focus on results, not activities. For example, improving your search ranking is good, but the real goal should be the increased number of leads or conversions that results from that activity.

Just remember to set a time frame to measure your progress—typically six or twelve months into the future. And make sure your goals are achievable; there's no point in planning for the impossible.

Marketing Strategy

As the title implies, this section of the plan sets forth your company's overall digital marketing strategy. It refers to the preceding section, and describes how your company will pursue the identified opportunity. This section should include direction for each type of digital media, and how that ties into your overall marketing objectives.

 Note

The Marketing Strategy section is the strategic section of your plan; it's not where you discuss specific tactics. In other words, this section describes the *what* you're doing, not the *how* you're doing it.

I particularly like tying in each type of digital media to the five stages of the B2B buying continuum (Reach, Acquisition, Conversion, Retention, and Loyalty), as we've discussed throughout this section of the book (see Figure 8.1). You might want to devote subsections to each part of the customer life cycle; you can then discuss the digital media strategy for each of the life cycle stages, and how they'll help you achieve the goals for each stage.

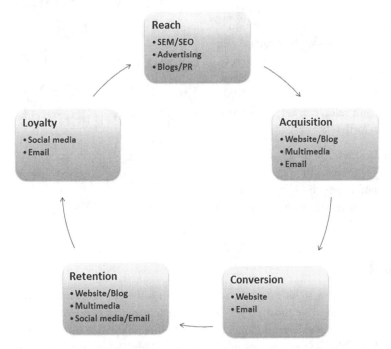

Figure 8.1 *Define your digital marketing strategy for each stage of the B2B buying continuum.*

Action Plan

The Action Plan section describes specific tactics you'll use to implement the marketing strategy set forth in the previous section. This is where you get down to the nitty-gritty of which digital marketing activities you'll be undertaking, and how much you'll be spending on each one.

Think of the Action Plan as your marching orders, a set of step-by-step instructions you can hand to your staff to implement. It's the most detailed section of your entire marketing plan.

When writing the Action Plan for your digital marketing activities, you should devote separate subsections to individual activities—website design, search engine marketing, social media marketing, and the like. You can then link each activity to the stages of the customer life cycle, as described in the Marketing Strategy section of your plan.

For each overall digital marketing vehicle, you should describe the exact activities you expect to undertake, along with a timeline (typically by month or quarter) for these activities. Describe each event, present its timing, estimate its costs, and then detail the event's goals and objectives (page views, visitors, dollar or unit sales, market share gains, and so forth).

You can then roll up all your marketing activities into a master time-table and master budget—the latter of which demands its own section of the plan.

> "Think of the Action Plan as your marching orders, a set of step-by-step instructions you can hand to your staff to implement. It's the most detailed section of your entire marketing plan."

Budget

The final section of your digital marketing plan is the one that your financial people will pore over the most, so you have to make sure that everything adds up. This section is your master marketing budget, detailing how much money you expect to spend over the plan period—typically one year. This Budget section should include all the normal financial reports that accounting types like to see, so make sure you work with your finance department accordingly.

Writing Your Marketing Plan

Now that you know what goes into a full-featured digital marketing plan, how do you go about writing that plan?

First, the good news. An effective marketing plan doesn't have to be a massive document. I know that there's a lot of information that needs to be presented, but (depending on the needs of your particular company), you can present a lot of it in bullet points. It's important that your audience (senior management, typically) get the gist of what you're proposing; presenting them with a novel-length document probably isn't the best way to go about it.

That said, you do need to include all the pertinent information, in as much detail as is necessary. That means doing your homework ahead of time, and a lot of it; then you can decide how best to present each piece of data. Some information should be presented in text format; other information can be presented visually, typically in a table or graph. Use the format that works best for you.

It's easy to get overwhelmed by all these details and lose sight of what you're trying to achieve. To that end, I like to think of a marketing plan as a discussion; writing the plan, then, simply entails documenting that discussion.

Here's how I like to approach it. Imagine that you're sitting in a coffeehouse or bar, talking with a colleague about your marketing activities. You talk your friend through what you're doing and what you'd like to do, and that becomes your marketing plan. In the course of your conversation, you cover the following points:

- Why you're doing what you're doing, in just a sentence or two. (This is the Mission section of your plan.)

- What's happening in the market, and with your company. (This is your Situational Analysis.)

- What opportunities you think there are in the current market. (This is the Opportunities and Issues section.)

- What you think you can accomplish with your digital marketing activities. (These are your Goals and Objectives.)

- How you plan to accomplish these goals. (This is the Marketing Strategy section.)

- What specific activities you want to undertake. (This is your Action Plan.)

- How much money you'll need to spend to accomplish your goals. (This is the Budget section.)

That doesn't sound too daunting, does it? Just a normal conversation, something you can talk through in ten or fifteen minutes or so over a cup of coffee or bottle of beer. That's all you need to do.

Creating your plan, then, is simply writing down what you'd say and then filling in a few blanks and making it all look pretty. It doesn't have to be any more difficult than that.

Putting the Plan into Practice

So, you spend the requisite number of hours creating a detailed digital marketing plan, present it to your management, and get the necessary approvals to do what you want to do. Then, in all too many cases, the plan gets put on

> "Even the best-written marketing plans are worthless if they're not followed. If you don't follow your own action plan, what's the point of planning at all?"

a shelf—where it stays, unread, until the following year, when you start the entire process over again.

Even the best-written marketing plans are worthless if they're not followed. If you don't follow your own action plan, what's the point of planning at all?

The key to a successful marketing plan is not so much the plan itself, but rather what you do with it. If you put it on the shelf and ignore it, you probably won't achieve your goals. (If, in fact, you even remember what your goals are.) If, on the other hand, you treat your marketing plan as an active document, a set of instructions for your day-to-day marketing activities, you stand a good chance of accomplishing what you set out to do.

I like to revisit the marketing plan on a regular basis—at least quarterly, ideally monthly. You can then gauge your progress on an ongoing basis, and know when you need to shift gears or reassign priorities. If things aren't going to plan, there's no shame in changing those goals midstream; better to do this after three or six months than to be a year down the road and discover that you're not going to get there.

In other words, make your marketing plan a living document. Follow the action plan you set forth, constantly measure your progress to plan, and adapt your plan as necessary throughout the year. This is the way to ensure success—and make the entire planning process worthwhile.

The Bottom Line

A marketing plan serves two purposes. First, it helps to gain approval from management for your marketing activities. Second, it serves as a roadmap, a set of instructions that guide you and your staff in the coming months.

A digital marketing plan should contain the same sections as a traditional marketing plan: Executive Summary, Mission, Situational Analysis, Goals and Objectives, Marketing Strategy, Action Plan, and Budget. Consider the creation of your marketing plan to be similar to carrying on a conversation about your marketing activities; what you might describe to a colleague becomes your written plan.

9

B2B Website Marketing

All digital marketing revolves around one essential element: your website. That's right, everything you do online, from the keywords you target to the blog posts you make, centers your home on the Web. If you don't create an exceptional website experience, nothing else matters; all the advertising and promotion you do is wasted if there isn't an effective home to drive customers to.

Your digital marketing, then, has to start with the design of your website. But what makes for a great B2B website? It's all about giving current and potential customers what they need—and making what they need easy to find.

Why Your Website Is Important

It should go without saying that your website is your company's home base on the Internet. It's not only where everything important is stored, it's where all your other activities point to.

In addition, it's where both potential and existing customers expect to find key information. If they want to find out more about your company, where do they go? If they want product info, where do they go? If they need support, where do they go?

The answer to all these questions, of course, is your company website. Yes, they can search online for information (and will, to some degree); yes, they can go to industry-specific sites for certain data. But when it comes to getting important information straight from the horse's mouth, as it were, they want to get it from you—on your website.

Just how important is your website? When it comes to influencing potential B2B customers, it's the most important thing out there, side-by-side with word of mouth from other customers. As digital marketing firm Mediative (formerly Enquiro) found, your website is more important than any other marketing vehicle—online or off[1] (see Figure 9.1).

"...your website is more important than any other marketing vehicle— online or off..."

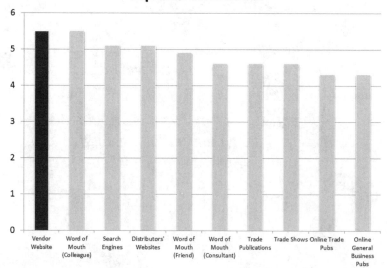

Figure 9.1 *Top influences on B2B buying decisions (Courtesy Mediative, www.mediative.ca).*

1. Enquiro (Mediative), "Business-to-Business Survey 2007"

Designing Your Website for B2B

When it comes to website design, there's really little difference between a B2C and a B2B site. Yes, the target audience is different, which means the content is different. But the thinking behind the site—the quest for good design—should be the same. It all revolves around giving the customer what he wants, and making that something easy to find.

Keeping It Simple

I've been dealing with website design since the advent of the Web in the mid-1990s, and here's something I've come to expect. Call it the Internet equivalent of entropy; over time, web pages and websites become more complicated—and as they become more complex, they become less useful. I'm not sure why this is; perhaps it's because companies can't resist adding more and more things to an existing design, or maybe it's because multiple masters keep getting their way. In any case, there are numerous examples of once easy-to-use websites becoming overly cluttered—and less easy-to-use—over time. It just happens.

> " ...over time, web pages and websites become more complicated—and as they become more complex, they become less useful."

This clutter can take many forms. Sometimes it's multiple content modules, all competing for attention. Sometimes it's an overabundance of design elements, each getting in the way of the others. Sometimes it's technology gone wild, with too many moving elements going nowhere. Whatever the cause or causes (and it can be more than one), the result is a website that many visitors find too confusing to use.

It doesn't have to be this way. In fact, some of the most popular sites on the Web are the most simple—Google and Wikipedia being among the most noted. These sites have resisted the temptation to clutter up their home pages, and instead present a very simple and clear message to their visitors.

On the B2B front, take a look at the Swarovski Gems website (see Figure 9.2). It's sophisticated looking but extremely simple. There are top-of-page links for Brand, Products, and Vision (each of which expands to display additional submenu items); bottom-of-page pop-ups for three major events; a top-right search box; and fine-print links to other necessary stuff at the very bottom of the page. Nothing cluttered, nothing really in your face, just quick links to the content you need most.

Figure 9.2   *The sophisticated, uncluttered B2B site for Swarovski Gems (www.swarovski-gems.com).*

Easy enough to praise this site, I'm sure you're saying, but your site is different. You're catering to a specific type of B2B customer and need to present more information in more different ways. You have to put more content on the page.

Now, that may be the case; I'm sure your business is uniquely complex. But you can still present multiple pieces of information—or multiple pathways—in a simple, easy-to-navigate fashion. It's all a matter of knowing what your customers want to find, and how they want to get there.

The point is to make it easy to find what customers want to find, without overwhelming them with unwanted content. That might mean presenting one primary item and other items in a subsidiary fashion. It might mean cutting back on the number of items you display on a page. It might even mean relegating some items to smaller links or placement on navigational menus. Not everything can take primary position; not everything is of equal importance.

Just remember, the Internet's top sites—Google, Twitter, Wikipedia, and the like—all have relatively simple gateway pages. There's a reason for that.

Minimizing Technology—and Design

While we're on the topic of keeping things simple, let's consider all the fancy technological and design elements that many websites use today. I'm talking Flash animations, videos, and those things that in general exist to "wow" site visitors.

In other words, all the things that visitors hate.

That's right, all those fancy elements your design and technology people love are roundly despised by many web users—especially business users. Website visitors just want to do what they want to do; they don't want to be interrupted in their quest. And trust me, animations and movies and things that go "pop" are interruptions—unwanted and unnecessary interruptions. They get in the way of getting to where one wants to go.

As a user yourself, I'm sure you've experienced this. You go to a site, and before you can even visit the home page, you're greeted with some sort of animation or video. You're forced to sit through this thing, which takes several seconds (or more) to load and then just as long to play, before you can start looking for the information you want. It's a huge roadblock, one which many visitors simply click away from without ever visiting the site beyond.

Now, why would a website do this? It's the online equivalent of making customers to a bricks and mortar store wait outside while you put on a little play; you don't let them the front door until the production is finished. If you did this in your physical offices, most of your visitors would just walk away. So, why would you do this online?

It's the same thing with other technological and design gimmicks. Yeah, they're fun, and I'm sure you and your design and technology staffs really like them. But do they truly serve your site visitors, or merely annoy them? That's the question to ask—and most of the time, the right answer will be to avoid these doodads completely.

Yes, simple, straight ahead text content may be technologically boring, but it provides visitors with the information they're looking for. Don't force anything else on them that they don't want or need.

Providing the Right Content

What really matters when constructing a website is the content. In fact, it's the only thing that matters. You could have the worst-looking website in the world but if your content was useful and unique, you'd still provide real value to your customers. Not that design should be totally ignored, but your primary focus should be in providing that content that your customers want.

> "What really matters when constructing a website is the content. In fact, it's the only thing that matters."

What sort of content should you include on your site? Whatever it is that your current and potential customers want and need! That probably includes information about the products and services you offer, as well as support for those same products and services. Your website is a great place to offer instructions and manuals, how-to videos, and the like—the sorts of things that actually reduce your customer support load. You should also use your site to include all the brochures and catalogs and other collateral material you offer, in easy-to-navigate format. And if you let your customers place their orders online, you definitely need a product ordering/shopping cart/checkout path.

In addition, you can add to the customer experience (and enhanced retention and loyalty) by offering discussion forums, blogs, and the like on your site. Use your site to promote customer feedback and interaction—but then make sure you manage these elements and respond to customer comments.

In short, your website can do lots of things for lots of people. It's all about the content.

Keeping the Content Simple—and Accessible

It's important that the content you put online is both simple and accessible. That's because you never know just how or where they content will be viewed—or by whom.

B2B buyers tend to prefer content in either straight text format or in Adobe PDF format (for brochures and the like). The reason for this is that the person accessing your website is seldom the only person in that organization who is involved in making the buying decision. The content the first person finds on your site is likely to be passed around to others in the company, and the easier it can be passed around, the better.

To this end, information that you present in rich media formats—videos, Flash animations, and the like—are more difficult, if not impossible to download and share. I happen to like using videos to present certain types of product information, but realize that only visitors to your website will be able to view them; they can't be downloaded and passed around like you can with a PDF-format brochure.

Putting Content on the Page

When you're putting that content on the page, consider that web users don't like to scroll all that much. You might get one or two down-scrolls out of them, but not three or four. It's the online equivalent of putting newspaper content above the fold.

To that end, think in terms of short pages—which means short blocks of text. If you have something longer to present, break it up into multiple pages. Believe it or not, visitors are more likely to click to a second (or third) page than they are to scroll down a single page.

Of course, writing web copy is an acquired skill. Not only should you keep your pages short, you should also write in short sentences and paragraphs, and then introduce each section with a heading or subheading. Website visitors tend to graze more than read, and your copy needs to recognize this. I call it "chunky" content—both on the page and in pages on your site. Don't be wordy, and don't be overly complex. You don't have to insult your audience, just remember that nobody's visiting your site for the deathless prose.

 Note

Copywriting for websites is very similar to direct response copywriting. You have to describe what you're providing in words, not pictures—and, if you're selling something, provide a strong "why to buy" message.

Providing Content for Search Engines

One more thing about website content. It's not just your human visitors you need to consider.

That's right, your content is also browsed by robots—software robots, to be exact. These programs, called *spiders* or *crawlers*, are sent out across the Internet by Google and the other search engines, in search of relevant pages to add to their search indexes. As such, these programs need to be able to figure out just what a page is about, which they do by examining the content of your copy, especially those keywords you include.

It's all in service of what we call *search engine optimization*, and it means you have to be of two minds when writing your website copy. Yes, you have to provide readable, compelling copy for your human visitors, but at the same time incorporate all the necessary keywords and phrases that matter to the search engines—and in the fashion that influence how the search engines rank a page. You don't want to sacrifice one for the other; never make your page less readable just to cram in another keyword. Go for readability first, and then incorporate the keywords as you can.

It's not that easy to do, which is why some professional web copywriters earn big bucks. And those bucks are well spent; a well-optimized web page will rank higher in Google's search results, which leads to more new visitors to your site.

 Note

Learn more about search engine optimization in Chapter 10, "B2B Search Engine Marketing."

Providing Easy Navigation

All the content you provide on your site has to be easily found. That means coming up with some sort of navigational scheme that makes sense to your site's visitors. You can't just put it all out there in a list and expect people to find what they need.

Potential customers need to be able to quickly click to product information. Current customers need a quick link to support resources and other material. And everyone needs immediate access to contact information, whether in the form of a web contact form, clickable email addresses, or honest-to-goodness real-world telephone numbers.

In this respect, consider navigation to be in service to your site's content—and a necessary service. This means devising some sort of easy-to-understand organizational hierarchy, using the model of directories and subdirectories and even sub-subdirectories. The key is to figure out what visitors are looking for on your site, and then make it easy to get there. Minimize the number of clicks that have to be made; it's always better to get there in one click than two or three.

To that end, your navigational system must be easy to find and easy to figure out. That probably means a set of pull-down menus or links across the top of the page, or along the left side; that's where most people look for navigation.

Your menus don't have to be fancy, either. In fact, they probably shouldn't be fancy; better to use easy-to-understand text instead of impossible-to-comprehend graphics. Don't make it difficult on your visitors; just point them to where they want to go.

Take, for example, Airclic, a company that offers logistics software for businesses (see Figure 9.3). You can easily navigate this site by either products or industry; everything you need is found on or under the menu items at the top of the page. Additional features, such as live chat and live call, are accessible from the very top of the page; featured news items are displayed below the main content.

Figure 9.3   *Navigate Airclic's site (www.airclic.com) by product or industry.*

I also like the navigation on Tyco's website (see Figure 9.4). You have a nice menu bar near the top of the page, complete with pull-down submenu items; featured content in the middle of the page (in an iTunes-like flip display); a scrolling bar of featured customers just beneath the main content; and news and videos at the bottom. Everything is up front and easy to find—which is what you want.

Figure 9.4   *Tyco's easy-to-navigate website (www.tyco.com).*

Key to devising an effective navigational structure is to *think like the customer*. How are your current and potential customers likely to look for specific items on your site? Instead of focusing on internal departmental divisions or the way you or your bosses think about your products or services, organize your content the way your customers think about it.

Considering the Look and Feel of Your Site

Finally, we come to the design of your individual web pages—how your pages look. This is, of course, a matter for the design team, but as a marketer, you need to have significant input.

First, the design has to be in service of the content. No design for design's sake. Every element on the page has to serve a purpose; the design has to be efficient and make your page more effective. (This might be tough for the designers; sorry.)

Next, and equally important, your site has to present your company or brand identity. A potential customer visiting your home page should know at a glance what company or product he's dealing with. Content is important, yes, but visual identity must be maintained.

Finally, your site design has to be of a whole with the rest of your corporate and brand image. You don't want a red background on your website if your corporate image is all about blue, for example. You want to include the same branding elements on your site as you do in all your promotional materials. It all has to look like it came from the same place; customers will be confused by any inconsistency in identity.

I wish I could offer more specific design advice, but every company and every website is unique. What works for IBM might not work for Dell, and definitely won't work for an accounting or consulting firm. Work with your designers to create a site that looks and feels like your product, your company, and your other sales and marketing activities. Keep it as simple as possible, and make sure that the design doesn't get in the way of the content or the navigation. It's not easy; you'll devote a lot of discussions to this part of the project. But if you do it right, your customer base will recognize your website as your company's home base on the Web—which is what it should be, after all.

✉ *Note*

Some designers like to create a *wireframe* or blueprint of each web page, before doing the actual coding. This is rough sketch of the page design, showing where text blocks and graphics go.

CONSIDERING COLOR

One more thing about page design. I know you want to stick to the colors that your company brand is known for; I also know that your web designers will be pestering you to accept a particular color palette for your site. But if you go too wild with color, you can create readability problems—and if you make your site hard to read, people won't visit.

When it comes to readability, nothing beats good old black text on a white background. That's how you're reading this book, after all, and it works pretty well; you get good contrast without hurting your eyes.

Next best is black text on a light neutral background, like beige or light gray. After that, a light color background is probably okay—light yellow, light blue, or light green, for example.

What you want to avoid are dark or brightly colored backgrounds. Black text on an orange background, for example, will be pretty much unreadable. Weird color combinations, such as green text on a purple background, are also bad.

For that matter, you should avoid reverse text (white text on a black background), with a few exceptions. You can use reverse text for short text blocks; it's actually good to convey emphasis. But you shouldn't use reverse text for long blocks of text because it's very hard on the eyes.

And, just as you shouldn't put dark text on a dark background, you also shouldn't put light text on a light background. It's all about contrast, and light on light (and dark on dark) doesn't give you enough. If you find it hard to read, your customers will, too.

The point is that you want to make it easy for visitors to read your content. Make the text pop from the background—and consider using a larger font size, especially if you have a lot of older visitors to your site. (Which you will, if you're trying to serve an upper management clientele.)

Creating Unique Landing Pages

It's not just your site's home page that's important. You need to design every page on your site with the same intensity of focus.

That's because you don't know on which page a visitor might enter your site. Not everyone types your home page's URL into their browsers; some visitors come via links found elsewhere on the Web.

To that end, you'll need to consider some pages on your site as dedicated *landing pages*—those pages that visitors land on when entering from another site. Some landing pages might be obvious—product pages, for example, or pages devoted to a particular brand or customer segment. These pages should be treated as if they were home pages.

Other landing pages are devised to serve other web marketing activities. For example, if you create a pay-per-click advertisement, you need to create a unique landing page that potential customers see when they click that ad. You don't want customers clicking from a product-specific ad and landing on your site's general home page; you want them landing on a page that follows directly from the advertisement they just clicked.

Landing pages of this type are all about presenting a consistent image to potential customers. The more products or services you offer, the more customer segments you service, the more marketing vehicles you use, the more activity-specific landing pages you need to create. Each landing page has to be product or service specific, and reference the ad or activity that led to the page. Each landing page must also continue your overall site branding, as every page on your site should. And use the landing page to continue the customer's journey; give them the information they clicked for, and provide a path to get even more info or purchase the product.

Choosing the Right Content and Features

General design aside, which specific content and features should you include on your website? Do you need a blog, live chat, downloadable presentations, a video library, or what?

What content and features you include depends a lot on what you're trying to achieve with your site. To that end, I like to break things up by the key website-related stages in the B2B buying continuum: acquisition, conversion, and retention. How much you focus on each of these stages will determine what you put on your web pages.

That said, it's always instructive to see what other B2B companies are doing with their sites. To that end, take a look at what MarketingSherpa recently found when it asked B2B companies about the effectiveness of various "design, management, and optimization tactics" on their sites (see Figure 9.5).[2] Not surprisingly, the most effective tactics include unique landing pages and optimizing content for conversions and search engines.

---

2. MarketingSherpa, "B2B 2011 Marketing Benchmark Report," 2010

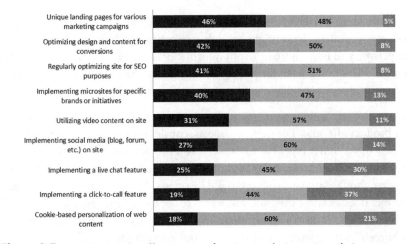

Figure 9.5 *Measuring the effectiveness of various techniques in website content and design.*

Designing Your Website for Acquisition

As noted, the content and features you include on your site depend on a large degree on how you're using the site. We've previously discussed the five stages of the B2B buying continuum or customer life cycle, and how website marketing can factor into three of these stages: acquisition, conversion, and retention. Let's focus first on how you can design your website to enhance customer acquisition.

Key to the acquisition phase is providing the appropriate information for potential customers to make a buying decision. You not only have to provide informative content, but make that content easy to find, read, and perhaps download.

Organization and Navigation

This challenge noted, start with your site's overall organization. How are potential customers coming to your site? Will they land on specific landing pages? Or will they come directly to your home page? Whichever is the case, you need to design the navigation from that entry point with the customer's informational needs in mind.

That probably means constructing some sort of universal navigation system that appears on all pages. Perhaps that's a top-of-page menu or toolbar, or a list of key topics or items in a sidebar. You need to make it clear where the customer is and then help him find where he wants to get to.

In doing this, realize that different customers think of themselves and their needs in different ways. You might have to create different paths to the core content on your site.

For example, some customers will want to go directly to information about specific products or services. They might have already seen a brochure or ad or talked to a salesperson, and need more in-depth information about what interests them. For these products, you'll need direct product navigation; help them go directly to a product or service page that contains the specific information they're seeking.

Other customers will know less about what you offer and thus need to be guided to your product offerings. For these prospects, consider some sort of organization by industry or customer type. For example, if you provide products for medical industry, you might have menu items for hospitals, medical offices, pharmacies, and the like; even though similar products might be offered for each customer type, the customer doesn't know this, and just wants to see those products that apply to him. With this sort of industry or customer organization, the customer can easily identify himself or the company and then see your relevant offerings.

You can also improve the "findability" of information on your site by including site-specific search. Place a search box prominently at the top of all your pages so that more savvy visitors can search for the specific information they need, instead of browsing for it. Remember, customers just want to find the information they want as quickly as possible; quick in, quick out should be your motto.

Note

What sort of information is a potential B2B buyer looking for on your site? It's the basic stuff—product information, prices, technical specs, and customer service and support information.

Content and Collateral

Now we come to the content you provide to potential customers. Here you need to be as liberal as possible, providing as much content as you can in as many different formats as possible.

What does this mean? Depending on your specific situation and what you have available, you might offer some or all of the following:

- Brochures
- Product spec sheets
- White papers

- Case studies
- Presentations
- Price lists
- Catalogs
- Videos (product overviews, company overviews, how-to videos, customer testimonials, and so forth)

This is in addition to the core information you place on the web pages themselves, of course. Remember—the more information you provide, the more comfortable buyers will be purchasing from you.

When presenting this content and collateral, you should consider how your customers want to access and use each item. Some buyers will simply want to read them onscreen. Others will want to print and save for future reading, or to distribute to others in their organizations. Still others will want to access from their mobile phones while they're out of the office. This means you might have to make items available in multiple formats. It's not about what's easiest for you, it's about what your potential customers need or will find most useful.

 Note

For collateral material, PDF format is probably the best way to go. This format is great for both reading onscreen and downloading to print; the item displays and prints as originally designed, you don't have to worry about conversion or compatibility or much of anything else.

Where should all these items be on your site? You probably want to provide multiple access points. For example, it's a good idea to provide access to all relevant materials for a given product from individual product pages. It's also good to list relevant materials on overall industry or customer type pages so that customers identifying themselves in that fashion can find what they want. You can also list all materials for all products on master "presentations" or "brochures" or "white papers" pages. Make it easy for customers to find what they want, however they're looking for it.

> "Make it easy for customers to find what they want, however they're looking for it."

Access for Everyone?

Here's a tough one: Do you let anyone visiting your site access and download your sales collateral without question, or do you require some information about a visitor before you let them download?

On one hand, the thinking goes that more information downloaded by more people is better. Making it easy (no questions ask) to download materials will result in less frustration for potential customers.

On the other hand, you don't want to let potential customers walk away without getting to say hello. If you require visitors to provide contact information before being allowed to download material, you now have an inquiry that your sales people can follow up on (see Figure 9.6). When someone clicks on a particular item, you present a contact form they have to fill in first. After they fill in the form, they can do the download thing—and you can send the information to your sales staff.

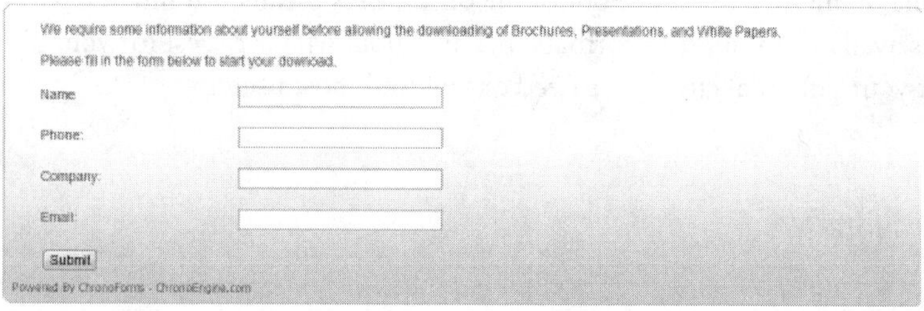

Figure 9.6 *Requiring customers to submit contact information before downloading collateral material.*

If you do choose the info-before-download route, you'll want to be sure you intelligently store and reuse the information visitors submit. The last thing anyone wants is for a customer to have to re-enter their contact information for each item they want to download; it should be an enter-once, download-many situation.

You'll also want to be clear that by submitting this information, you'll probably be contacting them—but that you won't be sharing their information with any other entities. Transparency is important.

FILLING IN FORMS

Although I understand the eagerness to collect contact information from site visitors, I'm not a big fan of this approach. I feel it turns off too many potential customers who don't want to be contacted just yet, or don't want to spend the time filling in a form. (Most people want immediate gratification; filling in a form, however short, delays that.)

Isn't your goal to get your product information in the hands of as many potential customers as possible? If so, why would you complicate that? This is why
I prefer allowing unfettered downloads—but providing a button visitors can
click if they *want* you to also contact them. That's the best of both worlds,
and a heck of a lot less intrusive.

Asking for More

As much information as you can provide on your site, some customers will have
even more questions. Or maybe they just prefer talking to a real live human being.
In either case, you'll want to provide mechanisms to put site visitors in contact
with your sales personnel.

There are many ways to do this, including the following:

- Include a "click for more information" button on product and collateral pages. This button should link to a web form where visitors can
  ask their questions, as well as provide their contact information.

- Include an "email us" link or button on product and collateral pages.
  This should open a new email message with your contact address
  already filled in.

- Offer live online chat with live personnel. This works only if you have
  someone available 24/7—and that person is well qualified to handle
  questions at the given level.

- Offer click-to-call functionality. This takes the form of a button on the
  page that, when clicked, opens either an Internet-based voice chat or
  initiates a traditional phone call. Again, you'll need to be appropriately
  staffed to offer this type of contact.

The point is to make it easy for customers to contact your customer service center
or sales people, and vice versa. Establishing a personal contact as early as possible
in the process will lead to successful acquisitions—and a higher possibility of conversion.

Designing Your Website for Conversion

Speaking of conversion, after you get past the acquisition stage, it's time to start
pressuring for the sale. You might or might not want to do this on your website;
many B2B companies prefer doing things the old school way, as do many potential
customers.

Is Online Conversion for You?

Whether or not you convert on your website depends to a degree on what exactly it is you're selling. Smaller and less expensive items are more likely to be ordered without personal attendance; larger and more expensive items tend to require more personal handholding during the purchasing process. In addition, the ordering of professional services are less likely to be accomplished online than product purchases.

It also depends, to some degree, on the size and status of the customers. Some B2B companies handle their large customers personally, but offer website ordering for smaller customers who don't get the personal treatment. Not that smaller customers are less important, but... well, actually, smaller customers *are* less important, from a financial standpoint. You don't want to ignore them, but you also might not have the human resources to handhold them. Online ordering for these customers might make more sense, cost-wise.

 Note

Consider that some customers might want to place their initial orders with a salesperson, but then find it more convenient place their reorders online. This argues for e-commerce functionality, even if it isn't used during the initial conversion process.

In other words, don't feel as if you have to provide online ordering, especially for first-time customers. If it fits with your particular business, great. If not, leave it to your inside or outside salespeople.

Designing for E-Commerce

If you do want to convert online, you'll need to enhance your website with e-commerce capability. That means building, buying, or renting an online shopping cart and checkout system, and integrating this system throughout your site.

You'll want to add "buy now" buttons to each of your product pages, and make sure it's easy to find each of those products on your site. It goes without saying that you'll need to establish a buyer-friendly navigational structure, as well as search functionality, so that customers can quickly and easily find the products they're looking for.

It also goes without saying that every product you offer for sale should have its own page on your site, unless you are catalog seller and have thousands of products. This needs to be a content-rich page, not just a flashy advertisement. You need to include one or more product photos, a detailed description, all relevant dimensions and sizes and colors and such, as well as any other information that a customer might need to place an informed order.

When a customer purchases a product, that product needs to go into that customer's shopping cart—the online equivalent of a physical shopping cart. The cart holds multiple purchases and then feeds into your site's checkout system, which then interfaces with your online payment service.

This checkout system needs to integrate with your inventory management system. This way, a product sale will automatically update both your inventory database and the availability information on your product pages.

Naturally, you'll also need to include some sort of payment system. This might actually be an automated purchasing system that ties into each customer's line of credit or the purchasing information they've previously provided. You might also want to offer credit card or bank draw payment for smaller or less frequent customers. This could be provided by your shopping cart provider, or you can always sign up with one of the major online payment services, such as PayPal or Google Checkout.

Providing Customer Service

Finally, remember that the purchasing process doesn't end when the customer places an order. It's inevitable that some customers will want to contact you with questions or issues, either before or after they place an order. This argues for similar contact functionality as discussed for the acquisition process—contact forms, email links, online chat, and click-to-call options. You want to make it easy for customers to contact you.

In addition, you'll want to contact your customers with purchase confirmation and shipping information. It's best if you can automate all these customer communications using web-based forms and email marketing.

Designing Your Website for Retention

Your website can also be an ongoing focal point for customers after the initial sale. You want to support your customers after the sale, as well as provide information that might lead to additional purchases. It also doesn't hurt to provide an online community for your customers, where they can help support each other—and recommend additional products and services.

Providing Support

The first post-conversion feature you need to consider is some form—or a variety of forms—of customer support. Customers will have questions, they will have problems, and you will have to help them. Whether you do that in person (via a call from a sales or support person), over the phone, via email, on your website, or what, depends on your company's support policy and budget.

There are lots of ways you can provide customer support on your website. Consider some or all of the following:

- Downloadable instruction manuals and materials, ideally in PDF format
- List of frequently asked questions (FAQ) and answers
- List of common problems and solutions
- Interactive troubleshooting guide
- Videos showing how to install, configure, and use your products
- Email link to the support department
- Web form to submit questions/suggestions
- Text listing of support contact information, including toll-free number
- Click-to-call functionality to your support staff
- Live chat with support staff, via instant messaging technology (either text, audio, or video)

Note

Some or all of these items might be isolated in a password-protected area of your site devoted exclusively to your paying customers. Or you can put these items on the public portion of your site, figuring that some or all of them can also function as pre-purchase information for potential customers. (This is particularly so with instruction materials.)

These support features should be easy to find on your site. I like hosting them on a dedicated customer support page or section, but also pointing to them from the appropriate product pages. You might also link to them from your customers' account pages. The point is to let this web-based support alleviate the load on your traditional support staff; you're both serving your customer base and reducing your costs.

Providing Additional Information

You can also use your website to suggest future business from your existing customers—and to cross sell related products. To that end, make sure to point customers to pages devoted to other things they may be interested in:

- Similar items
- Replacement items
- Accessories
- Related services

For example, if you sell computer systems, you might assemble a page presenting cables, monitors, mice, keyboards, and the like. You could also use this page to offer service or warranty plans for the system(s) just purchased.

If you sell HVAC equipment, you could assemble a page presenting furnace filters, air conditioning covers, add-on humidifiers and dehumidifiers, and the like. Naturally, you'd also plug your service and warranty plans on this page.

You get the idea; your website should be a continuous selling tool. Just because a customer placed an order doesn't mean your job is over—you should always be suggesting the *next* thing to purchase.

Providing Community

Another important way to encourage retention (and, ultimately, loyalty and referrals) is to build a customer community on your site. To do this, you need to provide one or more means of both one-way and two-way communication. You want to talk to your customers, yes, but you also want them to talk back to you—and to each other.

How can you build community on your site? There are a few things you can do.

First, consider creating a corporate blog where you present information (about your company, products, industry, or employees) to your customer base. Naturally, you should encourage comments to your posts; you might also want to enlist select customers to create special posts on occasion.

You should also consider adding a web-based message forum to your site. The forum should be organized into specific topic areas, perhaps around specific products or services you offer, perhaps around different industries or customer types. This forum is where customers can ask questions of you and associate with other customers.

If you do your job right, the community aspects of your site will keep customers coming back on a regular basis. You'll encourage participation and make customers feel like they're part of the family—all of which should lead to additional sales and recommendations.

OTHER IMPORTANT WEBSITE ELEMENTS

We've talked a lot about specific marketing-oriented features of a B2B website. But that's not all you need on your site; there are some other important features you need to consider. These fairly standard features include the following:

- **About Us**—You definitely need a page or so on your site that talks about who you are. Consider including a corporate overview, company history, and bios of key management.

- **Investor Information**—If you're a public company, you'll want to include a page or section targeted at investors. This can include some of the same information as in the About Us section, along with key financial documents, a stock price history, and so forth.

- **Press Room**—I like creating a virtual press room for interested media. This section of your site should include press releases, product photos, fact sheets, and other information that members of the press (including bloggers) can access if they're writing about you.

- **Privacy Statement**—This is kind of a boilerplate thing, but important. You need to tell visitors to your site just how you might be using any information they explicitly submit, as well as how you might use any cookies you create.

- **Contact Info**—You definitely want to tell visitors how they can get in contact with you. Include your corporate addresses (along with a map of and directions to key locations), phone numbers, email addresses, you name it.

You can include links to all these subsidiary elements at the bottom of your home page. These elements probably aren't important enough to warrant inclusion in your main menu system, but still have to be accessible to those who want them.

The Bottom Line

Your website is an essential marketing vehicle for the acquisition, reach, and retention phases of the B2B customer life cycle. Use your website to provide pre- and post-purchase information about your products and services, as well as offer ongoing support to your customer base—and do so in a way that makes all these items easy for your site visitors to find.

10

B2B Search Engine Marketing

When it comes to achieving reach—that is, getting the attention of potential customers—nothing beats your friendly neighborhood search engine. More customers, in both the B2C and B2B worlds, start the purchasing process by searching than by using any other digital marketing vehicle. That's right, it's likely that the majority of new customers you find online will come from Google, Yahoo!, Bing, and other web search engines.

So, although you can purchase pay-per-click (PPC) ads, seed influential blogs, and work the social networks, more new prospects will find you because they're searching for something, and your site came up in the search results. And because you can't buy placement in these results, how you rank is a function of how well your site matches what potential customers are searching for. It's all about search engine marketing—and optimizing your site for search.

Why Search Engine Marketing Is Important

It's a fact—search engines drive the majority of new traffic to most websites (see Figure 10.1). That's even true in the B2B world, where more than half of B2B customers turn to a search engine before any other information source when they want to find out about a product or service.[1]

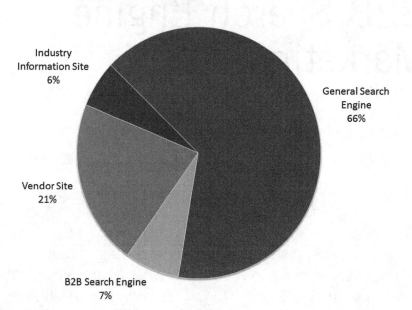

Source of Initial Online Awareness

Industry Information Site 6%

General Search Engine 66%

Vendor Site 21%

B2B Search Engine 7%

Figure 10.1 *Where do B2B customers gain initial awareness of a company? (Courtesy Mediative, www.mediative.ca)*

Because search engines drive so much traffic to B2B websites, you want to ensure that your site ranks as high as possible in the results for all the major search engines. This activity is what we call *search engine marketing*, and it involves optimizing your site to rank higher in these search results.

 Note

Most marketers consider search engine marketing to include both search engine optimization and pay-per-click search advertising. Although definitely related, I prefer to treat them separately because the former involves website design and the latter is really just another form of paid advertising.

---

1. Enquiro (Mediative), "Business-to-Business Survey 2007"

Why is a high ranking in the search results important? Don't searchers read the entire page of search results and then go onto the next?

Unfortunately, no. Most people, business buyers included, don't read through entire pages of search results; instead, they just graze the top results. That's right, most don't even scroll down to the bottom of the first page of results, let alone click to the second or third results pages.

So, if you want to be seen—and get the clicks—you have to rank in the top five or ten sites that pop up when someone searches for a given topic. Any lower and the number of visitors you attract decreases rapidly.

Understanding Search Engine Optimization

Search results are what we call *organic*. This means they happen naturally; you can't buy them. The major search engines generate their results based on which sites they feel best match a particular query; Google and the other search engines don't accept money for placement. You just can't buy your way to the top.

> "Google and the other search engines don't accept money for placement. You just can't buy your way to the top."

Because search results occur organically, you have to find other ways to affect your ranking. If you have the right content and site design, users searching for a given topic will see your website among the top search results. That results in click-throughs to your site, which is how you acquire new prospects (and hopefully convert them into paying customers). This is what search engine marketing is all about—doing whatever it is you have to do to improve your ranking with Google and the other search engines.

To improve your search engine rankings, then, you need to optimize your site for these very same search engines. This process, not surprisingly, is called *search engine optimization*, or SEO.

What does SEO entail? In general, SEO requires you to focus the content of your site to best match the terms or keywords that your desired customers are searching for. You have to identify the keywords they use in their queries and then feature those keywords throughout your site—in the visible copy and behind the scenes in the appropriate HTML code.

SEO also requires you to organize your site in such a way that search engines can more effectively determine its content. That also affects web page design—there are design techniques that can improve your search ranking and those that can cause the search engines to ignore you completely.

SEO is all about hard work and smart design. It's more about the time and effort you spend rather than the money you spend. A bigger budget doesn't necessarily lead to better results.

Understanding Web Search

To better understand how search engine marketing and SEO work, you need to understand how the search engines work—what they search for and how. A short lesson ensues.

How a Typical Search Works

Searching a site like Google, Yahoo!, or Bing is deceptively simple. The user enters a search query, clicks the search button, and then waits for the site to display a list of matching results.

A typical search of this type takes less than half a second to complete. That's because all the searching takes place on the search engine site's own web servers. That's right; a user may think that he's searching the Web, but in effect he's searching a huge index of websites stored on the search site's servers that was created over a period of time. Because the user is only searching a server, not the entire web, his searches can be completed in the blink of an eye.

 Note

Many of the major search engines are now augmenting the use of compiled search indexes by real-time results from Facebook, Twitter, blogs, and other social media. So, you get some real-time results mixed in with the indexed web pages.

Of course, the user is unaware of what happens behind the scenes; he simply types his query into the search box on the search site's main web page, clicks the search button, and then views the search results page when it appears. Where the results are stored and how they're served is irrelevant.

How a Search Site Builds Its Database—And Assembles Its Index

So, searching Google or another search engine really means searching the index to that site's in-house database of web pages—not the Web itself. These databases hold literally billions of individual web pages. That's not necessarily the entire Web, but it is a good portion of it.

How does a search site determine which web pages to index and store on its servers? It's a complex process with several components.

First and foremost, most of the pages in the site's database are found by special *spider* or *crawler* software. This is software that automatically crawls the web, looking for new and updated web pages. Most spiders not only search for new web pages (by exploring links to other pages on the pages it already knows about), but also periodically recrawl pages already in the database, checking for changes and updates. A complete recrawling of the web pages in a search site's database typically takes place every few weeks, so no individual page is more than a few weeks out of date.

The search engine's spider reads each page it encounters, much like a web browser does. It follows every link on every page until all the links have been followed. This is how new pages are added to the site's database, by following those links the spider hasn't seen before.

The pages discovered by the spider are copied verbatim into the search site's database—and copied over each time they're updated. These stored web pages are used to compile the page summaries that appear on search results pages.

To search its database, the search site creates an index to all the stored web pages. This search engine index is much like the index found in the back of this book; it contains a list of all the important words used on every stored web page in the database. After the index has been compiled, it's easy enough to search for a particular word and have returned a list of all the web pages on which that word appears.

And that's exactly how a search index and database work to serve search queries. A user enters one or more words in a query, the search engine searches its index for those words, and then those web pages that contain those words are returned as search results. This is fairly simple in concept but much more complex in execution—especially given that each search engine indexes all the words on several billion web pages.

Examining the Major Search Engines

Okay, you're convinced—search engine marketing is important. Which search engines, then, should you target?

The number-one search engine today, in terms of searches and users, is Google (see Figure 10.2). In any given month, depending on who's doing the counting, Google (www.google.com) is responsible for about 65% of all web searches made in the U.S; its market share is even higher in some other countries (approaching 90% in the U.K, for example). That makes Google an extremely dominant player; no other search engine has half its market share.

Figure 10.2   *Google, the web's most popular search engine.*

The new number-two search engine today is Bing (see Figure 10.3). Bing (www.bing.com) is the latest iteration of Microsoft's search engine; it was formerly known as Live Search, Windows Live Search, and, before that, MSN Search. Officially launched in June 2009, Bing has been gaining market share on a month-by-month basis. Last time I checked (May 2011), Bing's share was around 17%.

Figure 10.3   *Bing, number two with a bullet.*

The number-three search engine today is Yahoo! (see Figure 10.4). Yahoo! (www.yahoo.com) has been around quite a bit longer than Google, but long ago lost the number-one position to its chief competitor. Today, Yahoo!'s search market share is in the 14% range and declining—still important, but less than it used to be.

Figure 10.4   *Yahoo!, the number-three search engine.*

 Note

Interestingly, Yahoo! has contracted with Microsoft for Bing to power Yahoo! search results. Although users will still see separate interfaces and possibly different search rankings, the search database and index will be the same for both sites.

Fortunately, the same SEO techniques work for all of these "big three" sites—and for smaller search engines, as well.

B2B SEARCH SITES

Although most B2B buyers will use one of these "big three" search engines to start their online research, some purchasers will also access B2B-specific search sites, especially when compiling information pertinent to the final negotiation. These B2B search sites are often specific to a given industry, and include the following:

- Alibaba.com (www.alibaba.com)
- Business.com (www.business.com)
- GlobalSpec (www.globalspec.com)
- Jayde (www.jayde.com)
- KnowledgeStorm (www.knowledgestorm.com)
- Masterseek.com (www.masterseek.com)
- ThomasNet (www.thomasnet.com)
- Zibb (www.zibb.com)

This type of B2B-specific search is a growing area—and a bit different from the traditional web-based search. Many of these sites don't search the Web per se, but rather are directories of relevant sites, with information assembled by a team of editors. You might need to manually submit your site to these B2B sites for inclusion; visit each site separately to determine what it takes to get listed.

What Search Engines Look For

How do Google and the other major search engines decide what pages appear at the top of a search results page? It's all about determining what a page's content is about and how that content relates to the search at hand.

The goal of a search engine is to provide the most accurate results to its users. The search engines don't care so much about the individual websites in their databases; they care about giving their users a more effective and efficient search experience.

"When a search engine ranks search results, it's with the intent of delivering the one best answer to that particular user's query."

When a search engine ranks search results, it's with the intent of delivering the one best answer to that particular user's query. Ideally, then, if someone is searching for a particular topic, those sites that best cover that topic will rise to the top of the search results.

But how do the search engines know what content is on a given page? There are a number of things the search engines look for—which happen to be the very things you'll want to optimize on your site.

Keywords

A search engine doesn't yet have the human capacity to read sentences and paragraphs and understand what it reads. Current technology enables a search engine to pull specific words and phrases from a page's text, but that's about it; the search engine has no way of knowing how well those words and phrases are used.

To determine what's important on a page, search engines look for *keywords*. A keyword is a word or phrase entered as part of a search query; the search engine tries to find the keyword on a web page and then determines how important that keyword is on the page.

The search engine does this by noting where on the page the keyword appears and how many times it's used. A site with a keyword buried near the bottom of a page will rank lower than one with the keyword placed near the top or used repeatedly in the page's text. It's not a foolproof way of determining importance and appropriateness, but it's a good first stab at it.

For example, if someone is searching for "consulting" and your web page includes the word *consulting* in a prominent position—in the first sentence of the first paragraph, for example—then your page is a good match for that search. If, on the other hand, you have a page about business services in general that doesn't include the word *consulting* at all or only includes it near the bottom of the page, the search engine will determine that your site *isn't* a good match for that searcher. Unless you use the keyword prominently and relatively often, you won't rank high for that particular search.

The major search engines, when they examine your pages, are going to look for the most important words—those words used in the page's title or headings, those words that appear in the opening paragraph on the page, and those words that are repeated throughout the page. The more prominently you include a word on your page, the more important a search engine will think it is to your site.

Conversely, giving prominent placement to the *wrong* words can hurt your search rankings and provide less relevant results. For example, if your site is about consulting but you for some reason include the words *packing* and *shipping* multiple times on the page, it will likely be viewed as a site about shipping services. This not only drives the wrong visitors to your site, but also lowers your search ranking in general because you're now one of the less useful spots listed.

Note

Search engines have a hard time analyzing—or even recognizing—images, videos, Flash animations, and other nontext content on a web page. This means you want to avoid presenting key information in images only; if you want the search engines to see something, it better be in text format.

HTML Tags

A search engine looks not just to the visible text on your site, but also to the page's underlying HTML code—specifically, the *metadata* in the code. This metadata includes your site's name and keyword "content," which is specified within the **<META>** tag. This tag appears in the head of your HTML document before the **<BODY>** tag and its contents.

A typical **<META>** tag looks something like this:

```
<META NAME="KEYWORDS" CONTENT="keyword1, keyword2,
keyword3">
```

It's easy enough for a search engine to locate the **<META>** tag and read the data contained within. If a site's metadata is properly detailed, this gives the search engine a good first idea as to what content is included on this page.

Beyond the **<META>** tag, search engines also examine the **<TITLE>** tag in the code. The search engines figure that the words you use in your page's title define, to some extent, the key content on the page. For this reason, you want to make sure that each page's **<TITLE>** tag includes two or three important keywords, followed by the page's name.

The search engines also seek out the heading tags in your HTML code—**<H1>**, **<H2>**, **<H3>**, and so forth. For this reason, you should use traditional heading tags (instead of newer Cascading Style Sheet coding) to emphasize key content on your pages.

Inbound Links

Google was the first search engine to realize that web rankings could be somewhat of a popularity contest—that is, if a site got a lot of traffic, there was probably a good reason for it. A useless site wouldn't attract a lot of visitors (at least not long-term), nor would it inspire other sites to link to it.

So, if a site has a lot of other sites linking back to it, it's probably because that site offers useful information relevant to the site doing the linking. The more links to a given site, the more useful that probably is.

And it's not just the quantity of links; it's also the quality. That is, a site that includes content that is relative to your page is more important than just some random site that links to your page. For example, if your business sells security solutions, you'll get more oomph with a link from another security-related site than you would with a link from a site about computer systems in general. Relevance matters.

Optimizing Your Site's Content

How do you optimize your site for higher search results? Well, there are lots of SEO tricks and tools you can employ, but the most effective thing you can do to improve your search ranking is to improve your site's content. Everything else you do is secondary; when it comes to SEO and improving your search ranking, content is king.

> "...when it comes to SEO and improving your search ranking, content is king."

What Is Quality Content?

How do the search engines define quality content? Pretty much the same way you and I do. It's content that fills visitors' needs and relates to and answers the questions at hand.

Quality content is useful content. It's informative, and it's accurate. It's grammatically correct, it's punctuated properly, and it reads well. It's original, it's lean and mean, and it's on point. It is relevant to the topic at hand and, most important, it is authoritative.

Quality content informs the reader without being self-serving. It answers important questions without leaving more questions unanswered. It serves a useful and practical purpose.

In short, quality content distinguishes your site from competing sites. When a potential customer says, "I found something important there," you know you have quality content.

Why Does Quality Content Matter?

As to why quality content matters, it's all about delivering relevant results. All the major search engines want to provide searchers with sites that best answer their users' queries; they don't want to serve up sites that leave their users still asking the same questions.

There are other reasons for improving your site's content, of course. First and foremost, the better your site's content, the more satisfied your customers will be. In addition, the better the content on your site, the more likely it is that other sites will link to it—and these inbound links are also important to your site's search ranking. If your site's content disappoints, other sites won't link to you; if your content excels, you'll get a lot of links without having to ask for them.

 Note

Experts dub content that attracts links from other quality sites as *linkworthy*. If your site is just like all the others out there, it's not linkworthy— that is, there's no reason for other sites to link to yours.

Writing Engaging Copy

Now we come to how you present the information on your web pages. There's a lot to be said for presenting your information in a grammatically correct, properly punctuated, engaging fashion.

 Note

Engaging copy involves more than just including all the keywords you've identified—which could be viewed as *keyword stuffing*. This is a technique wherein the site owner inserts multiple instances of a keyword onto a page, often using hidden, random text, in an effort to increase the keyword density and thus increase the page's apparent relevancy of a page. Most search engines today view keyword stuffing as a kind of search-related spam and employ sophisticated algorithms to detect the technique.

What does this mean? Well, it means utilizing your own copywriting skills or hiring an experienced copywriter. In fact, there's a whole army of web-friendly copywriters out there, and they know how to fine-tune copy for the particular needs of the web audience, as well as incorporate SEO techniques into their copy (which we discuss next). It's just like traditional marketing copywriting, except different.

Bottom line: Facts alone don't make for quality content. You have to present your facts in a way that is readable and easy to follow—just as you do in any medium.

Crafting SEO-Friendly Content

Your site's content not only has to be authoritative and engaging, but it also has to be presented in such a fashion that search engines notice it. This means making your content SEO-friendly—which may be a new skill for you.

Just what is SEO-friendly content? Here's a list of things that can make or break the way search engines interpret your site's content:

- **Use words, not pictures**—It bears repeating that today's search engines only look at the text on a web page, not at a page's images, videos, Flash animations, and the like. If you have important content to present, present it in the body text on your page.

- **Include keywords in your copy**—When you're presenting your core concepts, make sure you work in those keywords and phrases that your potential visitors will be searching for. If a keyword doesn't exist in a page's copy, search engines won't return that page as part of the relevant search results.

- **Repeat keywords and phrases naturally**—It's not enough to include your most important keywords and phrases once on a page. You need to repeat those keywords and phrases—but in a natural manner. It can't look as if you're keyword stuffing; the words have to flow organically in your text.

- **Make the important stuff more prominent**—Whether we're talking keywords or core concepts, the most important information on your web page should be placed in more prominent positions on the page where it will be more easily found by search crawlers. This might mean placing the information in one of the first two or three paragraphs on your page. It might also mean placing key concepts in your page's headings and subheadings.

- **Break up the copy**—It's always a good idea to modularize the content on your page. Instead of presenting a long train-of-thought block of text, break up that block into short chunks, no longer than 10 lines of formatted text, each chunk introduced by its own prominent heading or subheading. Make it easy for readers—and search crawlers—to find the information they want on your page.

Remember, though, that the way you present your content is secondary to the content itself. You have to start with authoritative content and then work from there.

Optimizing Your Site's Keywords

To some degree, all search optimization revolves around the use of keywords and key phrases. Whether you're talking the content on a page or the code that underlies that content, you use keywords to give your content and code more impact.

It's vital, then, that you learn how to create a list of keywords and key phrases relevant to your site and how to include them in your site's coding and content. It all starts with learning how to *think like the customer*; you need to get inside searchers' heads to determine which words they'll use in their queries.

Performing Keyword Research

The art of determining which keywords to use is called *keyword research*, and it's a key part of SEO. When you know which keywords and phrases that your target customers are likely to use, you can optimize your site for those words and phrases; if you don't know how they're searching, you don't know what to optimize.

Although you can conduct extensive (and expensive) market research to determine how your target audience is searching, or even guess as to what the top searches are, there are simpler and more effective ways to get smart about this. Several companies offer keyword research tools that compile and analyze keyword search statistics from all the major search engines. You can use the results from these keyword research tools to determine the most powerful keywords to include on your site.

These keyword research tools work by matching the content of your website with keywords relevant to that content; they've already searched through hundreds of thousands of possible keywords and phrases on the most popular search engines and mapped the results to their own databases. You enter a word or phrase that describes what your site has to offer, and the research tool returns a list of words or phrases related to that description, in descending order of search popularity.

Some of the more popular keyword research tools include the following:

- **KeywordDiscovery** (www.keyworddiscovery.com)
- **Wordtracker** (www.wordtracker.com)
- **WordZe** (www.wordze.com)

These tools don't come cheap; expect to pay $35 to $70 *per month* to subscribe.

Fine-Tuning Keywords for B2B

One challenge that B2B sites face is filtering out unwanted consumer visitors. The total number of site visitors you attract is much less important than attracting the *right* visitors—specifically, businesses that are interested in your products and services. You don't want a lot of general consumers hitting your site; not only is this wasted bandwidth, you might end up fielding a lot of irrelevant questions and requests from individuals who will never become part of your customer base.

How, then, do you filter nonbusiness traffic from your site? The first step is making sure that only potential business customers find your site when searching—and that your site does *not* come when nonbusiness buyers search.

You can accomplish this by the careful use of selected keywords. Select the right keywords and you'll show up in business searches but not general consumer searches. Pick the wrong keywords and everybody and their brother will find you, and waste your time and resources.

Determining the right keywords for B2B purposes is a tricky business. You have to choose keywords that are *selective*; you want to be exclusive rather than inclusive.

Here's an example. Let's say your company provides enterprise-level computer security solutions. You might think that *computer security* would be a good keyword phrase; it describes what you do, after all, and what your customers are likely to be looking for.

Unfortunately, *computer security* is also something that general consumers look for—quite frequently, as a matter of fact. Use *computer security* as a keyword and you'll end up ranking alongside Norton and McAfee and other companies offering consumer-oriented security and anti-malware solutions. This is bad for a number of reasons; not only will you have hordes of home PC users clogging up your site, you'll also be competing with those consumer security companies for that keyword, which will drive up your cost per click. Not a good situation.

What you need to do is come up with keywords that mean something only to your targeted business buyers. That might mean adding the word *corporate* or *enterprise* or *business* to your keyword phrases. It might also mean using industry jargon instead of more common phrases to describe what you offer.

Now, I'm generally not a fan of industry-speak and buzzwords, but when it comes to SEO, they can be useful. Take our "computer security" example. Instead of using the keyword phrase *computer security*, you might use the buzzier *information security* or *IT security* or *secure enterprise computing* or *site protection services* or *data leakage protection*. (I love that last one!) You get the idea—use words and phrases that the business market will know, but general consumers won't.

This will require some work. You'll probably have to try a variety of keywords before you find the right combination that delivers business traffic and not consumer traffic. But then, successful SEO requires constant fine-tuning; this is especially so when optimizing for B2B search.

Determining the Right Keyword Density

After you've generated a list of keywords, you now have to use those keywords on your web pages. Let's start by examining how and how often you should include keywords in your page's copy.

First, know that the more often you use a keyword in your body text, the more likely it is that search crawlers will register the keyword—to a point. Include a keyword too many times, and crawlers will think you're artificially stuffing the keyword into your phrase, with no regard for the actual content. If you're suspected of keyword stuffing in this fashion, don't be surprised to see your search ranking actually decrease or your page disappear completely from that search engine's search results. (As I've mentioned, search engines don't like keyword stuffing.)

Thus, you need to determine the correct keyword density when you're optimizing the content of a web page. What is an optimal keyword density? That depends. If you have a lot of different keywords on a long page, you could have a density of 20% or more and still rank fine. If you have only a handful of keywords on a short page, a 5% keyword density might be too much. The key is to make sure your page is readable; if it sounds stilted or awkward due to unnecessary keyword repetition, chances are a search engine will also think that you're overusing your keywords.

 Note

Keyword density is the number of times a keyword or phrase appears compared to the total number of words on a page.

Writing Keyword-Oriented Copy

So, what's the best way to incorporate keywords into your site's content?

First, know that web copywriting is very similar to direct response copywriting. You have to describe things in words, not pictures, and if you're selling something, provide a strong "why to buy" message. The big difference between direct response copywriting and web copywriting is that with web copywriting, you have two different audiences: the site's visitors and the search engines.

This means you have to provide readable, compelling copy for your customers, while at the same time incorporate all the necessary keywords and phrases that matter to the search engines. You don't want to sacrifice one for the other; never make your page less readable just to cram in another keyword. Go for readability first and then incorporate the keywords as you can.

One way to improve both readability and search optimization is to break your copy into small sections or chunks of text and then introduce each section with a heading or subheading. As you learn shortly, search crawlers look for keywords in your heading tags; headings also help readers identify important sections on your page. So, chunking up your text has benefit for both your audiences.

> "...never make your page less readable just to cram in another keyword. Go for readability first and then incorporate the keywords as you can."

Two other good places to include keywords are in your page's first and last paragraphs. Not only do search crawlers look more closely at the beginning and end of your page and tend to skip the middle parts, readers look to the first and last paragraphs to introduce key ideas and then summarize your page's content. It's just like in writing a newspaper article; it's the first and last graphs that are most important.

Of course, when you incorporate keywords and phrases into your text, you have to do so in a natural fashion—while using the word or phrase verbatim. So, if one of your key phrases is *enterprise solutions*, you have to use that exact phrase and in a way that doesn't sound forced. This is a definite copywriting challenge but one that can be met.

One last thing. On the Web, there's little benefit to short copy. Not only do readers want as much information as possible, longer copy provides more opportunity for you to place your keywords and phrases without overly increasing keyword density. Let's face it, if you have 10 keywords to include, it's easier to do so on a 1,000-word page (organized into shorter reader-friendly chunks, of course) than on one that includes only 100 words total. (Put another way, a shorter page is more likely to sound keyword-stuffed than a longer one.)

So, write more copy if you need to—but make sure you chunk into shorter sections for the reader. Use the extra words to add more keywords and phrases to your page, and to provide more useful information to your site's visitors.

Optimizing Your Site's HTML Tags

Another important use of keywords is within your site's HTML code; most search crawlers scan specific HTML tags for information they use in indexing a page. Insert your keywords and phrases into these tags, and you'll improve your site's results for that search engine.

Which HTML tags do you need to focus on? There are a few, but they're relatively easy to work with—assuming you know a little HTML.

<TITLE> Tags

We'll work our way down from the top, starting with your page's title. The title is the text that appears in the title bar of a web browser; the title should present your page's official name and provide a glimpse to its content. It's also an effective place to use your chosen keywords.

That's because the page title is one of the first places that search crawlers look to determine the content of your page. Crawlers figure that the title should accurately reflect what the page is about—for example, if you have a page titled "Accounting Services," the page is most likely about accounting services. Unless you mistakenly or purposefully mistitle your page, the search crawler will skim off keywords and phrases from the title to use in its search engine index. In addition, when your page appears on a search engine's results page, the title is what the search engine uses as the listing name.

For all these reasons, you need to get your most important keywords and phrases into your page's title—which you do via the HTML **<TITLE>** tag. This tag appears in the head of your document before the body text. It's a simple tag that looks something like this:

```
<TITLE>Insert your title here</TITLE>
```

✉ *Note*

As with all HTML tags, capitalization is not important. For example, you can enter this tag as either **<TITLE>** or **<title>**; it works the same either way.

Just insert your chosen title text between the **<TITLE>** and **</TITLE>** tags. Whatever is between the tags is your page's official title and is what appears in the web browser's title bar.

What's the ideal length for a title? Well, a title can't exceed 64 characters; any additional text is truncated. So, you have to keep the 64-character limit in mind but aim to include from three to ten words total. This makes the title both readable for users (short enough to scan) and useful for search engines (long enough to include a handful of keywords).

What should you put in your title? Your page's official name, of course, but also one or more of the most important keywords for your site. It's best if the name includes the keywords, but you can always add the keywords after the name, following some sort of divider character—a colon (:), or semicolon (;), perhaps a vertical line (|), or dash (-), or even a simple comma (,).

For example, if your site's name is New Energy Sources, you might enter the following <TITLE> tag:

```
<TITLE>New Energy Sources: Wind, Solar, Geothermal, Tidal,
Biomass</TITLE>
```

That's 59 characters and 8 words, both of which fit within our guidelines. Users will see the name of the site in their title bars and in the search results, and search engines will link this page to queries regarding all types of new energy.

 Note

When counting characters, remember that a space counts as a character, same as a letter or number or special character.

<META> Tags

The <META> tag is actually several tags, each with its own specific attribute that conveys so-called metadata (data about your page) to the search crawlers. You can insert multiple <META> tags (one for each attribute) into the head of your document, like this:

```
<HEAD>

<TITLE>Accounting Services</TITLE>

<META NAME="DESCRIPTION" CONTENT="Accounting services for the manufac-
turing industry">

<META NAME="KEYWORDS" CONTENT="accounting, accounting
services, manufacturing, finance">

</HEAD>
```

As you can see from this example, there are two primary <META> attributes—**DESCRIPTION** and **KEYWORDS**. (There are actually more than two attributes, but these are the important ones for SEO.) Each attribute is defined by the **NAME** attribute, as in **NAME="ATTRIBUTE"**. Then the **CONTENT** attribute is used to define the content for the description or keywords. It's all fairly straightforward.

> ✉ *Note*
>
> The only problem with <META> tags is that they've been so overused that many search engines now ignore them (for example, Yahoo! recognizes the <META> KEYWORDS attribute, but Google doesn't). That said, you can't ignore <META> tags because they do feed information to some search engines.

Let's continue by looking at the **DESCRIPTION** attribute. The text assigned to this attribute is used by some search engines as the description for your web page in their search results. This means you want to think of the **DESCRIPTION** text as a short promotional blurb that describes what your page is about.

The tag works like this:

```
<META NAME="DESCRIPTION" CONTENT="Insert your description here">
```

The variable text is the bit between the quotation marks. It's read as a complete text string—a block of text, as it were. (And it's okay to include commas in the **DESCRIPTION** text because they're treated as-is.) Within this descriptive text, you should make sure to include as many keywords or phrases that fit naturally (avoid keyword stuffing).

The second important <META> tag uses the **KEYWORDS** attribute. As you might suspect, this attribute is your opportunity to tell the search engines which keywords your page is targeting.

It's easy to add this tag to your page's HTML code. Just use the following template:

```
<META NAME="KEYWORDS" CONTENT="keyword 1, keyword 2,
keyword 3">
```

Separate each keyword or phrase by a comma. You can include as many keywords or phrases as you like, and capitalization doesn't matter. And this is important—the keywords you include in this tag *don't* actually have to appear on the web page.

Note

One good use of the **KEYWORDS** tag is to include common misspellings of
legitimate keywords used on your site. For example, if you use the keyword
"accounting," you might use the **KEYWORDS** tag to include the misspellings
"acounting," "acconting," and "accountining." Similarly, you can use the
tag to list synonyms for your actual keywords—such as "financial services"
and "bean counting."

Header Tags

A header is a heading or subheading within your body text, kind of like a newspaper headline or the headings between sections in this book. The HTML standard
lets you use six different levels of headings, from <H1> to <H6>, in descending
order.

Headers are important because most search crawlers look in these tags for content information. They figure that if a topic or keyword is important enough to
be included in the header, it probably describes your page's content and that it's
important enough to index.

So, first of all, you have to organize the information on your page into short
chunks of text and then introduce each text block with its own header. Include in
the header text as many keywords and phrases as you can that describe the given
text in an organic fashion.

The form of this HTML code is simple:

```
<H1>This is the header text.</H1>
```

Obviously, insert your own text between the "on" and "off" tags, and use the other
header tags (<H2>, <H3>, <H4>, and so on) for lower-level headers.

 Note

Many cutting-edge web designers have switched from the older **<H1>**-style
heading tags to Cascading Style Sheet (CSS) **<DIV>** and **<SPAN>** codes.
That's unfortunate because most search engines look for the traditional
heading tags to determine the content of a page. If you want to optimize
your ranking in most search indexes, you'll have to include both CSS coding and the traditional **<H1>** and **<H2>** tags.

Anchor Text

Keywords are also important for the *anchor text* on your page—the text that accompanies your web links.

The anchor text is one of the elements that search engines evaluate to determine the value of a link. You can increase the value of an outbound or intrasite link by including keywords in the anchor text. This lets the search crawlers know that the site you're linking to is related to the keyword—and thus a more relevant link.

For example, if one of your top keywords is *microprocessor* and you're linking to the Intel website, the anchor text that links to the website should include the word *microprocessor*. In this instance, you might write and link from the following sentence:

```
We exclusively use Intel microprocessors in our systems.
```

Although you could limit the link to the word *Intel*, the anchor text would not include your keyword *microprocessor*. Better, then, to format the entire sentence—including the word *microprocessor* as the anchor text for the link.

Obviously, you create the link for the anchor text using basic HTML code. This sort of linking is done automatically by most HTML editing or web page creation programs, or you can code the text manually, like this:

```
<a href="http://www.intel.com">We exclusively use Intel
microprocessors in our systems.</a>
```

The takeaway here is to always include one or more keywords in the anchor text you use to link to related sites.

Optimizing Your Site's Design and Organization

When it comes to SEO, content is king, but design is also important. A good design can help search crawlers identify key content, whereas a bad design can negatively affect how your site ranks. In fact, some designs can actually make your site *invisible* to search crawlers. Assuming that you want your site seen and indexed, you need to pay attention to a few design basics.

To that end, let me present some tips you can use to optimize the individual pages on your website. These are universal tips that work on any type of page on any type of site.

Put the Most Important Stuff First on the Page

Search crawlers start at the top of a page and then read downward. Like human readers, they might not read the entire page, so it's essential to put the most important elements at the top of your page, in the main headings, and in initial paragraphs. A search crawler will see your leading content and register it as important; content lower on the page will be registered as subsidiary if it's noted at all.

Use Headings and Subheadings

Another way to tell a search engine that something is important is to include it in a heading or subheading on the page. As we've previously discussed, your page's heading tags are singled out by most search crawlers on the assumption they highlight the most important content of your site. So, you need to use headings to separate and highlight content on your page and to highlight your most important keywords and phrases.

Use Text, Not Pictures (or Videos or Flash...)

Although I've mentioned this before, it bears repeating: Search crawlers read text and nothing but text. They don't read images, they don't read Flash animations, and they don't read videos. Every element on your page other than text is essentially invisible to search crawlers. It's only the text that matters.

This is important if your website designers (or even the techie guys) insist on presenting important content via nontext elements. The most glaring example of this are sites that use nothing but Flash animation on their introductory pages, which not only annoys many users but also causes most search crawlers to skip completely over them—and perhaps the rest of the site.

The reason this is bad is that a page made up completely of Flash elements is basically a blank page as far as the major search engines are concerned. If the page is completely in Flash, the search engines have no idea what the page is about. They can get some idea of the content from the page's <TITLE> and <META> tags, but that's not nearly as good as reading the site's actual content—which they can't because there's no text to read.

The same thing goes with pages that rely on images or videos for the bulk of their content. A search crawler can't look at an image or view a video; it has no way (short of a file's **ALT** tag) to determine what the image or video is about. Again, the page appears blank to the search crawlers.

So, the first thing you need to do is overrule those designers who want to Flash up your site and take a back-to-basics, text-based approach. You don't need to get rid of all images, animations, and videos, but they need to be downplayed on the page—and supplemented by well-written, descriptive text.

Optimizing Inbound Links

As you've learned, Google bases a large part of its search ranking on how many and what kinds of sites link to your pages. It assumes that the more authoritative and relevant your content, the more inbound links you'll have.

It's imperative, then, that you work on increasing the inbound links to your site. You need to work not just on the quantity of these links, but also their quality; the more relevant and authoritative the sites that link to yours, the higher the import that search engines will assign to those links.

What are quality inbound links? For a B2B site, you want to encourage links from up and down the supply chain. That means getting links from your suppliers (up) and your distributors and customers (down). It's also good to get links from other sites in your industry, including industry groups, blogs, and web-based publications.

How do you get other sites to link to your site? It all starts with the content—and then you can always ask.

Creating Linkworthy Content

The most important part of attracting inbound links is having site content that other sites want to link to. It's a matter of building a "linkworthy" site; if you have quality content, websites and blogs will link to you.

The keys to creating linkworthy content are to be authoritative, creative, and add value not found in competing sites. Your site needs to fully address the chosen topic and offer unique content. If related sites find your content to be both valuable and unique, they'll make the links.

Getting the Word Out

Of course, for a website or blog to link to you, it has to know about you. The old adage of "if you build it, they will come" is viable only if they actually hear about what you're doing.

There are many ways to get the word out about your site. Probably the most popular approach is to employ traditional public relations techniques. Issue a press release (paper or electronic), make some phone calls, fire off some emails to relevant blogs and forums—anything you have to do to create a buzz about your site.

When other sites and blogs start talking about your site, you'll attract interested visitors, some of whom will find it worthwhile to link to your site.

The nice thing about generating links in this fashion is that they're truly organic. The links come from sites and blogs that are interested in your content and are thus highly relevant. They link because they want to, not because they're asked to or paid to. They're quality links—just what Google and the other engines tend to rank high.

> ✉ *Note*
>
> When you attract links organically, you should experience a trickle-down effect—that is, other sites will link to your site when they see the link on another respected sites. Quality links beget more links.

Making Link Requests

This isn't to say that you can't directly ask other sites to link to yours. In fact, making link requests is an important part of any SEO strategy, but sometimes you have to be a bit aggressive in creating new inbound links.

How do you ask another site to link to yours? It's as simple as identifying the site or blog (based on its relevance and quality) and then sending an email to the site's webmaster or author.

At that point, the targeted site either will or won't make the requested link. If the answer is yes, you're good to go. If the answer is no (or, more likely, if you don't receive an answer), there's no harm in asking again.

Engaging in Link Trading

Then there's the issue of link trading, or reciprocal linking. There are two ways to do this, one of which generates higher-quality results than the other.

The best way to trade links is directly with another site. That is, you identify a site or blog that you'd like to have linked to yours and email that site. In your email, you offer to place a link to their site in yours if they reciprocate with a link back to your site. You both benefit from the link exchange.

The more suspect way to trade links is via a link exchange service or program. These services, such as GotLinks (www.gotlinks.com) and Link LinkMarket (www.linkmarket.net), can provide hundreds of sites to link to your site in exchange for links from your site to theirs. The only problem with these link exchanges is that the linking sites are not necessarily high-quality sites; they're often not even sites relevant to your site's topic. In some instances, the links you get are from obvious link farms—not sites that help you increase your search ranking.

> ✉ *Note*
>
> I'm not a big fan of automated link exchanges. I am, however, a fan of active link trading. There's no harm at all in exchanging a link on your site for a link from a relevant website. One good turn deserves another, as the saying goes—sometimes it takes a link to get a link.

Purchasing Links

Finally, we come to the controversial topic of link purchasing—paying for links back to your site. This could involve sending another site a one-time check or perhaps agreeing to share some portion of your site's ad revenue.

Some marketers view link purchasing as a black hat technique, somehow less pure than trading links or generating links organically. But there are some good reasons to consider this approach.

For example, if the only way you can get a link from a relevant, high-quality site is to pay for it, that might be better than not getting the link at all. And some high-volume sites only sell their links, which means you have to pay to play.

Bottom line? Paying for links shouldn't be your first approach, but you shouldn't rule it out, either. Sometimes it's the only way to get the inbound links you need.

Optimizing Links Between Pages on Your Site

There's one last type of link to deal with—those links from one page on your site to another. These internal links are important for a number of reasons.

First, and perhaps most important, internal links help the individual pages on your site to get noticed by the various search crawlers. Search crawlers actually look for internal links; they use these links to identify further pages on your site. For this reason, you should include links to all your important pages on your site's home page, as well as in your site's menu and navigation system.

Second, using a keyword or phrase in the anchor text accompanying an internal link helps to build the relevancy of the linked-to page. It's a simple thing; search crawlers look to the anchor text for targeted keywords. The more anchor text you create via internal links, the more keywords get noticed.

This also increases the ranking of your site's internal pages with that search engine. The closer a page is from your site's home page, in terms of number of clicks, the higher that page will rank with the search engine. Include a direct link from your site's home page, and you'll ensure a higher ranking for the linked-to internal page.

For all these reasons, you need to pay as much attention to your site's internal links as you do to building inbound links from external sites. There's no getting around it—every link is important, whether it's inbound or internal!

Optimizing Images

As you've hopefully learned by now, search crawlers pretty much ignore images, videos, and other media files on a web page. They crawl a page's text and look at certain HTML tags, but that's about it—which means, of course, that any content on your site that isn't text is essentially invisible to the search engines.

But what do you do if you use a lot of images and videos on your web pages, instead of text? (Some designers are insistent, after all... .) Well, there are ways around the crawlers' limitations, as you'll soon learn.

Using the ALT Attribute

Images are inserted into a web page via the following bit of HTML code:

```
<IMG SRC="image.jpg" WIDTH="XXX" HEIGHT="XXX" ALT="description"
TITLE="title">
```

In decoding the code, the <IMG> tag says that there's an image to insert, the **SRC** attribute defines the location of the image file, and the **WIDTH** and **HEIGHT** attributes define the size of the image (in pixels)—all pretty standard stuff. It's the **ALT** and **TITLE** attributes, however, that deserve closer inspection.

The **ALT** attribute defines what a web browser should display if, for some reason, the image file isn't available or doesn't display on a page. Instead of seeing the chosen image, the user would see the text entered between the quotation marks in the **ALT** attribute.

More important, the **ALT** attribute is what search crawlers read to determine the content of an image file. Because they can't view the actual content of an image file itself, they rely on the text description in the **ALT** attribute to tell them what the image is about. It's an inexact science, of course; there's no law, unfortunately, prohibiting a site designer from describing an image of a wrinkled old man as a "hot babe."

Limitations noted, the **ALT** attribute is how you get the search engines to recognize your page's images as valid content. This means you need to enter descriptive text into the **ALT** attributes for each and every image on your website. Make sure the attribute text not only describes the image, but also includes (you guessed it!) important keywords and phrases. In other words, use the **ALT** tag to reinforce your site's keyword scheme—while still describing how an image looks.

Using the TITLE Attribute

The final attribute for the <**IMG**> tag is the **TITLE** attribute. This attribute assigns a title to the image, which is what displays if a user hovers his cursor over an image.

Although the **TITLE** attribute isn't crawled as often as the **ALT** attribute, it still represents an opportunity to describe your image in words. Follow the same approach as you do with the **ALT** attribute; use the **TITLE** attribute to hold a description of the image, along with important keywords and phrases.

The Bottom Line

For most B2B marketers, search engine marketing is the most important part of their digital marketing strategy. That's because search engines drive the majority of new customers to most B2B sites; the higher your site can rank in the search results, the more prospects you'll attract. For that reason, you need to optimize your site for search. You do this by providing relevant content, choosing the right keywords to describe that content, and then using those keywords throughout your site (and its underlying code) in a fashion that the search engines like. It's a bit of a trial-and-error process, but when you get it right, traffic—and potential customers—will follow.

11

B2B Online Advertising

How do you reach new B2B customers? Obviously, search engine marketing plays a big role, but you can also attract the attention of prospective customers via online advertising.

You probably do some degree of advertising in traditional media—probably in targeted periodicals and industry publications. Well, online advertising is similar in its effect, especially when you target customers by keywords or demographics. The big difference is that you can tell exactly how well each ad is working—all you have to do is track the clicks.

How Effective Is B2B Online Advertising?

B2B advertising, both online and off, is all about reaching out to prospective new customers and alerting them to your products and services. B2B ads, when targeted at the right audience, both enhance brand awareness and help you generate new leads.

Are online ads as effective as search engine marketing? No, they're not, even in the B2B milieu. Online users, even those who are professional business buyers, tend to trust organic search results more than paid placements. So, given the choice between a high ranking on a search page and a text ad on the same page, potential customers are going to be more influenced by the search result, and somewhat discount the paid placement. That's just the nature of the beast.

That does not mean, however, that online ads have no value. They do. Online ads can reinforce your organic search results, as well as reach potential buyers via careful placement on targeted websites and blogs. It's certainly possible an online ad can reach buyers that might not otherwise find you via search.

> "Online users, even those who are professional business buyers, tend to trust organic search results more than paid placements."

Online ads can also be targeted to specific purposes. For example, you can use ads to support your current promotions, or to encourage prospects to attend a web seminar.

And, when compared to traditional advertising, online ads have the benefit of being a direct response medium; customers can act directly on online ads, simply by clicking the ad. Because of this, it's much, much easier to track the effectiveness of online advertising; you can track not just how many people view an ad, but how many click the ad, go to your website, and then submit an inquiry or initiate a purchse. That introduces a level of accountability unheard of in more than a century of traditional advertising.

Perhaps this is why B2B marketers continue to increase their spending on online advertising. In fact, B2B marketers increased their online advertising expenditures by double digits every year from 2005 to 2010 (see Figure 11.1).[1] For the average B2B company in 2010, online advertising made up 13.1% of their total marketing budget.

---

1. eMarketer, "B2B Marketing Online," 2011

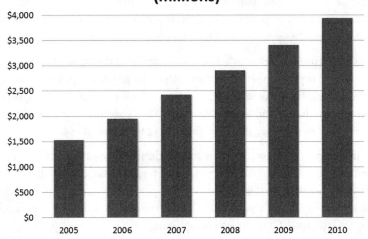

U.S. B2B Online Ad Spending (millions)

Figure 11.1   *B2B online advertising spending from 2005 to 2010. (Courtesy eMarketer, www.emarketer.com)*

That said, not all B2B marketers are enamored of online ads. Many have experienced diminishing returns from their online advertising programs, especially from the pay-per-click component; indeed, ROI from all forms of online advertising is diminishing as many business buyers ignore the paid ads that appear alongside the organic search results on Google, Yahoo!, and Bing. So, you should be constantly monitor the performance of your online advertising campaigns, and be prepared to shift funds if things aren't working out as well as you'd hope.

How Online Advertising Differs from Traditional Advertising

In many ways, online advertising is quite similar to advertising in traditional print media. An ad is an ad, after all; it's nothing more than a paid display of your promotional message.

With traditional advertising, you pay for space on the printed newspaper or magazine page or you pay for time on radio or television airwaves. With online advertising, you pay for space on a web page.

So, the pay for placement thing is pretty much the same. What's different about online advertising is that you have a lot more say over where your ad gets placed and who sees it, which is important for B2B companies. You also can track each ad's performance with a level of granularity not possible in traditional advertising—right down to the individual person clicking an ad.

Targeted Placement

Let's tackle the placement part of the equation. When you're advertising online, you place your ad on a web page. In most instances, you can dictate both where on the page your ad appears and on what websites.

When you're running a display ad, you typically have the choice of several page placements. Many sites offer advertising along the top of the page (so-called *banner advertising*), along the left or right sides, along the bottom of the page, or in a box somewhere in the middle. Not all sites offer all positions, of course, but you'd be surprised at what's available if you're willing to pay for it.

Page placement is less assured when you're running pay-per-click advertisements. We discuss the mechanics of this type of ad in more detail later in this chapter, but in general know that the higher you bid for a per-click price, the more likely your ad will appear higher on a page. Bid lower, and your ad will likely appear lower on the page. It's a kind of pay-for-placement deal.

Equally important for B2B marketers, you can easily place display ads with just those websites that meet specific targeting requirements. You can choose specific sites where you want to appear (such as industry-related sites) or identify sites by their traffic or demographic profile.

With pay-per-click ads, on the other hand, you let the ad network determine which sites to use; you identify (and pay for) certain keywords, and your ad appears on sites with content that matches those keywords. Although that might not be as desirable as choosing specific sites for your ads, you could discover new sites for promotion that you wouldn't have found on your own.

The point is, online advertising is more about narrowcasting than broadcasting your message—which is ideal for B2B marketing. Traditional media tend toward the broadcast model, where your message goes out to a large audience with a lot of waste, and you end up overshooting your target audience, even when advertising in industry-specific publications. In contrast, online media are very targeted. If you only want to reach IT decision makers in Fortune 500 companies, you can do it; you don't have to show your ad to everyone and their brother in the consumer world.

✉ Note

Although it's relatively easy to target online ads demographically, it's not always so easy to target regionally. That is, many ads on the Web are viewable by users anywhere in the world. You want to make sure you don't waste resources following up on inquiries from outside the area where you normally do business.

Improved Tracking

There's an old saying among advertisers that you know that only half of your advertising works, but you don't know which half. Well, with online advertising, you can quickly and easily determine which half of your advertising is working—down to a specific ad on a specific website.

That's because online, you can track when an ad is clicked; when someone takes action with an ad, you know it. There's no guessing as to whether this ad or that drove a given person into a store to make a purchase because the data tells you precisely which ads delivered the most traffic back to your website. (And from there, you can track further actions—including sales.)

This puts a lot more responsibility on you as an advertiser, of course. There's no more waffling about a given ad enhancing your brand image or gaining some nebulous type of "exposure." Online, an ad either gets clicked or it doesn't. You know immediately whether your advertising is working by tracking the traffic from the ad to your website. The more clicks you get, the more effective the ad is. (At attracting viewers, in any case—not necessarily in increasing sales.) If you don't get any or many clicks, you know a particular ad is in the half that doesn't work.

This ability to track ad results clearly distinguishes online advertising from its offline brethren. With traditional advertising, there's no way to know how effective any single ad is; sure, you can tell if sales go up during the course of a campaign, but you don't know which ads in which media truly drove those sales. With online advertising, there's no way *not* to know how each ad is performing; you get near-real time data that can help you fine-tune your future ad content and placement.

Efficiency of Investment

This combination of relevant placement and improved tracking makes online advertising a much more efficient investment than traditional B2B advertising. You don't have to engage in broad placement when you want to target only a narrow audience. You don't have to put up with half your ads not working when you can easily determine which ads are pulling customers and which aren't.

The upshot is that you can typically get better results with less investment online, especially if you properly target where you advertise; you don't have to pay for unwanted broad reach. You can create very targeted ads for a very targeted business audience, which will likely result in higher response rates. In other words, you can target the exact audience you want, and pay only for those results.

Different Payment Models

All this talk about online advertising makes it sound like there's only one type of ad, which isn't the case. There are lots of different types of ads you can run and several different payment models to choose from for those ads.

Let's look at the payment models first. There are two primary forms of payment for online ads—you can pay for impressions, as with traditional media, but you can also pay for performance.

CPM—Cost-Per-Thousand

Let's start with the payment model you're probably most familiar with, the good old cost-per-thousand impressions (CPM) model. It's simplicity itself; you pay a certain price to get your ad in front of a thousand eyeballs.

 Note

The "M" in CPM comes from the Latin word *mille*, or thousand. If Latin isn't your thing, know that some people refer to this payment method as CPT, or literally cost-per-thousand.

For example, you might make an ad placement with a $50 CPM. That is, you pay $50 for each 1,000 impressions. This might be measured in terms of 1,000 copies printed of a newspaper or magazine or 1,000 viewers of a television program. In any case, you apply this $50 CPM rate to the total number of impressions—the total print run or the full viewership. So, continuing the example, if you place your ad in a magazine with a 100,000-copy print run, you pay $5,000 total for your ad—that's 100,000 divided by 1,000, times the $100 rate.

With this traditional model, you're paying for exposure, not for results. It doesn't matter if don't make a single sale from the ad; you still pay the full cost of the ad. The only thing the host medium guarantees is the eyeballs; what the bodies connected to those eyeballs do after viewing your ad is totally up in the air.

Although this payment model is not the dominant model on the Web, it is still used for some online advertising, notably online display ads. In this instance, an ad network guarantees placement on a selection of websites that deliver a specified amount of traffic; you apply the CPM rate to the website traffic, and you get how much you pay.

Know, however, that with the online CPM model, there is no guarantee of any sort of driving traffic back to your website. You're paying solely for placement, not for results.

> ✉ *Note*
>
> Cost-per-view (CPV) advertising is a uniquely online version of traditional CPM advertising. Instead of charging for ephemeral "impressions," CPV advertising charges for distinct views of an advertisement or website. It's kind of the same thing but measured with web-specific page view metrics.

CPC—Cost-Per-Click

Instead of paying for impressions or views, most online advertisers opt for a more performance-oriented payment method. The most popular online payment method, then, is cost-per-click (CPC), a hallmark of pay-per-click (PPC) advertising. With CPC/PPC ads, the advertiser pays only when a user clicks an ad. The advertiser does not pay for the placement of the ad itself, so the number of impressions or views is mostly irrelevant.

> ✉ *Note*
>
> Of all the different payment models, CPC is far and away the most prominent in online advertising.

The actual cost-per-click is typically determined by how much the advertiser is willing to bid on a specific keyword. That is, you choose a keyword to associate with your ad, and your ad is displayed on websites that have similar content or on search results pages when someone searches for that keyword on Google, Yahoo!, or other search engine. How often your ad is displayed or how high up on the search results page are factors of how high you bid for that keyword in relation to how high competing advertisers also bid. If you bid more than your competitors, your ad will be seen more often and more visibly. If you're cheap about it (that is, if you get significantly outbid), your ad will be less visible.

As to that CPC bidding, how much you actually end up paying is a factor of what you bid versus what your competitors for that keyword bid. You don't necessarily pay the full bid price; if you outbid the competition, you'll be charged only slightly more than the next-highest bid. So, if you bid $2 per click and the next-highest bid is $1 per click, you might only be charged $1.10 per click or so. In any case, you'll never be charged more than your specified bid amount.

And remember, you pay only when someone clicks your ad. Even if your ad gets displayed on a website that has 100,000 visitors per day, if only one of those visitors clicks your ad, you pay just for that single click. (Of course, if you only get one click from a 100,000-visitor site, there's probably something wrong with your ad—or you're advertising on the wrong site.)

Given that you never know in advance how many clicks an ad might receive, how do you know how much you'll spend for CPC advertising? That's simple; you establish a budget up front. The ad network will run your ad until you've hit your budget level and then cease all further display. You're never charged more than what you budgeted.

Most online ad networks work with a daily CPC budget level. So, for example, if you set a $100 daily budget and bid $2 per click, your ad will run each day until you've received 50 clicks. (That's the $100 total budget divided by $2 per click.)

The advantage of CPC payment is that you're truly paying for results. You don't pay if no one takes action on your ad. It's that simple—and that powerful.

For this reason, CPC is the dominant payment method for online advertising, both to consumers and to businesses. Certainly, all the text ads you see on the search sites are CPC in nature; much display advertising is also moving to the CPC model.

Both the CPM or CPC payment models can be used with any type of online advertising. There are two primary types of ads used by B2B marketers—text ads and display ads. We'll discuss both next.

Using PPC Ads

The most popular type of web advertising today is pay-per-click (PPC) advertising. If you're just starting out with an online advertising program, you'll probably want to start with PPC ads.

How PPC Advertising Works

With PPC advertising, you don't pay for placement; you pay only when someone clicks the ad. At that point, you pay the agreed-upon (or previously bid) cost-per-click rate.

The typical PPC ad is a small text ad, placed contextually on a search results page or website with similar content. There are other types of PPC ads, of course; PPC merely explains the payment method, not the look or feel of the ad itself.

These text ads typically consist of three or four short lines of text but no images. The first line is a clickable headline, followed by one or two lines of body copy, and a final line consisting of the target URL. Short but sweet, these ads are; you have to write some powerful and efficient copy to encourage customer clicks.

PPC ads are most often found on the results pages of the major search engines—Google, Yahoo!, Bing, and the like. These ads are typically listed alongside the organic search results in a separate section of the page (see Figure 11.2).

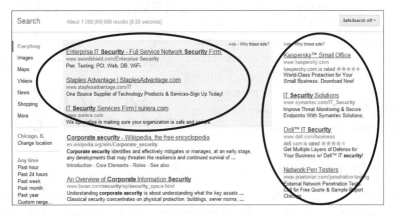

Figure 11.2   *Text ads at the top and side of Google's search results page.*

Text ads can also appear on third-party websites. In most instances, these third-party sites are part of the ad network run by the major search engine. So, if you advertise with Google's AdWords network, your text ads will appear on Google's search results pages, as well as on websites that belong to the AdWords network.

Understanding Context-Sensitive Ad Placement

PPC ads are different from traditional ads in that they're highly relevant to the pages on which they appear. That is, PPC ad networks don't display any old ad on a web page; instead, they try to serve up the right ads for the right potential customers. To do this, PPC advertising networks utilize *keywords*—those words and phrases that users search for on Google and other search engine sites.

In essence, PPC ads are *contextual* or *context-sensitive* in nature. This means that the ad is served only to websites with content that is directly related to the ad's content—or, more precisely, to those keywords purchased by the advertiser. As an advertiser, this works to deliver more targeted impressions for your ads; if you're advertising business shipping services, for example, your ad will be served to sites related to business shipping, not general purpose consumer sites.

This context sensitivity also dictates ad appearance on search results pages. When you purchase a keyword for a PPC text ad, your ad will appear on search results pages when someone searches Google, Yahoo!, or Bing for that particular keyword.

Take the business shipping services example again. You purchase the key phrase *business shipping services* for your ad, and when someone searches Google for "business shipping service," your ad appears on the resulting search results page. Someone searching for "stamps" won't see your ad; you get visibility to only those businesses looking for what you're offering.

> "...PPC ads are *contextual* or *context-sensitive* in nature. This means that the ad is served only to websites with content that is directly related to the ad's content..."

Paying by the Click

Now to the PPC part of the equation. The reason it's called pay-per-click advertising is that an advertiser pays the ad network only when prospects click the link in the ad. If no one clicks, the advertiser doesn't pay anyone anything. The more clicks that are received, the more the advertiser pays.

As noted, PPC ad rates are calculated on a cost-per-click (CPC) basis. That is, the advertiser is charged a specific fee for each click—anywhere from a few pennies to tens of dollars. The actual CPC rate is determined by the popularity of and competition for the keyword purchased, as well as the quality and quantity of traffic going to the site hosting the ad. As you can imagine, popular keywords have a higher CPC, whereas less popular keywords can be had for less.

This varying CPC rate is determined by having advertisers bid on the most popular keywords. That is, you might say you'll pay up to $5 for a given keyword. If you're the high bidder among several advertisers, your ads will appear more frequently on web pages that contain that keyword, or higher on a search results page for that keyword. If you're not the high bidder, you won't get as much visibility—if your ad appears at all.

✉ Note

A given PPC ad probably won't appear on every search engine results page for the keyword purchased. That's because page inventory for a given keyword is limited, whereas advertisers are theoretically unlimited. For this reason, ad networks typically rotate ads from multiple advertisers on its search results and affiliated websites.

Bidding for Keywords

> "Pick keywords that no one is interested in, and your ad won't appear anywhere; pick more general keywords, and your ad will appear more often..."

As a B2B advertiser, it's important that you pick the most effective keywords for your PPC ads. Pick keywords that no one is interested in, and your ad won't appear anywhere; pick more general keywords, and your ad will appear more often—and, perhaps, on general-interest sites where you don't want the ad to appear.

The challenge, then, is choosing the right keywords that target potential business buyers and filter out unwanted general consumers. It's the same challenge faced when choosing keywords for search engine optimization of your website; you have to pick those words and phrases that people in your industry are familiar with, and that the general populace probably won't use. Pick too focused a word, and you might see little or no placement; pick too general a word, and you'll get placement on consumer sites that won't do you any good.

> **Note**
>
> Learn more about choosing B2B keywords in Chapter 10, "B2B Search Engine Marketing."

You also have the challenge of bidding on those keywords against competing advertisers. This competition for keywords among advertisers becomes, essentially, an online auction. Those advertisers who bid the highest amounts for keywords will "win" more and better ad placements. If you don't bid high enough on a popular keyword, your ad simply won't appear as often. In fact, if you bid way too low, your ad might not appear at all.

The temptation, then, is to bid high on the most popular keywords in an attempt to get more ads displayed and drive more traffic to your website. Be careful what you wish for, however, because this approach can result in higher-than-necessary advertising bills.

Note

PPC ad networks let you set a daily or monthly budget for your total advertising expenditures. Your ad will run only until your budget is maxed out; at that point, your ad is no longer in circulation.

That said, bid price isn't the only factor in determining how often an ad is displayed—at least not anymore. It used to be that the highest bidder got the most placements, but that didn't always ensure that the most relevant ads got placed. For that reason, the ad networks now utilize a "quality score" factor that attempts to determine the relevance of the ad's landing page—the page that the ad links to. If an ad's landing page consists of low-quality or largely irrelevant content, that ad gets a low quality score and won't rank high in the ad network's results. A landing page with high-quality, relevant content will rank higher and thus be displayed more frequently.

To maximize your ad placements, then, you need to consider a number of factors:

- Keywords
- Bid price for those keywords
- Content of the linked-to landing page
- Effectiveness of your ad copy

In other words, you have to bid on keywords that are both popular and relevant; bid the going rate for those keywords; create a high-value landing page for your ad; and write an ad that encourages users to click it. Fall down on any of these factors and your ad will be less than fully successful.

Choosing a Bidding Strategy

When you bid on a keyword for a PPC ad, you enter the maximum CPC you're willing to pay. The actual amount you pay might be less, however.

That's because most PPC ad networks manage your CPC bids so that you don't have to pay more than you have to. This works by the ad network's automatically lowering your maximum bid to a penny or so more than the next-highest competing bid. So, if you bid $2.00 for a keyword but the next-highest bid is $1.50, you don't pay the full $2.00; instead, you pay $1.51.

Knowing this, you can adopt one of several bidding strategies, depending on the goals you set for your PPC ads. These strategies include

- **Bid whatever it takes to be number one**—If you want to always win the keywords you choose, you can—but it'll cost you. All you have to do is consistently bid higher than all competitors. This can, of course, be a costly strategy, especially if you get into a bidding war with another advertiser following the same strategy; when two advertisers are both intent on being number one, the price for a given keyword can skyrocket. That said, the key to this strategy is constant monitoring of your ad's position—at least daily. If your position starts to slip, that means someone else is outbidding you, and you'll need to increase your bid.

- **Bid for a specific position**—The problem with bidding for the number-one position is that it's costly—and apt to get more costly over time, as other advertisers also bid for those same keywords. For many advertisers, a better approach is to bid for a lower position—something in the 3–6 range, for example. These positions will cost you a lot less than the number-one position, but still land you on the first page of the search engine's search results page—which typically results in a good click-through-rate (CTR) for a much lower CPC. The key to this strategy is to fine-tune your bid after your campaign is running to find the sweet spot you want. It's a time-consuming process, but one that guarantees a decent ROI over time.

- **Bid the bare minimum**—The thinking here is that you can waste a lot of money trying to get the top positions; your budget might be better spent bidding low for your traffic, especially if you have a high quality score that can pull up your position compared to lower-performing competitors. Now, you'll probably never rise to the top spot, but you might end up on the first page of search results—which isn't bad. If you decide to go this route, you need to always bid at the lower end of the suggested range. You should also consider *not* bidding on keywords estimated to have a high CPC; you might get better results bidding on less popular keywords.

- **Bid high—and then lower your bid**—There's a quirk in most PPC systems that can work to your benefit, cost-wise. As you know, many ad networks use a "quality score" to help determine your ad's position, and one key component of the quality score is your ad's click-through rate (CTR). You get a higher CTR, and your quality score goes up; your quality score goes up, and you get a better position; you get a better position, and your CTR goes up; and a higher CTR makes your quality score go up again. The key here is to realize that if your ad is working and your CTR is going up, thus improving your quality score, you can maintain the same ad position at a lower cost; you end up at the same (or higher) position at a lower cost.

To use this strategy, start by bidding at a higher level to strongly establish your position. After your position has been established, you can then lower your bid. Naturally, you'll want to monitor your average position and quality score on at least a daily basis and then use your best judgment on when to change your bid.

Writing Effective Ad Copy

The final component of your PPC ad campaign is the ad itself. Given that most PPC ads are text ads, this means writing effective ad copy.

In most PPC ad programs, a text ad consists of four lines of text. The first line is the headline or title, with a relatively short character count. The next two lines contain the body of the ad, often a product description, which can hold more characters but still not a lot. And the final line is the URL of the site where you're driving traffic.

As you might suspect, the most important part of any text ad is the title. This is because some ad formats on third-party pages display *only* the title and URL, skipping the two description lines. So, your title has to do the heavy lifting; it has to grab potential customers at a literal glance. You can then fill in more details in the next two lines, but the title must be able to stand alone if necessary.

Naturally, the headline must inform customers of what you're selling or trying to accomplish; in this aspect, it needs to be informative. But the headline should also trigger specific customer behavior—in most instances, a click-through to your chosen landing page.

Of course, the two lines of descriptive or body text should also persuade potential customers to click through to your landing page. To this end, you should use words that appeal to the customer's emotions. Even business buyers want to be excited or comforted or entertained; your copy should fulfill these emotional needs.

In addition, your copy needs to solve a problem or answer a question the potential customer might have. What does the customer need to do that your product does? That's the solution to push in the body of your ad.

> ✉ *Note*
>
> Because you only have two short lines of copy to work with, you don't have space to talk about your product's features. Instead, you must focus on the benefits—that is, how the customer will benefit from buying what you're selling. If you're selling copy paper, don't talk about its unique ink-retaining properties; tell people that they'll "print cleaner and clearer." Tell readers what's in it for them.

You also want to include your primary keywords in both your ad's headline and body copy. That's because people look for the keywords they've queried when they're viewing search results. If someone searches for "accounting," he's going to scan the search results page for the word *accounting*. He's more likely to click an ad that contains that word than one that doesn't because of the implication that an ad that contains *accounting* in its headline or copy is relevant to his search.

Finally, because PPC ads link to the advertiser's website, you want the potential customer to do something. We're not talking generic image advertising here; PPC ads should result in a specific action—that you need to ask for.

To that end, your ad copy needs to include a strong call to action. You have to ask the customer to do something before they'll do anything at all.

What's a good call to action? Here are some common ones:

- Order now
- Buy now
- Download your free trial
- Sign up
- Get a quote
- Learn more
- Read our brochure
- Request more information
- Browse our site
- Join us today
- Start now

Notice what's *not* on this list: the phrase *click here*. Asking someone to click your ad is not a good call to action for a number of reasons. First, it's implied in all PPC ads; the title is a hyperlink, after all. Second, most ad networks don't like it and might reduce your quality score and your ad placement if you include it. Third, clicking isn't really what you want users to do; you want them to get more information or buy now or something similar. Focus on that.

In addition, some of the highest responses rates in B2B advertising come from the offer of content that delivers information of value to the prospect. I'm talking white papers, reports, technical reviews, and the like. Construct a PPC ad around the offer of a free white paper and you might be surprised at the response rate.

Remember, you want the customer to do something specific, beyond just clicking the ad—and you have to tell them what that is. Without a call to action, your ad is just a bunch of words on the page.

Creating PPC Image Ads

Most PPC ad networks let you create both text and image ads. While text ads are most prevalent, clickable context-sensitive image ads are also popular among some advertisers.

A PPC image ad is like any web-based display ad; it just falls under the CPC payment method. That is, instead of buying the ad space on a web page, you pay only when a user clicks the ad. In most instances, the click takes a user back to your website, where you can provide more information or try to make a sale.

Like display ads, PPC image ads are available in a variety of sizes and formats. You can create horizontal banner ads, vertical skyscrapers, or simple squares or rectangles. Typically, the whole of the ad consists of the image you provide.

 Note

Some PPC ad networks also let you place rich media ads containing audio, video, Flash animations, and the like.

The big drawback to PPC image ads is that they typically don't display on search engine results pages. So, if you want to advertise directly to people searching Google or Yahoo!, you need to use text ads. PPC image ads display primarily on third-party websites affiliated with the PPC ad network—and not on all of them. (Websites have the option of accepting either text ads or a mix of text and image ads; not all webmasters choose the image ad option.)

What makes for an effective PPC image ad? Pretty much the same thing that makes for an effective display ad, as we discuss in the next section. But because you want customers to click the ad, you also need to include a call for action and ask for the click, in so many words. It's a display ad that isn't a brand ad; you want the customer to click through and visit your website.

Using Display Ads

When it comes to online ad spending, display ads, like the one in Figure 11.3, are the visual opposite of text ads; these are ads that display images, animation, even videos. Display ads can be big, like the banner ads you find at the top of many web pages, or small, like graphical versions of text ads. These ads are designed to attract the visitor's attention and, in some instances, to click for further information.

Figure 11.3   *A typical display ad at the top of the IT News site.*

Understanding Display Ads

In the early days of the web, display ads—typically in the form of banner ads—were all there were. Over the next decade, PPC text ads became the advertiser's chosen format as Google took over the search advertising market. But in recent years, display ads have made a bit of a comeback, especially for B2B advertisers.

Display ads can be sold on both a CPM and CPC basis. CPM used to be the more popular method and is still common in larger ad sizes. CPC is gaining ground, however, as advertisers embrace the higher accountability model; it's the de facto standard in smaller, text ad–like sizes and is even becoming popular in larger sizes.

One of the benefits of display advertising is the variety available. For example, if you're into PPC advertising but don't want to be relegated to a bland text ad, you can create a small PPC image ad instead. This type of ad is the same size as a text ad but conveys the advertising message in a graphical format; with most of these PPC image ads, the entire ad is clickable.

Larger display ads tend to be more popular among big advertisers. The best-known type is the so-called banner ad that stretches across the top of a web page, although "banners" can also run along the bottom of a page or down either side. (A vertical banner ad is more accurately called a *skyscraper*.) This type of ad can even sit in a box in the middle of a page.

✉ *Note*

Some websites display more than one banner ad per page, either from the same advertiser or from multiple advertisers. Some sites will even rotate banners every few seconds or display different ads each time a visitor reloads the page.

Examining Rich Media Ads

When it comes to display advertising, there's no one single type. Today's display ads can be image ads (that is, they consist of a static graphic image) or rich media ads. And when it comes to rich media, the sky's the limit.

What is rich media? It's anything that moves or plays or that delivers dynamic content to the targeted audience. In short, you can look at ads that offer any or all of the following:

- Voice narration or music
- Video playback
- Animated elements
- "Frame-breaking" construction, where elements of the ad break out of the traditional ad frame and move across the underlying page
- Expandability, where the ad itself shrinks or grows dependent on some action
- Dynamic content, such as live Twitter or blog feeds inserted into the ad
- User interaction

A plain image ad, in contrast, is just a picture. A *still* picture. That isn't necessarily a bad thing, especially from a technological standpoint. There are several issues with rich media ads, concerning both download time (audio and video files can be rather large and slow to download over a slow Internet connection) and compatibility (not all users have the state-of-the-art technology installed to play back all rich media ads). If you want to guarantee a no-hassle experience with all users, ditch the rich media and stick with a simple image ad.

On the other hand, rich media ads can really pull viewers into your message. Watching a character walk across the web page while talking directly to the viewer can be a compelling experience. And some people will always stop to watch a video on any web page.

The real benefit of rich media ads, of course, is their effectiveness—which is measurable. By most accounts, rich media ads typically have a CTR two to four times that of simple image ads, which means moving from a 1% (or less) CTR to something in the 3% range. That's significant.

So, if you want to stretch your imagination, stand out from the pack of static image ads, and increase your CTR, by all means incorporate rich media into your display advertising. You won't be alone; by most accounts, more than 40% of all display ads incorporate some form of rich media content.

Choosing a Display Ad Format

Whether you go with a plain image ad or a fancy rich media one, you also have to decide on the size of the ad you want. For many years, display ads were synonymous with banner ads, those horizontal ads that stretch across the top of the page. But there are places on a page other than the top where you can place an ad, and that placement will to some degree determine the size and shape of the ad.

Display ads can, of course, be horizontal banner ads. They can also be vertical skyscrapers or smaller square or rectangular ads. In fact, the Interactive Advertising Bureau (IAB) has compiled a list of 18 common web ad formats of various shapes and sizes, as detailed in Table 11.1 and shown in Figure 11.4. Pick the format that works best for your particular message.

Table 11.1   IAB Recommended Ad Units

Ad Unit	Size (Width × Height, in Pixels)	Recommended File Size
Leaderboard	728 × 90	40KB
Pop-Under	720 × 300	40KB
Full Banner	468 × 60	40KB
Large Rectangle	336 × 280	40KB
Half-Page Ad	300 × 600	40KB
Medium Rectangle	300 × 250	40KB
3:1 Rectangle	300 × 100	40KB
Square Pop-Up	250 × 250	40KB
Vertical Rectangle	240 × 400	40KB
Half Banner	234 × 60	30KB
Rectangle	180 × 150	40KB
Wide Skyscraper	160 × 600	40KB

Ad Unit	Size (Width × Height, in Pixels)	Recommended File Size
Square Button	125 × 125	30KB
Skyscraper	120 × 600	40KB
Vertical Banner	120 × 240	30KB
Button 1	120 × 90	20KB
Button 2	120 × 60	20KB
Micro Bar	88 × 31	10KB

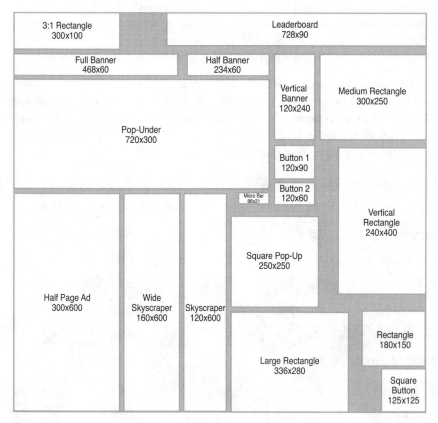

Figure 11.4 *Standard web display ad sizes, as recommended by the IAB.*

Of course, you're not limited to a single ad format. You can employ different formats on different sites or even place multiple ads in multiple formats on the same page. This particular approach can be effective; if you don't get their attention with a top-of-page banner, the smaller rectangle ad further down the page might just do the trick. Or, even better, the two ads work together to reinforce your message. It's an increasingly popular approach.

Creating Effective Display Ads

Want to create an effective display ad? To do so, you need to consider not only ad media and size, but also position, content, and all sorts of other stuff. Here are some tips for ensure display advertising success:

- **Bigger is better**—When it comes to advertising effectiveness, bigger is better. It should come as no surprise that wider ad formats tend to outperform narrower formats—even if the narrower ad is also taller. It's all about readability. Visitors can read more at a glance with a wider ad than they can with a taller one. Obviously, you should experiment with different ad sizes, as well as ad positions, to find the ones that work best for your ads. But there's nothing like size for getting you noticed.

- **Keep it small**—While we're talking about ad sizes, you also need to consider the file size of the ad—the size of the image or video or Flash file that loads when the ad is displayed. In general, you want to keep file sizes as small as possible—for most formats, under 40KB. Anything larger and you will affect the viewership of the ad.

- **Choose the best position**—You don't always get a vote in where your display ad appears on a page. But if you can choose your ad position, where should you place it? There are some variables to consider, but in general the best position for a display ad is nearest the page's core content that can be seen without scrolling. That typically means near the top-middle of the page, either above, to the left, or below the main content. Other good positions are directly after the end of an article, blog post, or other editorial content; between other elements, such as between articles or blog posts; and near navigational elements, such as menus and back/up buttons. Bottom line: Top is better than bottom, left is better than right, and butting up against important content is best of all.

> "...the best position for a display ad is nearest the page's core content that can be seen without scrolling."

- **Include a call to action**—It should go without saying that if you want a prospect to click your ad, you need to make that clear. Include some sort of call to action, such as a "submit" or "click for more information" button. Without such a call to action, most readers assume a banner ad is like a billboard, not meant for interaction.

- **Keep it short**—If you have an animated display ad, keep the animation relatively short. Surveys show that viewers spend less than 10 seconds looking at the top of a web page. You have to display all your content within this time frame, including—and especially—your call to action. Dispense with long animations and get your message out there as quickly as possible.

Finally, don't assume that you'll get everything right on the first try. You should always include a period of testing for different display ad approaches. You can test different sizes, placements, content, and the like. Evaluate responses on a regular basis and go with the ads that perform the best. You might be surprised how something small, such as changing the font or background color, can improve an ad's performance.

✉ *Note*

Most display ads are designed for brand building, not direct response. So-called *brand response ads*, however, combine brand and direct response models by including URLs and other contact information in what is otherwise a brand-oriented ad.

Getting to Know the Big Ad Networks

When you want to place an online ad, chances are you'll be dealing with one of the major online advertising networks. These networks will take your ad and place it with their network of affiliated websites. Most networks also offer assistance in ad creation if you need that.

Who are the big players? Table 11.2 details the major online ad networks working today.[2]

---

2. comScore Media Metrix, June 2011

Table 11.2 Top Ten Online Advertising Networks

Ad Network	URL	Unique Visitors
Google Ad Network (AdWords and Display Network)	www.google.com/ads/displaynet-work/adwords.google.com	214,474,000
Yahoo! Network Plus	advertising.yahoo.com	198,995,000
AOL Advertising	advertising.aol.com	184,132,000
ValueClick Networks	www.valueclick.com	172,212,000
24/7 Real Media Global Web Alliance	www.247realmedia.com	167,563,000
Specific Media	www.specificmedia.com	162,548,000
Tribal Fusion	www.tribalfusion.com	160,443,000
AdBrite Exchange	www.adbrite.com	159,861,000
Collective Display	www.collective.com	159,429,000
Burst Media	www.burstmedia.com	147,678,000

 Note

Google's ad network consists of two parts. AdWords handles all the PPC ads, whereas DoubleClick (purchased by Google in 2007) handles all the display advertising.

Most of these ad networks work in a similar fashion. You create or submit your ad and decide on the payment model you want—typically CPM or CPC. You settle on a budget and either choose a list of keywords for your ads or desired website demographics. In some instances, you can choose the specific sites where you want your ads displayed.

You pay the ad network when the ads run or when they're clicked if you chose the CPC model. The ad network splits the ad revenue with their affiliated sites—or keeps it all for themselves if the ads are run on search results pages or on their own company-run sites.

Which of these ad networks should you utilize? If you're interested in reaching across the Internet, there's no reason you should limit yourself to a single ad network; you could (and probably should) utilize multiple networks to get your ad seen on as many sites as possible.

Maximizing Effectiveness with a Custom Landing Page

A landing page is the page that appears when a prospect clicks your ad. The landing page could be your site's home page, it could be a product page for whatever it is you're advertising, or it could be a page specially designed to accompany the specific advertisement.

Why Landing Pages Are Important

Here's the deal. Most people, businesspeople included, don't view more than the first page of the resulting web page when they click an ad. If they don't like what they find, or if the landing page doesn't contain the information they want, they leave immediately.

For this reason, you need to set up a well-structured landing page to greet those users who click your ad. The more effective your landing page, the more clicks you will convert to sales.

The best landing pages display content that is a logical extension of the advertisement. Depending on the nature and intent of the page, it should provide additional information, ask for the customer's contact information, or in some instances, ask for the sale.

Why You Need a Separate Landing Page

As we've discussed, you could link to your site's home page, but that generally isn't a great idea. That's because most home pages are rather general in nature; they advertise your company or brand, not necessarily the specific product or service mentioned in your ad. That is, they don't follow directly from your ad—which could be confusing to potential customers.

Likewise, linking to any existing page on your site might not be the best approach. Remember, if you're looking to acquire leads rather than just generate raw clicks, your landing page has to further the acquisition process. That means that you shouldn't point to a generic brand or product page; customers need to see a page that displays the product or service you talked about in the ad. Going to any non-specific page requires unnecessary work on the part of the prospect to learn more about what's advertised and to ask for more information; response rates dramatically fall off the more clicks the prospect has to make.

The best approach, then, is to link to a page on your site custom-designed for readers of your PPC advertisement. This page should display information about only the product promoted in your advertising—and include some sort of lead-generating mechanism to ask for the customer's contact information.

Why design a special landing page for each ad you create? It's simple: You want to make it as easy as possible for buyers to ask for more information or give you're their contact info. If you just dump potential customers on your site's home page, they could get lost. Or they might have trouble finding the product they want and give up. In any instance, you don't want them randomly browsing your site; you want them to immediately respond to your specific offer.

Creating an Effective Landing Page

Although you can create a different landing page for each ad you place, you might be able to get by with a single landing page for all the ads in a campaign. In any instance, some custom page design is in order.

The connection between your ad and the landing page is of utmost importance. That means that your landing page *must* discuss or display the product or service promoted in the ad. It probably shouldn't display any other products or services; you don't want to confuse potential customers. Remember, a prospect clicks your ad to find out more about what the ad talked about. He expects to click to a page that follows seamlessly from what was discussed in the ad.

For this reason, your landing page needs to be consistent with your advertisement, both in terms of content and presentation. That means using the same terminology employed your ad—talk about the same product in the same way. Don't change things up or get greedy about presenting other products. There will be time enough for that later if the customer decides to continue the purchasing process.

And if you're designing a landing page for a PPC image ad, the page should convey the same look and feel of the ad itself. Obviously, this is less important if you're running a text ad, which really doesn't have a visual design. But a landing page for an image ad should look and feel like the ad the customer just clicked.

 Note

Remember that customers see your ad because they're interested in particular keywords. Make sure to include those keywords not only in your ad but also on your landing page.

Naturally, the landing page can and should include more information than you had space to present in the ad. After all, you now have a lot more than three lines to work with. So, the landing page should include detailed information about the featured product, as well as more detailed product photos. It should be a very informative page.

Asking for the Lead

The purpose of your online ad and the associated landing page is to acquire a customer lead. To that end, you need to include a form (or a link or button that links to a form) that asks for the prospect's contact information. The landing page has to work toward convincing the prospect that it's worth talking to you.

That means that you have to provide enough information to make the prospect comfortable with your company and your products and services. The landing page, then, needs to include links to additional product information, collateral materials, and the like. You have to get and keep the prospect interested in your product, and then entice the prospect to leave his contact information.

You then have to make it easy for the contact to enter the asked-for information. To this end, don't ask for any more information than is absolutely necessary; resist the temptation to ask for overly detailed information about the buyer's company size and purchasing plans and what not. The more you ask for, the lower your response rates will be. Maybe all you need is the prospect's name, company name, and email address. If you want or need more data, you can ask for it after you make the initial contact.

Note

Be cautious about asking for phone numbers in this initial contact. Most prospects will be okay providing an email address, but much less comfortable handing out their office or home phone number. They just don't want to deal with an unwanted (at this point) phone call.

TRENDS IN ONLINE ADVERTISING

The online advertising industry is one of almost constant change. What was standard operating procedure ten years ago are quaint practices today; even the major players are constantly in flux. As such, it helps to know which way the winds are blowing. With that in mind, here are some of the more important trends to keep abreast of:

- **Mobile advertising**—Online advertising isn't all about the Web; users with iPhones, Android phones, and other smartphones also use their devices to connect to the Internet. If you want to reach this increasingly important mass of mobile users, you have to include mobile advertising as a major component of your online advertising plans.

- **Social media advertising**—Equally important as the mobile Internet trend is the social networking trend. Facebook, Twitter, and the like are major destinations for a large number of web users; advertising to the users of these sites makes increasing sense for most advertisers.

- **Application advertising**—Speaking of the mobile Internet, here's a relatively new form of promotion—developing your own application as an advertising mechanism. This is increasingly common on the iPhone/iPad and Android platforms, where advertisers are building their own customer-focused apps. It's a great way to entice customers to your brand.

- **Going direct**—You don't have to place your ads through an ad network; many B2B advertisers prefer to place their ads directly with host websites. Going direct is a good way to cut out the middle man, reduce your advertising costs, and guarantee better placement. It's also popular among the big websites, who can book more of the ad revenue themselves. This trend seems like a win-win for everyone—except the major ad networks.

- **Nonstandard ads**—In an effort to break out from the typical blandness of display advertising, more and more advertisers are requesting ads in nonstandard sizes. (The standard sizes, of course, being those dictated by the Internet Advertising Board, or IAB.) This trend might even find favor among website publishers, who can customize ad placement for their own content.

- **Bigger, more intrusive ads**—Along the same lines, some advertisers are looking for a more dominant web page presence, which results in bigger, more intrusive ads. This trend is also being pushed by some of the ad networks, who are looking to make up for lost revenue by selling bigger, more expensive ads. This isn't necessarily a good trend, however, as it goes against what most website users want.

The Bottom Line

Online advertising can be an important part of a B2B company's online marketing strategy. You can choose from either small PPC text ads, where you pay by the click, or larger display ads with either PPC or CPM payment models. In either case, you can specify where the ads appear, either by choosing the appropriate keywords or choosing specific websites.

12

B2B Email Marketing

Email is a central component of many B2B marketing programs. It's fair to say that email is more important to B2B marketers than it is to their B2C cousins.

Why is B2B email so popular? It's versatile, of course; you can use email in just about any part of the B2B buying continuum. It's also relatively low cost, which always has appeal. Bottom line, email marketing is a great way to make contact with both current and potential customers at relatively low cost.

Understanding B2B Email Marketing

If you're doing any digital marketing at all, chances are that email is part of your mix. That's how key email marketing is in the B2B community; it's right up there with website marketing and search engine marketing in terms of acceptance.

And, contrary to what might be happening in the B2C world, B2B email continues to gain in use. A recent survey by eMarketer and *BtoB Magazine* revealed that 68% of B2B marketers intend to increase their budgets for email marketing in 2011 over the previous year.[1] That's a level of increase second only to investment in companies' websites (and five points higher than the investment in social media), which shows a real commitment to the medium.

Email Marketing Is Direct Marketing

When it comes to defining exactly what email marketing is and what it does, the most obvious observation is that it's a form of direct marketing. Email marketing is not (or should not be) mass marketing, as web advertising is, displayed blindly to hundreds of thousands of unwitting recipients. Instead, email marketing is targeted marketing, aimed directly at specific prospects or customers. It's just like those marketing pieces you send via postal mail, except better; the recipients of your email promotions have to agree to receive your mailings, which means they have a built-in receptivity to your marketing messages.

It's that one-to-one communication that makes email marketing so effective. Unless you're engaging in spam activities, you send your email messages only to existing customers or to active leads who've opted in to your mailings. They're willing recipients, less likely to view your emails as unwanted junk. As such, you get a higher response rate than you do with other marketing vehicles.

Email Marketing Is Database Marketing

Key to successful email marketing is the ability to manage large databases of information. Done right, you're managing more than customer names and (email) addresses. You're also managing information about each individual customer. The databases you assemble include data about what each client has purchased in the past, what they've looked at on your website, the communication they've made with you, and so on. It's this data that holds the value; without it, you're just carpet-bombing a bunch of anonymous email addresses.

---

1. eMarketer/BtoB Magazine, "2011 Outlook: Marketing Priorities and Plans," 2011

With this detailed data, however, you can tailor your mailings to each individual customer. That means tailoring not just the content of each message, but also the timing and frequency. Manage the database correctly, and you can put relevant messages in front of interested customers when they're most likely to buy. That makes each message you send more valuable to the recipients and should increase the response rates.

For this to work, you have to do a bit of database management. You have to create the right type of database, populate it with the right data, and then extract that data in an appropriate fashion. This isn't a simple mail merge like what you can do in Microsoft Outlook; it's sophisticated database management, often involving multiple databases.

To that end, frequent email marketing might not be something you can do in-house. Many B2B companies engage the use of professional email marketing firms. These firms can help you develop an email schedule, create your promotional emails, build and manage your customer databases, and create and send your email messages—or any subset of those. Database management expertise is imperative; if you don't have it, hire it out.

Email Marketing Is Targeted Marketing

If you manage your email database smartly, you'll find that you can slice and dice your mailing list to an almost infinite degree. You can sort and filter names on any number of criteria—size, location, previous orders, products/services purchased, stage in the B2B customer life cycle, you name it.

This ability to segment your customer base lets you send email promotions to selected customers or groups of customers in your database. You don't have to (and probably shouldn't) send the same generic email to every customer name you have. Instead, target specific customers or groups of customers with offers that are relevant only to them.

Email Marketing Is Proactive Marketing

Another thing I personally like about email marketing is that it's proactive rather than reactive. That is, instead of waiting for a potential customer to find you (as is the case with search engine marketing, for example), you're taking your message to your customer base. You reach prospective and current customers when you want to reach them, on your terms—and at your speed.

To that end, it also helps that email marketing is extremely fast marketing. You can get an email into the hands of a buyer within seconds, compared to the days or weeks it might take to place an offer with traditional media. You can come up with a promotional idea and blast it out to your email list the same day—you think it, they see it.

Email Marketing Is Inexpensive Marketing

In the old world of postal direct marketing, you were on a budget; you could only do so many mailings each year because you had to pay for paper and envelopes and (of course) postage. But with email marketing, you don't have any of those costs—which means you can, in theory in least, send out as many emails as you like.

What's the cost of an email mailing? You have to manage your database of names, of course, but that's an ongoing cost. You might also pay for an outside firm to develop your mailings or just to develop a template that you use going forward. But you don't have to pay for names (assuming companies proactively sign up), you don't have to pay for the individual emails themselves (no paper or ink involved), and you don't have to pay to have the emails delivered.

To this end, it doesn't matter whether you send out one email or a hundred thousand or if you send them once a month or once a day. Whatever the quantity or frequency, your costs are essentially the same.

Basically, email marketing does not incur media or delivery costs. Yes, you still have creative costs, and you have the cost of managing the database. But beyond that, the incremental costs are minimal. For most businesses, then, the resultant cost of an email campaign is only about 5% of the cost of a similar direct mail campaign.

This makes email marketing ideal for B2B companies who want frequent contact with their customers. It's also ideal for companies with a complex message that would otherwise require multiple printed pages to get across; a short email message costs the same as a long one.

Like much online marketing, email marketing is also a great leveler, providing a somewhat level playing field for B2B companies large and small. This introduces a kind of "marketing democracy" to the game in that a small company can be just as professional and persuasive as a larger one.

Although you don't need a huge budget to be competitive with email marketing, you do need a certain level of intelligence and creativity. To that end, a smaller company can actually be more competitive than a larger one. A smaller company that is more receptive to new ideas and faster on its feet can run rings around a larger company with too many entrenched political systems in place.

Email Marketing Is Permission Marketing

Let's be clear about one thing, however. Legitimate email marketing is opt-in marketing; that is, you've received the customer's permission in advance to send out your email messages. If you send out emails without this prior permission, you're a spammer (and spamming is not part of any legitimate marketing mix).

The theory is that emails that users consent to receive will be better received than those unsolicited messages that arrive blind in their inboxes. If you're providing true value in your emails, you'll find that your recipients look forward to receiving your emails once a week, once a month, or on whatever schedule you have them set to be sent out.

Permission marketing typically involves some sort of regular communication with your customers. This could be a weekly or monthly email newsletter, a list of weekly deals, a list of weekly new releases, or something similar. It can (and probably should) also include personalized mailings, with offers or messages specific to that prospect or customer. You can make your communications as close to 1:1 as best fits your needs.

✉ *Note*

Email frequency depends on the degree of relationship between you and your customer. The closer the relationship, the more frequently you can make contact.

How do you build your database of companies that willingly agree to receive your mailings? There are a number of ways. Many B2B companies request permission to send mailings when they make their first purchase or sign on as a customer. Others encourage prospects to sign up for mailings when they're evaluating a purchase; for most companies, getting email contact info counts as acquiring a lead.

However you garner permission, it's important to tie your database of names with other databases that hold additional customer information. That way you can trigger emails based on customer characteristics, such as items they've purchased or expressed an interest in.

You can also program your databases to send out mailings on a regular schedule; this is useful for monthly announcements, for example. Do your programming work well and you can have your entire message put together automatically, dropping in the right notices and products for each customer in your database.

AVOIDING SPAM—AND BACON

When we're talking email marketing, we're talking emails sent with the explicit permission of the recipients. Emails sent without this permission are unwanted commercial emails (UCEs)—otherwise known as *spam*.

Nobody likes spam—especially busy businesspeople. So, why does spam exist? Because it's cheap (remember, it costs almost the same to send out a million spam messages as it does to send a thousand legitimate ones) and because, to some degree, it's profitable. That's right, some small percent of people who receive this junk actually click on the spam messages and order stuff. Even a miniscule response rate can be profitable when you send out millions of unsolicited messages at no or low cost.

Legitimate marketers, of course, don't engage in spam, and reject any connection to the junk email industry. They go to great lengths to stress the opt-in nature of their mailings and feature large and noticeable "unsubscribe" links in their mailings so that anyone who no longer wants to receive emails can be removed from future mailings. Legitimate email marketing is all about giving recipients only those emails that they want to and expect to receive.

That said, you need to make sure that your email marketing efforts do not violate those anti-spam laws that are on the books. In the U.S., that means reading up on and adhering to the terms of what is known as the CAN-SPAM Act of 2003. (That stands for—take a deep breath here—Controlling the Assault of Non-Solicited Pornography and Marketing.) You can read the entire thing online at http://uscode.house.gov/download/pls/15C103.txt; like most official government documents, it's scintillating reading. Although it's true that B2B emails are generally exempt from the CAN-SPAM permission requirements, it's still best to adhere to the spirit of the law, if not the letter.

Even better, work with an established email marketing firm and let them sweat the details. But the best advice is to not do anything that would annoy you as a consumer. You don't want to receive emails in your inbox that you don't want; tailor your email marketing campaigns appropriately. You have worked hard to meet CAN-SPAM regulations, but sending bacon to your recipients could be just as damaging as spam to your email program.

But even if you do everything by the book, spam-wise, you still might find your company accused of sending out unwanted emails, or what some call *bacon*. This type of bacon has nothing to do with pigs; instead, it's spam's somewhat legitimate cousin. Where a spam email is totally unsolicited, a bacon email is one that the recipient actually requested at one point in the past, but no longer finds useful.

You generate bacon when your email doesn't deliver on its original promise. Even when customers sign up to receive your email, if you send out too much of it or if it doesn't contain useful or relevant information, it can be annoying as traditional spam. Research shows that 61% of email subscribers delete these now-unwanted messages, and another 14% report the messages as spam. That doesn't speak well for email marketing effectiveness.

There are a number of ways to avoid the bacon problem. First, you can simply decrease the frequency of your email mailings. Second, you can give recipients the tools they need to sift out the messages they want from the other messages you send out. And finally, you can make sure that you always— *always*—include useful and relevant information in your mailings. Give your customers something worth reading and they'll read it, it's as simple as that.

Using Email to Reach New Prospects

You can use email in any stage of the B2B customer life cycle. Although it's more commonly used after you've made the first contact with a customer, you can also use it for making that initial contact—if you do so gingerly.

The challenge with using email during the reach phase is that you don't have the prospect's permission to email them. Sending out an email without prior permission is, as you're well aware, the very definition of spam. And spamming a prospective customer is not a good way to begin a new business relationship.

> "...spamming a prospective customer is not a good way to begin a new business relationship.

That said, many B2B companies do use email to solicit new customers, just as they used direct mail for that task in the nondigital world. For some reason, junk mail is less negatively received than spam email is, but I'll leave that for the sociologists and psychologists to ponder why. All I know is that you stand a good chance of permanently souring the customer relationship if you're perceived as a spammer.

 Note

Interestingly, traditional direct mail is typically viewed as a neutral communication, where email is often considered intrusive. This is why emails— particularly unwanted ones—tend to trigger more annoyance than direct mail pieces.

Sharing Names

What you can do, with caution, is buy, rent, or share the names of prospects who signed up for other companies' email lists and also gave permission for their names to be shared with additional companies. This sometimes takes the form of a "would you like to receive special offers from our partners" sort of option, which a surprising number of people check. Names gathered in this fashion can be sold or rented to other companies—which is where you get all those new names to solicit.

This use of names and addresses from prospects who opted in at another site is called *co-registration*. It can be effective if you choose your partners carefully. That is, if you share names from a site that has a similar demographic or target customer to yours, you'll stand a better chance of success than if you use a random list. In this respect, list sharing is one area where quality is much more important than quantity.

> ✉ *Note*
>
> Most co-registration comes in the form of either list swaps (you share yours and they share theirs) or list rentals. It rarely takes the form of list purchases. In fact, most lists offered for sale are spam lists, constructed without the owners' permission or knowledge. You should avoid purchasing spam lists; not only will you get a very poor response, you'll risk the ire of those people who receive your unsolicited mailing (along with hundreds of others).

You can send two types of mailings to these shared names:

- Special offers, where you try to sell directly to recipients
- Sign-up offers, where you instead use the mailing to solicit recipients' approval for you to send them further mailings

The second type of mailing is the one most preferred by B2B marketers. This is a legitimate approach to acquiring leads and building your mailing list. Know, however, that your response rate from this type of unsolicited mailing will be much lower than what you get from a typical mailing to your own list of customers.

Best Practices for Email Lead Solicitation

If you do decide to use email to solicit new prospects, here are some best practices to follow:

- **Send it from someone important**—If you want your email opened, make it look as if it's coming from someone important. Include a title along with a name in the From: line—and use an upper-management title to get more attention.

- **Make the subject matter**—Work the Subject: line so that recipients can quickly determine the email's importance. You need to break through the clutter of similar email and get the attention of the recipient.

- **Make it short and sweet**—Don't assume that the recipient will read a longish email; he or she probably won't. (Length is even more critical when recipients are reading their emails on an iPhone or Blackberry...) Say what you want to say quickly; get to the point and offer your value proposition before the recipient hits the Delete key.

> "Say what you want to say quickly; get to the point and offer your value proposition before the recipient hits the Delete key."

- **Offer something of value**—If you want the recipient to become a solid lead, you'll have to offer something of value for his time. That could be additional information, a free white paper, a discount on future orders, free admission to an upcoming conference or webinar, maybe even a free gift.

- **Use text, not images**—Rightly or wrongly, emails with embedded images is most often viewed as spam. In addition, many corporate firewalls screen out HTML emails from non-listed senders. For that reason, it's often better to go with an all-text approach.

The point is, for this type of initial solicitation email to work, it has to be short, to the point, and offer something of value. General introductions don't cut it, nor do generic offers. Be specific, and make sure you tell the recipient what comes next.

Using Email for Customer Acquisition

After you've made initial contact with a prospect, you can then use email to move toward the acquisition phase. That is, email becomes a vital tool in providing essential information that prospective customers need to become solid leads.

In practice, this typically means that your marketing department or salesperson sends marketing material and other information to prospects via email. What kinds of materials are we talking about? Here's the list:

- Brochures
- Catalogs
- White papers
- Presentations
- Videos

And, of course, answers to specific questions and requests.

You can send some materials as file attachments, although you have to be cautious of sending files that are too large—more than 2MB or so is probably too big. It might be more prudent to send links to where these materials can be downloaded from your website, instead.

The point is to utilize email to keep the conversation going until the prospect is ready to commit—and convert. To that end, we're talking personal emails rather than form mailings, coming from a real human being instead of your company's generic "marketing department." You want email to enhance the development of the personal relationship, not function as sterile, automated communications.

Using Email for Conversion

Time passes. Information passes. Questions and answers pass, back and forth. Eventually, if you do your job right, that prospect becomes a lead and then becomes a customer.

The endgame is the conversion process, and email can play a part. It doesn't have to, and doesn't always, but it can.

Many companies prefer to keep conversion personal, and that's great. Others will try to automate conversion via website ordering, and that's okay, too—especially for smaller customers.

However your company approaches conversion, it's likely that email can play a part in the process. Obviously, email is a primary means of communication between you and your clients, and that's the case during the conversion process, as well. You can use email to ask questions, solicit information, send forms that need to be printed and returned, even to send contracts. It's not uncommon for some customers to send purchase orders via email. Whatever works.

✉ *Note*

> What you should *not* do is ask your customers to send confidential company information via email. I'm talking things like bank account numbers, credit card numbers, passwords, and the like. Email simply isn't secure enough to ensure the safety of this type of information; hackers often target B2B emails to extract this type of important data. Instead, take confidential information over the phone, or direct customers to a secure page on your website to submit this data.

Using Email for Customer Retention

We've paid a lot of attention for using email for reach, acquisition, and conversion. But the majority of B2B email marketing should be customer retention marketing—messages sent to existing customers. These are individuals and companies who have previously purchased something from you and agreed to receive future emails. They're proven customers and willing customers, ripe for further engagement.

Getting Permission

As most smart marketers know, it costs much less money to sell an additional item to an existing customer than it does to create the first sale from a new customer. And for B2B companies, the primary means of contacting your customer base is via email.

The key, of course, is to get your customers' permission to let you send them emails. You can do this when a customer places an order online, by including a box for email address as well as an option they can check to receive email messages from you in the future. You can also just ask for it when talking to the buyer over the phone or via email.

Different Types of Mailings

What kinds of emails can you send? B2B customers like to know about upcoming sales and promotions. They also like to know about new products. They're also big fans of things that work with or accompany things they've already purchased—add-on sales, in other words.

So, when it comes to devising emails for customer retention, consider these approaches:

- **Regular mailings**—These are emails you send out once a quarter, once a month, or even once a week. If you do it right, customers will look forward to receiving these mailings—and the information or offers they contain. You can use regular mailings for weekly or monthly specials, company news, new product announcements, service tips, and the like.

- **Newsletters**—A newsletter is a special kind of regular mailing, which can be a great promotional tool—even if it doesn't promote any specific items. Newsletters are typically delivered on a somewhat regular schedule—once a month, typically, although quarterly and even weekly newsletters also work in some instances. (Daily is too frequent in the B2B world.) You can use your newsletter to let your customers know what's new with your business or in your industry. That might be new products or services, new routes or destinations, new locations, new hours, new employees, new you name it. Naturally, you also use your newsletter to announce sales and other promotions, but you don't have to. A newsletter can be strictly news, or it can be a mix.

- **Related items mailing**—This is a promotional email that offers something to customers related to something else they've purchased or looked at. The best example of a related items mailing is one offering accessories or service plans for an item the customer recently purchased. Another type of related items mailing promotes items that a customer was considering or looking at on your website; you know a customer is interested in that product, so push the heck out of it.

- **Notification mailing**—This is an email that notifies the customer about something they should be doing. For example, an HVAC supplier might send out emails to customers notifying them when their filters need to be changed or their systems serviced. Naturally, a notification email can also include promotions on the given product or service; there's nothing wrong with drumming up a little business along the way.

- **Promotional blast**—This is a sales mailing, pure and simple; it promotes one or more items or services at a special price. Although there are many different ways to use promotional blasts, what's common is that these are occasional mailings, not regular ones. You can use promotional blasts to promote a once-a-year sale or clearance, a special purchase that you're promoting, or a sale targeted to a special event. It's not a mailing that drops into inboxes once or twice a month; it's truly something special.

Best Practices for Customer Retention Emails

A successful email program for customer retention always delivers timely and relevant information to the customer. To that end, here are some best practices you can employ:

- **Target your mailings**—Don't send generic emails to everyone on your customer list. Target your email content to specific customers or customer types; make each email highly relevant to its recipients.

- **Segment by behavior**—When it comes to targeting specific email customers, analyze which links your customers are clicking in your emails. When you segment your list based upon which links are clicked, you know which products or categories specific customers are interested in.

> "Target your email content to specific customers or customer types; make each email highly relevant to its recipients."

- **Track performance**—Not only should you track the response to individual emails, you should also track the website content that your customers link to from your emails. It's a matter of finding out what interests your customer base, and what doesn't—and then fine-tuning your future email content accordingly.

- **Develop modular content**—Chances are you send out a variety of different emails targeted at different parts of your customer base. That doesn't mean you have to write all-new content for each email you send. Develop specific content modules that can be dropped into different emails or newsletters, as appropriate.

- **Ask for input**—You can analyze the performance of your existing content, but how do you know what else your customers might like to see? It never hurts to ask them, in the form of an online or telephone survey. Use the collected data to drive new content in your emails and newsletters.

- **Update customer preferences regularly**—When you first signed up a customer for your email programs, he determined what kinds of emails in which he was interested. Interests change, so it makes sense to reach out to your customers once a year or so to encourage them to update their email preferences. For that matter, you can also include a regular reminder in the footer of your regular emails to that effect.

- **Clean your list**—B2B marketers, like their B2C cousins, face the challenge of dealing with email addresses that no longer work. You need to periodically weed through your list to identify past customers who are no longer customers, buyers who no longer work at their old companies, individuals who've moved to new positions, changed email addresses, and even companies that are no longer in business. In email marketing, list cleanliness is definitely next to godliness. Make sure you get the religion.

Using Email to Encourage Customer Loyalty

If you do your job with your customer retention emails, you'll create a base of very loyal customers. These loyal customers, then, will recommend you to other potential customers—thus starting the B2B buying cycle over again. Not surprisingly, email can play a key part in this loyalty/referral phase.

First, you need to remember that social media is an important way for customers to talk to one another. To that end, you should include links to your key social media in your regular emails and newsletters. If you have a Facebook page, link to it. Same thing if you have a Twitter feed. Use one medium to promote another.

Second, make it easy for customers to "like" or pass along interesting bits in your emails, especially in email newsletters. Include a Facebook "like" button, a Twitter "tweet this" button, or even buttons for Digg and other social bookmarking services. In this regard, you treat your newsletter like a real news medium, and encourage your readers to share your content.

Finally, you can use targeted emails to encourage customers to do the referral thing. Send out an email that includes some sort of reward or bounty for new leads—a discount on future offers, perhaps, or even a free pass to an upcoming conference or webinar. (Heck, you can even offer cash bounties, although that's less common—and perhaps frowned upon by some buyers' employers.) The point is to remind current customers that they can recommend you to their colleagues and friends in the industry—and to encourage that behavior.

Creating an Effective Email Preference Center

One important component to an active B2B email operation is the creation of an *email preference center*. This is a page on your website that lets your customers manage their email contact information as well as which mailings they receive.

A key component to a successful email preference center is that list of all the mailings you offer. You need to positively present all your different mailings, using benefit-laden marketing copy; you want customers to sign up to multiple mailings, after all.

To that end, an effective email preference center needs to include the following components:

- A description of each newsletter or mailing available
- A link to a sample copy of each newsletter or mailing
- A check box to sign up to receive each newsletter or mailing
- A check box to unsubscribe to each newsletter or mailing
- A single check box to unsubscribe to *all* newsletters and mailings
- Delivery preferences—plain text or HTML
- A box to enter or correct the recipient's email address
- A link to your privacy policy
- A "contact us" link to your customer support department, which either sends an email to you or opens a separate web form page where the customer can enter comments, complaints, and the like

✉ Note

Instead of calling them newsletters or emails, you might want to refer to your mailings as "special offers."

In addition, you can use this opportunity to ask for more information about the customer. This might take the form of a few check boxes related to specific activities or intentions; just don't overwhelm people so that they back off before they actually subscribe to your mailings.

Another popular option is a way for customers to recommend your mailings to other people. This typically takes the form of a "let your colleagues know about this" section with a text box for them to enter their associates' email addresses. If you go this route, however, you can't just automatically add these addresses to your lists; you'll need to send them an introductory mailing to convince them to sign up on their own.

It's important to note that giving customers the option to manage their email subscriptions is likely to result in higher retention rates than offering a simple "unsubscribe" option at the bottom of each email. It draws them back to your site and keeps them in the fold.

✉ *Note*

After a customer has made changes to their email settings, send out an immediate confirmation email. This confirmation should include a link back to the email preference center, in case they need to make additional changes.

THE FUTURE OF EMAIL MARKETING

Although email marketing is an established component of the B2B marketing mix, it's a marketing vehicle in flux. You can see this more clearly in B2C email marketing, where traditional approaches are beginning to garner diminishing results.

Part of this is due to the fact that younger consumers are using email less. Ask any recent college graduate how often she checks her email inbox, and you're likely to get a blank stare; the younger generation has mainly abandoned email in favor of communicating via Facebook and other social networks. If your business depends on using email to market to younger consumers, you need a change in strategy.

This shift away from email is less noticeable in B2B marketing solely because most companies, large and small, still depend on email as their primary means of inter- and intra-company communication. However employees are communicating in their personal lives, they're still using email when they're on the job—at least for the time being. Consumer behaviors almost always spill into the corporate world, so expect similar changes in your customer base at some point in the future.

Even though B2B customers can still be reached via email, it doesn't mean that they're checking their email on their computers. More and more businesspeople are using their smartphones—iPhones, Blackberries, and the like—for email, both in the office and on the road. If nothing else, they use their phones for triage, deleting unwanted and unimportant messages and keeping what's left for reading back on the office PC. That's as good a reason as any to incorporate mobile as part of your digital marketing strategy.

We'll talk more about adapting email marketing for mobile in Chapter 17, "B2B Mobile Marketing." Turn there to learn more.

The Bottom Line

Email marketing is an important component of any B2B digital marketing plan. You can use email to reach new prospects, acquire new leads, convert leads to customers, retain existing customers, and encourage loyal customers to recommend your business to others. It's all a matter of managing your email database and sending appropriate emails to each name on your list. Make sure you avoid sending unwanted emails, in the form of either spam or bacon—and always make your emails relevant and useful.

13

B2B Blog Marketing

Next up on our tour of B2B digital marketing vehicles is blog marketing. There are actually two types of blog marketing you can do—you can create your own corporate blog, and you can use other parties' blogs to promote your products and services.

Both types of blog marketing are important to your B2B digital marketing plan. You can use blog marketing in the reach, acquisition, and retention phases of the B2B buying continuum.

Why Create a Company Blog?

Blogging is, by most accounts, an integral component of most B2B companies' digital marketing strategy. Forrester reports that in 2010, almost half (49%) of B2B companies had their own corporate blog, significantly higher than the 32% who blogged two years' prior.[1]

There's a reason why half of all B2B companies blog—it works. And because it's a toss-up as to whether your competitors are blogging or not, there's still the opportunity to gain a competitive advantage by creating your own corporate blog.

Why Corporate Blogging Works

Just why are corporate blogs so effective? There are actually lots of factors, including the following:

- **Blogging generates leads**—Blogging is one of the most effective social media for acquiring new leads. HubSpot found that 57% of organizations with their own corporate blogs have acquired a customer through a blog-generated lead.[2] That compares to just 48% for those using Facebook, and only 42% for those using Twitter.

- **Blogging drives traffic to your website**—A visitor reading your blog should be encouraged to link back to your main website for more news and information. It's just one more source for website traffic.

- **Blogging provides fresh content for your website**—If you post to your company blog on a regular basis, and mirror your posts on your main website, all that blog content provides fresh content material for what might otherwise be a dreadfully static website. The goal is to keep your site's home page new and lively, and constant blog updates do that; there's always something new on your home page when you're making daily blog posts. The rest of the page's content—contact information, mission statement, pretty pictures of your corporate headquarters—can remain constant; new blog posts will still make your site appear fresh and relevant.

- **Blogging increases the effectiveness of other media**—In addition, blogging can increase the effectiveness of your other digital media marketing. For example, HubSpot also found that businesses with blogs have twice as many Twitter followers as those that don't. Put simply, a corporate blog can increase traffic to your other social media sites; they're highly synergistic.

---

1. Forrester Research, "B2B Marketers' 2010 Budget Trends," 2010

2. HubSpot, "The 2011 State of Inbound Marketing," 2011

- **Blogging improves search results**—A blog is one more item that search engines can index and display. Actually, it's more than one item because each blog post can become a search engine result. If your blog posts are timely and relevant, you can end up with multiple placements on a search results page—instead of single result from your static website.

- **Blogging enhances brand image**—Your corporate blog is a great vehicle to get your viewpoint out in a relatively controlled fashion. Unlike Facebook and other social media, you control all the content—which makes it great for branding.

- **Blogging demonstrates expertise**—What better way to convince prospects and customers that you're the leading authority in your field (what some would call a "thought leader") than by proving it with a series of informative blog posts? It's a perfect medium for proving that you're all you say you are.

- **Blogging grabs media attention**—If your corporate blog makes you an expert, the news media will take notice. Let's face it, the media wants to talk to thought leaders; newsworthy blog posts can result in increased media coverage.

- **Blogging humanizes your company**—One big advantage of a company blog is that the blog lets you establish a public face for your company, brand, or product. Instead of remaining a faceless, soulless corporation or empty brand, your blog lets you connect to customers on a person-to-person basis. Putting this personal face on your company or products will inspire more potential customers to purchase what you're selling—or help keep existing customers in the fold. B2B customers like the personal approach, which is exactly what a blog offers.

- **Blogging provides customer feedback**—A blog is also a great tool for gaining insight about your customer base. It's not just a one-way communication; comments left about your blog posts let you know what's on the minds of your customers' minds, especially those loyal trendsetters who follow your blog on a regular basis. That's invaluable research.

- **Blogging builds community**—Those comments on your blog posts also help build your online community and solidify customer relationships. You'd be surprised at the number of lively discussions that unfold at some corporate blogs; it's definitely proof that blogging is a form of social media.

- **Blogging disseminates news and information**—For many companies, one of the primary uses of a company blog is to get the word out about whatever it is you want your customers to know about. Maybe you talk about the new offices you're opening, or a new product line you're developing, or maybe a series of upcoming trade shows or seminars.

You can even talk about your current advertising campaign, changes in company policy, or what's new in your industry.

- **Blogging promotes products and services**—You can also use a company blog as a pure promotional tool. You can create blog posts to announce new products, upcoming promotions, big sales—you name it. All you have to do is post your promotional announcement as a blog post; that means couching ad copy as a news article, but that isn't so much different from writing a standard press release.

> ## ✉ Note
>
> It might be more effective to promote your products and services in a more subtle fashion on your blog. Instead of saying "Here's our new product!", you write an article about how a particular customer is using that product, or how a given company adopted your product line, or how easy it is to use your product in a particular situation. You get the gist of it; create a news event that features the product or service in question, and post talk about it on the a blog post.

- **Blogging heads off problems**—A company can also use a blog to address potential issues before they become big problems. Again, it's the human face thing. If you get a real human being in front of an issue, you can most likely defuse things before they get bad.
- **Blogging is low cost**—Your cost to create and populate a blog may be next to nothing. Indeed, HubSpot reports that 55% of businesses indicate that blog-generated leads have a below-average cost (see Figure 13.1); that makes blogging more cost-effective than social media, SEO, PPC advertising, direct mail, and trade shows. You can use a canned blog-creation service, such as WordPress (www.wordpress.com) or Blogger (www.blogger.com), or simply treat your blog as an addendum to your existing website. Content is free, provided you tap internal sources to post. There's no ad space to buy or other expenditures to make; it's truly low-cost digital marketing.

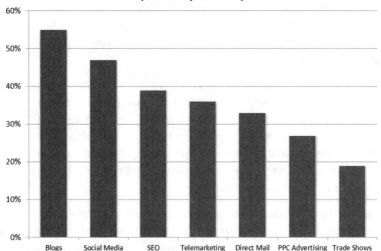

Figure 13.1 *More marketers believe that blogs have a lower cost per lead than other media.*

That's a lot of good reasons to establish a corporate blog—before we even address how you can best use a blog for reach, acquisition, and retention.

Blogging for Reach

The first stage of the B2B customer life cycle where blogging becomes important is actually the first stage—reach. A useful and informative blog can reach out to potential new customers and let them know that your company is an important player in the industry.

The key to using blogs for reach is to provide content that prospective customers want to read. Simply blogging about your new offices or internal promotions won't be of much interest; instead, you need to write about issues of interest to anyone in your industry, not just your loyal customers.

To this end, your blog should include a mixture of industry news, opinion, and advice. Yes, you can make some posts about the products and services you offer, and even about the people behind these products and services. But what will really draw the attention of potential buyers is your take on what's happening in the industry at large—and how these industry issues might affect them.

Blogging for Acquisition

Your corporate blog can also be useful when you're actively trying to turn interested readers into solid leads. Remember that during the acquisition phase, buyers are looking for information to feed their own decision-making process. Your blog can provide that information.

In this phase, we're talking less about general industry information and more about information specific to your company and the products and services you offer. This is where you can throw in posts about specific products and services—new products on their way, updates to existing products, and the like. You can also post case studies about how other customers are using specific products, answer some typical questions, and such. Use a variety of different types of posts to provide all sorts of information about what you offer.

You can also use your blog to get potential customers comfortable with your company. That means personalizing your company by featuring key staff in your posts—either by writing about them or letting them write their own blog posts. You can also do a little bit of corporate bragging, by creating short posts about any awards you've one, media exposure you've received, and such. There's also no harm in blogging about upcoming seminars, conferences, and the like.

The point is to try to draw prospective customers into your corporate orbit. Make them comfortable with who you are and what you offer—and help provide all the information they need to make an intelligent purchasing decision.

Blogging for Retention

After you've converted a lead into a paying customer, you can use your blog to help retain that customer. Here the focus is on making the customer feel like he's part of the family—and helping to foster a community among all your customers.

To some extent, the same types of posts that work for acquisition also work for retention. That means writing about the people behind the company—and about your customers, too. Case studies are always good, as are plain old customer focus pieces. For that matter, you might want to encourage key customers to contribute their own blog posts on occasion; it helps cement your relationship with the customer you ask to contribute, and provides a ringing endorsement from that customer to others.

It's at this stage of the B2B buying continuum that reader comments become particularly important. You want to build a community around your blog, and that happens when readers comment on your posts—and then other readers comment on those comments. Not only should you actively encourage comments, you should write posts that inspire comments. To that end, it's not bad to be a little controversial; strong opinions inspire debate. You can also use blog posts to query your customer base about company direction, potential new products and services, industry trends, you name it.

And remember, when readers comment on your posts, you'll need to respond. It's no longer a one-way communication at this point; your blog becomes a living, breathing community that requires constant attention. Apply the same focus to your blog community as you do to your social networking efforts; it's a great opportunity to actively engage with your customer base.

> "Not only should you actively encourage comments, you should write posts that inspire comments."

Running Your Blog

Maintaining a corporate blog makes sense for most B2B companies. But how do you set up and run such a blog?

Putting Together a Plan

It helps to do a little planning before you start blogging. There are several strategic issues you need to address.

First, you need to decide whether you want to include the blog as part of your existing website or set up a separate blog site. Perhaps the most common approach is to use a subdomain for your blog. For example, if your main domain is mybusiness.com, your blog might be located at blog.mybusiness.com. This keeps your blog separate from your website, but still tied to it.

You also have blog design issues to consider. The blog page itself is merely a container for your blog posts, but it's an important container. You should surround the posts with elements of use to both you and your customers. This includes links or buttons to share your blog's content with various social media sites, such as Facebook and Twitter; links to email blog content to other users; links to subscribe to the blog's RSS or Atom feeds; and links back to your website, either to the home page or to individual product pages.

Next, you have to develop a blogging strategy—that is, what you want to blog about and how often. Blog content can range from simple product announcements to in-depth articles about how your company works. Your blog posts define the character of your blog, and should reflect the brand or product image you want to convey; this includes not only the content but also the writing style. Should your blog be light-hearted or deadly serious? Should the articles be short and sweet or long and detailed? These are key strategic decisions you need to make.

When it comes to posting strategy, you can decide to post monthly, weekly, or even daily, if that makes sense. In general, you keep customers coming back with more frequent posts; certainly, anything less frequent than weekly isn't going to do the trick. If you have enough unique content to post several times a week, that's even better.

You also have to determine who should be doing the blogging. Should your posts come exclusively from a copywriter in the marketing department, or should you solicit input from throughout the organization? Do you want to go with consistent style and subject matter, which argues in favor of a single poster, or go for more variety in content, which you get if you use multiple posters? And what about soliciting posts from people outside the company, including customers? Again, important decisions must be made.

The goal, after all, is to use your blog to both entice new prospects and retain existing customers. Think of your blog as an extension of your existing digital marketing presence, and you'll be headed in the right direction.

Determining Who Contributes to the Blog

Let's deal with a few of the main strategic issues, starting with who in your organization should write your blog. It's not that easy a decision.

For example, some B2B companies assign blogging to the marketing department. This makes a lot of sense, especially if you view blogging as a marketing function, a kind of online PR activity.

Other companies leave blogging to the big shots. That is, it's the company president or CEO who handles the blogging chores. This certainly lends a bit of authority to the blog, but might not always be realistic. After all, how much free time does your CEO have to spend on the blog?

Other companies leave blogging to their product people, or to the sales department, or sometimes even to HR. There are certainly arguments to be made for each of these decisions.

But here's the thing. Blogging doesn't have to be assigned to a single person or department. Many companies are quite successful in incorporating contributions from multiple individuals throughout the organization—including, in some instances, key customers.

Personally, I like the multiple-blogger approach. When you go this route, you enable lots of people within your organization to talk about your business—about what they do, how they help customers, and the like. You end up providing multiple perspectives on your business, which really works to humanize the organization. That's a good thing.

It's also a good thing to draw on the expertise of individuals who do—and are expert in—different things. Let's say, for example, that you work for an auto parts distributor. You can assign one person to blog about new cars, one to blog about used cars, one to blog about service-related issues, and so forth. You get the idea; tap into the expertise of everyone in your organization. The more bloggers you have, the merrier.

Note

Some B2B companies even extend blog posting to some of their favored customers. There's nothing like adding a real-world customer perspective to flesh out your blog's content—and cement your relationship with those customers.

Deciding What to Write About

Of course, deciding who writes what depends to a large degree on what you want to write about. This is the big question: What is your blog about?

The first thing you need to decide is if you're writing for your existing customer base or to a larger base of potential customers. If it's the former, you're safe writing about things your company is doing—new products, personnel changes, and so on.

If you want to expand your base, however, you need to attract buyers who don't know that much about you, prospects who aren't insiders to your world. In this instance, your blog has to include posts that are interesting to casual readers. This means writing about more than just your company and products; you need to write about the world outside your company. This probably means writing about industry-related news and topics. You thus aim for your blog to become a valued industry resource.

That's not to say that you can never write about your company and products; you can and you should. But you need to do so in a way that engages both current and potential customers, and creates a community for these readers. Remember, your blog is your company's public face; it's the home base of conversations and content for and about your company and your customers.

Creating Powerful Titles

Now we come to the nuts and bolts of writing blog posts. We'll start at the top, with the title you assign to each post.

As you might suspect, the title of a blog post is extremely important, as it factors heavily into the post's searchability and, in many RSS and Atom feeds, might be the only part of the post that readers are first exposed to. Besides, the title of a blog post is like the title of a newspaper or magazine article, or even a print advertisement; it's what attracts the reader's attention and persuades him to read the text that follows.

> "...the title of a blog post is like the title of a newspaper or magazine article, or even a print advertisement; it's what attracts the reader's attention..."

To that end, you have to write powerful, compelling titles for all your posts. The title has to draw the reader into the post; it has to be interesting and informative in its own right, as well as descriptive of the post itself.

There are many ways to do this. You can, and probably should, communicate a customer benefit in the title ("Meet Our New A-9 Widget: Better Performance That Improves Your Bottom Line"). You can also pique the reader's interest by asking a question ("What's the Secret Behind the New A-9 Widget?"), or making a provocative statement ("Our New A-9 Widget Will Change the Face of Business in America").

You also need to include your most important keywords in your post titles. I'm talking keywords that describe the post content, of course, but also keywords that apply to the blog itself, or to your company or product. Now, you can't pack too many keywords into a title, so you have to choose judiciously. But titles are what count most when the search engines are indexing blog posts, so fitting in the primary keywords is essential.

The challenge in accomplishing all these goals is that the title of a blog post has to be relatively short. Although there are no practical limitations on the length of a blog post title, you need to know that search engine results pages will only show the first 65 characters or so of a post title. Anything past that 65-character mark simply gets truncated. So, you can go long if you want to, but a lot of people won't see the words at the end.

Writing Blog Posts

Effective blog writing is conversational yet direct. It has to reflect the personality of the contributor, while still getting across the company message. To that end, the author's voice is important; the writing needs to be personal, not corporate.

Getting that personal feel is important. A blog post shouldn't sound like a regurgitated press release, nor like a piece of catalog copy. It should sound like a letter from a trusted friend—a little chatty, perhaps, but full of useful and interesting information.

Blog posts also need to be relatively short. Not as short as a tweet or Facebook status update, of course, but not near as long as a magazine article, for example either. We're talking posts that are measured in paragraphs, not pages. Write too much and no one will read the complete post; write too little and the post won't be informative. You have to strike a middle ground fit for the short attention spans of today's web users—somewhere between 250 and 1,000 words.

As to how fancy the writing should be, the key descriptor is "conversational." You also need to know your customer base, and gear the writing to that level. There's nothing wrong with aiming at a fifth-grade reading level, which seems to be the American average these days (even for business writing), but you can probably notch it up a tad if you have a more educated or technical audience.

By the way, remember that a blog post doesn't have to be text only. You can include pictures and videos in your post, both of which can help to humanize the experience. There's nothing like a picture of someone making or using a product to grab the reader's attention and pull him into the process.

✉ *Note*

As you're using your blog to encourage customer retention and loyalty, you always want to keep your larger community of readers in mind. To that end, you should encourage comments to your blog posts—and then monitor those comments and jump in when necessary.

Determining the Right Frequency

How often should you post to your company blog? That's a good, strategic question. If you post too often, you could overwhelm readers with unwanted information. If you don't post often enough, your blog will appear stagnant and irrelevant. You need to strike a happy medium.

For most B2B companies, the optimal posting frequency is probably once or twice a week. It kind of depends on what actual news and information you have to convey, as well as the strength of the relationship you have with your customers. Obviously, the more you have to say, the more often you can legitimately post. And the more your customers are like fans, hanging on your every word and action, the more often they'll want to hear whatever it is that you have to say.

If you publish once a day or more, at least on a regular basis, you're probably going to start boring your readers. At some point, they're going to look at all the posts you make write and say, "Who cares?" I'm not sure exactly where useful information turns into useless blather, but you want to be someone on the useful side of that point.

On the other hand, if you post less than once a week, customers might forget you're there. You need to stay in front of them, and that means putting something out there on a somewhat regular basis. If your last post was a month ago, you just won't appear serious about this whole blogging thing. Your loyal customers will feel abandoned, and that's definitely not what you're going for. If you can't post more often than that, you're better off not having a blog at all.

So, aim for posting once a week or every few days. That leaves something new out there just about every day for interested customers to read; it keeps their interest without overwhelming them—and demanding too much of their time.

BLOGGING VERSUS SOCIAL NETWORKING

With the advent of Facebook, Twitter, and other more trendy social media, just how relevant are blogs today? After all, blogs were a really big deal a few years ago, but then social networking came along and stole some of the buzz. Should you still bother with doing your own company blog, or should you turn your attention more towards social networking?

That's a good question, at least on the surface—or if you believe that social networks have made blogs obsolete. But that doesn't appear to be the case because the blogosphere is flourishing like never before.

At least the business and professional areas of the blogosphere are flourishing. I'm not so sure about personal blogs; these do appear to have been affected by the rise of social networking. It's a lot easier to make one's personal opinions or activities known via a Facebook status update than via a post to a freestanding blog, after all. It takes zero skills and effort for friends and family to get set up on Facebook, whereas there is some work involved in creating a personal blog, even with the easy-to-use tools of Blogger and WordPress.

So, I definitely see a movement from personal blogs to social networking. But that movement doesn't apply to business and what I'd call professional blogs, which really can't be replicated via Facebook and other social networking sites. Naturally, your company can (and should) establish a Facebook presence, but that presence is nothing like what you get with a well-run blog. For B2B companies, then, social network marketing supplements and complements blog marketing. You need to do both.

Marketing to Other Blogs

Posting to your own corporate blog isn't the only way to include the blogosphere in your B2B marketing plans. You can also utilize third-party blogs to promote your company and products—by getting those bloggers to talk about you and what you offer.

Why Other Blogs Are Important

This approach incorporates the blogosphere as a key component of your public relations efforts. In the old days, you sent press releases to various press outlets, such industry magazines and journals. Today, however, that traditional press is supplemented by both professional and semiprofessional bloggers. In fact, you should consider some bloggers as part of the press; they function similarly in terms of informing the public, even if they don't have share the same journalistic code.

And here's the thing. Many companies are finding that blogs send more traffic back to their sites than do traditional media. Within any given industry or topic area, there are some blogs that are quite influential; they have a large readership that trusts the blogger's opinions. If such a blogger writes about your company or product, lots of traffic can result.

You need to expend effort, then, to get in front of (and in the good graces of) these influential bloggers. That means identifying these bloggers, of course, but also getting to know them, the same way your PR folks might get to know the most important magazine writers or columnists. This sort of thing is done on a personal basis, not just by sending out press releases or their electronic equivalent—although you still need to do that, of course, to hit the second- and third-tier bloggers. With the big guys, however, there's a lot of talking and cajoling involved; it's a relationship kind of thing.

If you can get in front of these bloggers, however, and get them to write about your products, you can then benefit from that implied endorsement. You can't always tell how many readers of a blog will act on the blogger's advice, but it's free placement that carries with it a legitimacy similar to true word-of-mouth marketing.

Directing your PR efforts to these influential bloggers is every bit as important as cultivating traditional media contacts,—and perhaps more so. It's the kind of exposure you just can't get from paid media.

How to Get Bloggers to Notice—and Mention—You

In some aspects, targeting bloggers is just like targeting any other member of the media—reporters, critics, and the like. You send information their way and, if you're persistent and a little bit lucky, they mention you or your products in their writings. Public Relations 101, as it were.

Except it isn't quite the same. You don't reach bloggers the same way you reach newspaper or magazine writers. And they're not looking for the same things, either. There are some subtle differences of which you need to be aware.

As with most PR efforts, reaching bloggers starts with you treating them as people, not just contacts on a list. Sending out blind emails or making cold calls isn't going to work; you have to establish a personal relationship with these folks. You have to learn a little about these bloggers, starting with their names. (The worst thing in the world is contacting a blog without having the name of the actual blogger.) Find out what they like and don't like, which is easy enough to do by reading their blog posts. (Yes, you have to read their blogs; that's how you get informed about what they're doing.) Get a judge of their temperament, what gets them excited, what they really hate, and so forth and so on. Get inside their minds.

After you're comfortable with how a blogger thinks, it's time to introduce yourself. Not via a press release or unsolicited email, mind you, but by leaving comments on the blogger's posts. That's right, you make yourself known by posting a comment or two or three. This establishes you as a participant in that blog's community, not as an outsider wanting PR favors.

So, you should get to know the blogger through his posts and let him get to know you through your comments. Then you can attempt a direct contact, typically via email. Introduce yourself, reference some of the aforementioned posts and comments, and let the blogger know you'd be glad to provide him with any information he might find useful. Plant the seeds, as it were.

Then, when it comes time that there's some news you want to publicize, call in your favors. Email the blogger and let him know what's cooking. Plug your product or service or whatever it is you're plugging, and suggest that the blogger might want to mention it in an upcoming post. Point out how the blog's readers might be interested in or benefit from this information. Make it sound like readers deserve to hear about this news. And offer to provide more information or resources if the blogger needs them.

✉ *Note*

For really influential bloggers, offer some sort of exclusive interview with a product person, member of the management team, or whatever—anything that the blogger can view as an exclusive to his blog.

Knowing how bloggers tend to work will help you in this task. Unlike traditional journalists who have a traditional 9-to-5 workday, bloggers don't necessarily keep the same hours. Some bloggers have day jobs and blog in their free time; so, it may be better to contact these bloggers in the evenings or on weekends.

Obviously, because you're both working online, you want to communicate online, as well. That means email instead of postal mail, and instant messaging instead of phone calls. Find out what the blogger prefers, and go that route.

As to what you send the blogger, a traditional printed press release or press kit is right out. Instead, put together an electronic press kit, something you can send to bloggers via email. The email message itself should probably serve as the press release; use attachments to send product photos and other key items.

That email press release, by the way, should include a link back to whatever it is you're promoting. That could be your company's home page, but more likely should be a dedicated landing page for this PR event. You want to send the blogger's followers to a web page that relates directly to whatever it is the blogger wrote; don't rely on generic links.

You should also include your own contact information in the email, so the blogger can contact you directly for more information. Most bloggers want to personalize the information they present, which means you shouldn't expect exact regurgitation of your press releases. Instead, help bloggers turn your message into something unique to their blogs.

By the way, bloggers (even business bloggers) tend not to react too well to traditional press releases. Instead, make the accompanying email conversational and personal. Use bullet points to highlight main topics, but always bring the content around to how it will benefit this blogger and the blog's readers. That means customizing your press releases for each individual blogger, but it's an effort well spent.

As to whom you should target, do your research and find out which blogs are read by your current customers or desired customers. Identify those blogs that are big in your industry, those that have the most followers and the most impact. These blogs are the ones that matter.

Once identified, you should treat these bloggers as you would members of the mainstream press. Treat them as friends, yes, but as very important friends.

These are also friends with their own unique worldviews and their own very definite opinions. Don't expect to tell a blogger what to write; you can suggest all you want, but in the end they'll do what they want to do and nothing more than that. Bloggers, in other words, are beyond your control. (In fact, most bloggers can't be controlled at all.) They're not corporate drones, and they don't work for you. They're important people with their own opinions, and should be treated as such.

Giving Bloggers Everything They Need

After you convince a blogger to mention your company or product, you need to provide him with everything he needs to create an effective blog post. Some of this stuff can be included in or attached to your initial email; other items can be linked to and downloaded from your website.

This means, of course, creating a section of your website devoted to the press and the media. This part of your site should include product photos at various resolutions; bloggers love to include pictures with their posts. Offer a variety of photos so that a blogger can choose the one best suited to his blog and readers.

In short, you have to give bloggers all the information and details they need to put up an interesting post. The easier you make it for them, the more likely they are to write about you.

The Bottom Line

Blogs are important in the reach, acquisition, and retention phases of the B2B marketing lifecycle. This means both creating your own corporate blog and influencing third-party bloggers to mention your company, products, and services. A company blog can be especially useful in establishing your company's role as a thought leader, and in developing a community of customers.

14

B2B Social Media Marketing

The biggest buzz in digital marketing today is social media marketing—marketing on Facebook, LinkedIn, Google+, Twitter, and other social networks. How important is social media to your B2B marketing strategy? What's the best way for your company to use these social media?

Social media marketing is a new thing for many B2B marketers. Read on to learn how to best incorporate social media marketing into your company's digital marketing plans.

Understanding Social Media

What is—or, rather, what are—social media? In a nutshell, social media are those websites, services, and platforms that people use to share experiences and opinions with each other. They cover everything from social networks (users share the details of their own lives) to social bookmarking services (users share the sites and articles they like), and include blogs, microblogs, and other forms of online communities.

Social media is differentiated from traditional media because of its two-way, conversational nature. Traditional media (newspapers, magazines, radio, television, and the like) are one-way; these media broadcast their static messages to the widest possible audiences. Social media, on the other hand, are interactive, encouraging two-way (or more-way) conversations between multiple parties. It's a participatory activity, not just a spectator sport.

It's this participation that makes social media of interest to B2B marketers. There are plenty of media available, both online and off, that let you broadcast your message to potential customers. But how many media enable you to engage your customers in an active conversation? That's where social media shine.

Not to complicate things, but there are many different forms of social media, all of which can be important to your online marketing efforts. Everybody divides them up a bit differently, but I tend to see them in this fashion:

- Social networks, such as Facebook, LinkedIn, and Google+
- Blogs
- Microblogging services, such as Twitter
- Social bookmarking and news services, such as Digg, Delicious, and StumbleUpon
- Media-sharing sites, such as Flickr and YouTube

In addition, you can probably throw in social review sites, such as Yelp, web-based message forums, and any number of topic-specific websites that create their own online communities. In other words, anyplace online where social interaction occurs has the makings of being a social medium.

Social Networking with Facebook, Google+, and LinkedIn

Social networking is, perhaps, the most popular social medium today, because it's a true online community; it's where friends, family, and business colleagues can hang out online and share their experiences.

In practice, a social network is a large website that hosts a community of users and facilitates public and private communication between those users. Social networks enable users to share experiences and opinions with each other via short posts or status updates.

Some social networks, such as school or alumni networks, are devoted to a specific topic or community. Other social networks, such as Facebook, are more broad-based, which allows for communities devoted to specific topics to develop within the overall network.

In short, social networks help people keep up-to-date on what others are doing, and keep others updated on what they are doing. They also help establish a sense of community based on shared experiences at school, in the workplace, or at play.

There are three major social networks active in the U.S. today:

- **Facebook** (www.facebook.com)—With more than 750 million users, it's the largest social network available, popular with both consumers and businesses.

- **Google+** (plus.google.com)—This is the newest social network on the block, Google's big entry into the social networking scene. Google+ garnered 20 million users in its first few weeks of operation, and has the potential to be a strong long-term competitor to Facebook.

- **LinkedIn** (www.linkedin.com)—This is the social network for professionals and businesspeople. LinkedIn has a smaller, albeit older and more affluent, audience than Facebook (100 million professional users), which makes it very popular among B2B marketers.

These aren't the only social networks out there, of course; others are smaller and more targeted, more popular in other countries; or, like the formerly dominant MySpace, on their way to an eventual demise. It's appropriate to focus your B2B marketing efforts on the big three players.

Blogging as a Social Medium

It might surprise you to think of blogs in the same breath as Facebook and Twitter, but it's true; blogging is a form of social connection. A blogger makes a personal connection with his readers, and a community is formed when those readers comment on the blog posts. (And on other comments, of course.)

As such, blogging is one of the key social media. Now, we've already covered blog marketing, so I won't repeat that information here. Know, however, that because blogging is a type of social media, you probably should consider blog marketing when you develop your overall social media marketing strategy.

Note

Learn more about blogs in Chapter 13, "B2B Blog Marketing."

Microblogging with Twitter

Then we have *microblogs*. As the name implies, a microblog is a little bitty blog—more accurately, a service that broadcasts very short blog posts, broadcast to a group of subscribers.

In reality, microblogging has more in common with social networking than it does with traditional long-form blogging. A microblog is what results when you separate the short text messages or status updates from a social network into a separate feed. Microblogs, typified by Twitter, exist solely to distribute short text posts from individual users to groups of followers. These posts are similar to traditional blog posts but are much shorter, typically in the 140-character range.

That said, a microblog is considerably different from both a social network and a traditional blog. Microblogs do not offer any of the community features found on larger social network sites; there are no topic-based groups, one-to-one private messaging, photo sharing, and the like. The only service a microblog offers is public message distribution. It's all about the tweets.

The most popular microblogging service today is **Twitter** (www.twitter.com), with more than 100 million users. A company creates a Twitter account and begins to post short text messages, called *tweets*. Other businesses sign up to follow the tweets of the first business; they are then notified when that business makes a new post. B2B companies use tweets to talk to their customer base, via new product announcements and other bursts of information.

Social Bookmarking with Digg, Delicious, and StumbleUpon

Social bookmarking services—sometimes called *social news* sites—represent a subset of features found on a social network. A social bookmarking service lets users save and share their favorite web pages with friends and colleagues online. It's all about finding something you like and then letting others know about it.

In operation, it's fairly simple. A user visits a website, web page, news article, or blog post that he or she likes, and then clicks a button or link to bookmark that site. This bookmark then appears in that user's master list of bookmarks on the social bookmarking service site; the user can share all or some of these bookmarks with anyone he or she designates.

Most social bookmarking services use tags to help users find bookmarked sites. When a user bookmarks a site, he adds a few tags or keywords to describe the site. Other users can then search by keywords to find the most popular matching book-marked sites—just as they search Google and the other traditional search engines.

Users can also vote on the bookmarks submitted, typically on an up or down basis; this helps quality and relevant bookmarks rise to the top of the list. Users can also add their comments to bookmarks, thus helping to create a thriving community.

The most popular social bookmarking services include **Digg** (www.digg.com), **Delicious** (www.delicious.com), **Reddit** (www.reddit.com), and **StumbleUpon** (www.stumbleupon.com). Although social bookmarking services are popular mar-keting vehicles for many B2C businesses, they're less important for B2B companies, simply because the scale isn't there; these services are designed for consumers, not necessarily for businesses. For that reason, I haven't found many B2B market-ers incorporating social bookmarking services into their digital marketing plans, although it certainly isn't out of the question.

Social Sharing with YouTube and Flickr

One interesting aspect of the social web is *social sharing*, the passing around of pic-tures, movies, music, and such between friends and family. Social networking sites, such as Facebook and Google+, offer media-sharing features; in fact, Facebook is probably the number-one photo-sharing site on the Web. But there are lots of sites dedicated solely to sharing specific types of media online.

All of these sites work in a similar fashion. Users upload their media—photos, movies, whatever—to the site. The uploaded media are made available either publicly to everyone on the site, or privately to selected lists of friends and family. Other users, invited or otherwise, then view the uploaded media as they wish.

Most media-sharing sites also offer some degree of community interaction, typi-cally by letting users share the media they find and like with others. YouTube, for example, makes it easy for users to email links to their videos, as well as embed videos in blogs and other websites. Flickr goes a step further by encouraging user-created groups devoted to particular subjects or types of photography. Most sites also offer private email-like communication between users.

In terms of photo-sharing sites, **Flickr** (www.flickr.com) is the big dog. In the video-sharing arena, it's **YouTube** (www.youtube.com) standing head and shoul-ders above the completion.

✉ *Note*

Learn more about YouTube and video sharing in Chapter 15, "B2B Audio, Video, and Interactive Marketing."

Social Location Sharing with Foursquare, Gowalla, and MyTown

Talking about sharing, if you take social networking mobile and local, you end up with something called *social location sharing*. This particular social medium helps consumers connect with one another—and with local businesses and location—while they're on the go. These services track your location via your iPhone or other smartphone, and either broadcast your location to other users or let you know if other users are in the neighborhood. They attempt to create real-world connections via the virtual medium.

Currently, the largest players include **Foursquare** (www.foursquare.com), **Gowalla** (www.gowalla.com), and **Loopt** (www.loopt.com). As you might suspect, social location sharing holds lots of promise for B2C marketers, especially local businesses. It's much less important for B2B marketers, if only because few businesses make spontaneous purchasing decisions while they're driving around town.

How Important Is Social Media Marketing for B2B?

There's an ongoing myth that B2B companies are less engaged in social media marketing than are B2C companies. Research disproves that myth.

For example, a recent Business.com survey showed that 81% of B2B companies had a company presence on social networking sites, compared to 67% of B2C companies. Similarly, 75% of B2B companies participated in Twitter, compared to 49% for B2C companies, while 66% engaged in online discussions, compared to 43% of B2C companies.[1]

This embrace of social media is also apparent in B2B marketing budgets. According to Outsell, B2B companies were expected to increase their social marketing expenditures 43% in 2010;[2] no other marketing media had that kind of increase in support.

---

1. Business.com, "2009 Business Social Media Benchmarking Survey," 2009

2. Outsell, "Annual Advertising and Marketing Study 2010: Total U.S. and B2B Advertising," 2010

There's a reason why B2B companies are embracing social media—it's where their customers are increasingly going to for information. The same Business.com survey cited previously found that 62% of businesses visited company social network pages for information, while 54% searched for information on social media sites (see Figure 14.1). If that's where your prospective customers are looking, you need to be there.

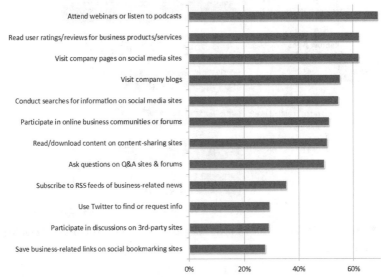

Figure 14.1   *The most popular social media sources for business information. (Courtesy Business.com)*

The reality is that social media might be more important to B2B companies than for their B2C cousins. That's because most B2B companies have a smaller potential customer base and a higher average price point than do B2C customers. With these dynamics, using social media to turn customers into advocates—which is what social media does—pays bigger dividends for B2B companies.

It's interesting how business professionals use the Internet to share information and build their network of industry contacts. Social networking sites are rife with professional communities that help their members solve problems and share their experiences and insights. Consider also how B2B buyers tend to rely on third-party feedback in making their purchase decisions, and you can see the value of social networks in various stages of the B2B buying continuum.

How exactly does social media marketing benefit your business? Certainly, social networking is all about nurturing relationships with your most loyal customers; it's a unique forum for two-way communication and community building. But beyond that, a strong presence in social media can benefit your other digital marketing activities; it can increase your business exposure, drive traffic to your website, and even improve your search engine rankings (see Figure 14.2).[3] It can also generate real leads.

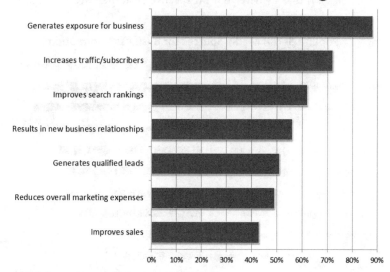

Benefits of Social Media Marketing

Figure 14.2 *Additional benefits of social media marketing. (Courtesy Social Media Examiner)*

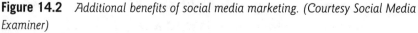 **Note**

It's also important to note that Internet users are increasingly replacing email with social media to communicate with others. This is particularly true with younger users, although less so in the business environment. Still, trends migrate upwards from youthful early adopters; Gartner Research predicts that by 2014, social networking will replace email as the primary vehicle for communication for 20% of all business users.[4]

And let us not ignore the cost factor. Social media is among the most cost-effective marketing vehicle in your arsenal. It's not free; in fact, it's somewhat time-intensive. But the actual upfront costs are minimal, which makes it ideal for smaller or cash-constrained businesses. Establishing a presence on most social networks takes nothing more than your time—which in itself is valuable. Indeed, you'll need to

3. Social Media Examiner, "2011 Social Media Marketing Industry Report," 2011

4. Gartner Research, "Gartner Predicts 2010: Social Software is an Enterprise Reality," 2010

determine just how much time to devote to social media marketing as opposed to other forms of digital and traditional marketing. Yes, you can get results, but you'll have to decide whether the time investment is worth it. Inevitably, there are tradeoffs to be made.

CAN YOUR CUSTOMERS ACCESS SOCIAL MEDIA?

One of the challenges faced by B2B marketers using social media is that some businesses don't want their employees "wasting time" on Facebook and Twitter, and thus block access to these and other social networks. It's hard to use social media to reach buyers when your buyers can't access social media.

How widespread is this issue? A 2011 survey indicated that 31% of companies with more than 100 employees prohibit all access to social networking sites.[5] That's a third of your potential customers who can't get your social media messages—at least at work.

It makes sense, then, to survey your customer base to see how many don't have work access to social media sites. If it's a big number, you might want to re-evaluate your social marketing plans. That said, just because a buyer can't access Facebook and Twitter at the office doesn't mean he can't access them at all; a lot of business work takes place at home, where social media access is not impeded by overzealous IT staff.

Which Social Media Should You Target?

As noted previously, the term *social media* actually encompasses several different types of websites and services. Some are more influential among business purchasers than others.

As to which of these social media has the biggest impact for B2B companies, it kind of depends on which survey you're reading. For example, an Outsell survey found that Facebook was most effective for 51% of respondents, with LinkedIn close behind at 45%, followed by Twitter at 35%.[6] In contrast, LinkedIn got the top spot in a HubSpot survey, dubbed effective by 45% of respondents; in this survey, Twitter was number two with 38%, and Facebook was number three with 33%.[7]

---

5. Robert Half Technology, 2011

6. Outsell, "Annual Advertising and Marketing Study 2010: Total U.S. and B2B Advertising," 2010

7. HubSpot, "2010 State of Inbound Marketing," 2010

Which social media is most effective might depend on the particular types of businesses you're trying to reach. In 2009, MarketingProfs conducted a survey of their members that broke out social media use by size and type of business (see Figure 14.3);[8] there are definitely differences between business types. For example, LinkedIn is going to be more important to you if you're targeting smaller businesses than if you target larger ones; Facebook is definitely more important to B2C companies than it is in the B2B universe.

Social Media Site Usage vs. Organization Type

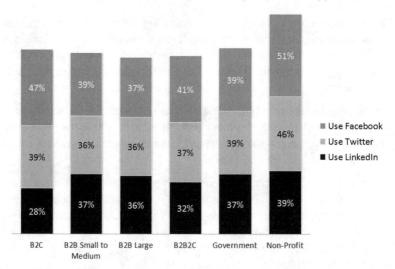

Figure 14.3   *Social media use by type and size of business. (Courtesy MarketingProfs)*

I think the takeaway here is that all the big three social networks (Facebook, LinkedIn, and now Google+) plus Twitter are worthy of your attention. Effectiveness might vary somewhat from one to another, but they all can help you build a thriving customer community—and, just perhaps, generate a few leads, too.

Developing a Social Media Marketing Strategy

What role should social media play in your digital marketing strategy? To that end, just how do you participate in social media? I won't kid you; there's a lot of work involved.

---

8. MarketingProfs, "MarketingProf's 2009 Fall Survey," 2009

Participating in Social Conversations

The most obvious way for a B2B company to participate in social media is to literally participate—to become part of the community. That means establishing pages for your business or products on all the major social network sites, creating a Twitter feed, and the like. You can use this type of presence to notify prospects and customers of upcoming products and promotions, as well as to connect one-on-one with your online customer base.

✉ *Note*

> In addition to letting you participate in social conversations, many social network sites also offer third-party PPC advertising. This advertising is typically contextual, meaning that you can target certain demographic qualifiers, such as age range or gender, and have your ads displayed only to users who match those demographics. Although this type of advertising is appealing to B2C marketers, it might not be an effective way to reach prospective B2B customers on these sites. Because many buyers will be logging in with their personal IDs, it's difficult to slice the demographics to target the people you want.

This participation should be two-way, of course. Not only should someone from your company monitor posts to your social pages, that person should also post to other pages on the social network—for both other businesses and key individuals. It's a matter of being an active participant in the community, not just hosting a passive web page.

Participation goes beyond your own pages and feeds, however; your company and products can be talked about anywhere online. For example, a disgruntled customer can tweet or post a Facebook status update that will be read by hundreds of his friends—some of which might be potential customers. For this reason, you should actively monitor the social media for conversations involving your company and products. This way you can be notified if your name is taken in vain (or justly praised), you have the opportunity to respond, and you're made aware of other groups and forums in which you should be participating on a more regular basis.

Responding to Online Comments

What do you do if you identify a social media conversation that mentions your company—and not in a positive way? It's your choice how you should respond, if at all.

Sometimes the better part of valor is to walk away from a potential flame war. Rather than engaging hostile commenters, it might be better to let the comments stand without response. That's not to say you should pretend the comments don't exist; even highly negative comments can prove useful for designing new products or formulating marketing campaigns. After all, if you know what people *don't* like, that can help guide you in producing something they do.

If you do decide to respond to a social conversation, keep a few things in mind. First, speed is of the essence. There's no point responding to comments made a month or two ago; you need to jump in while the conversation is fresh. This shows that you take the conversation seriously enough to respond quickly.

> "Sometimes the better part of valor is to walk away from a potential flame war."

You also need to respond positively, even to the most negative comments. Don't be defensive, and certainly don't be offensive; don't resort to name-calling or other insults. You need to be the adult in what might otherwise be a childish situation. Be professional, be calm, be cool, be collected. Don't let yourself get angry.

But don't be so calm, cool, and collected that you come off as being a PR flack. Yes, you probably should toe the company line, but you also have to genuinely respond to comments on a personal basis. Admit to mistakes, if there are any. Offer help or advice if any is to be given. Be sympathetic. Apologize. (You'd be surprised how far a genuine "I'm sorry for your problems" will go.)

If you're responding to more positive or general comments, your job is a little easier. Again, respond in a personal manner, friendly without losing sight of your corporate responsibilities. Most people will appreciate your getting involved, sometimes to the point of overwhelming you with additional comments or questions. Try to take it all in stride and be gracious with your input and comments.

There's a certain amount of acceptance involved in all this. You simply can't control what people say about you, no matter how much you (or upper management) might like to. You're always going to have some people saying bad things about your company, your products, and even your people. You can't take it personally. You have to accept that negative comments exist and learn to live with it. A thick skin is a must, but it also helps to develop an understanding of how people, even presumably professional businesspeople, use the Internet to amplify their petty (and more-than-petty) complaints. Remember, as a company you are a lot bigger than any single complaint or complainer.

Finally, you should log all the comments you find and all the responses you make for immediate action and future reference. For example, if you're getting a lot of comments about a particular product feature not working, you might have an actual problem on your hands that you need to address. If a lot of people are confused about a particular process, you might need to rethink that process—or at least your instructions for it. The social conversations you discover provide valuable feedback and information that you should put to use in your day-to-day operations.

Using Social Media for Customer Reach and Acquisition

Many marketing experts endorse social media for reaching new customers. I think that's certainly the case for B2C companies, but much less so for B2B. It all depends on where potential business buyers are looking for their initial information.

It's true that business purchasers are using social media; the data backs that up. But for what are they using it?

My experience indicates that social networks are great vehicles for connecting with your existing customers; it's relatively easy to get a customer to subscribe to your Facebook page or Twitter feed and participate thusly. It's much more difficult, however, to entice someone who doesn't know you to join your social community. After all, how likely are you to become a fan or subscriber to a company that you don't presently do business with? There are just too many things happening on these social networks to throw a speculative relationship into the mix.

That's not to say that some companies don't use social media to acquire new leads; it happens. Indeed, your social media presence is another good source of information for buyers in the decision-making phase of their purchasing process. But you're less likely to engage these pre-prospects in your social community than you are existing customers; potential buyers will read and download the information you have in your social media streams, but probably won't stick around much to chat.

What's important, if you're using social media to garner new leads, is to populate your content streams with information of interest to potential customers—facts about your products and services, notice of new products, links to third-party reviews and customer testimonials, that sort of thing. Prospects can thus read your stream and find information that might prove useful in their decision making—which does play into customer acquisition.

Using Social Media for Customer Retention and Loyalty

The more important use of social media marketing comes in the retention and loyalty phases of the B2B buying continuum. Social media are uniquely suited to building customer communities, forging strong relationships with your most loyal customers, and encouraging those customers to recommend your company to their colleagues.

Key here is establishing your online presence (company pages and feeds), posting regularly with information of value to your customer base, and then actively engaging your customers in the community. That means using your posts to start conversations and then following up with your customers' replies. You want customers to feel that you're listening to them, and that they're important members of your corporate family.

Obviously, part of retention marketing is encouraging customers to make repeat purchases. To that end, you can use social media to let customers know about new products, upcoming specials and sales, and so forth. You can even offer exclusive deals to your social media subscribers—items or discounts only they are aware of and can take advantage of.

As to the loyalty phase, you need to encourage your social media subscribers to enlist other businesses to subscribe to your pages and feeds. It's a matter of actively promoting your social network links and "like" buttons, so that customers get their friends and colleagues to sign up. Of course, you have to offer information that your customers think is worth sharing; if they don't like what they're seeing, they're not going to recommend you to others. But any new subscriber a customer brings to the social media table can become a viable lead or paying customer sometime in the future.

In this fashion, social media represents the ultimate in word of mouth marketing. You provide the forum for customers to gather and talk about you, and then let the word of mouth recommendations begin. You'll gain a stronger, more loyal customer base—and hopefully garner some new leads, in the bargain.

> "You provide the forum for customers to gather and talk about you, and then let the word of mouth recommendations begin."

Using Specific Social Media

Given that each social network is unique, let's look at how you can be using the big players in the social media world—Facebook, LinkedIn, Google+, and Twitter.

Using Facebook

Facebook (www.facebook.com) is the biggest social network, with more than 750 million users. Both B2C and B2B businesses have found success marketing on Facebook (see Figure 14.4).

Here are some tips on how to best market to other businesses on Facebook:

- **Create a page for your business**—Not a personal page, but what some call a "fan" page. (Facebook just calls them, somewhat generically, "pages.") This page is where all your posts (status updates) will appear, and can also host other content. Speaking of that other content...

- **Add photos to your page**—These can be pictures of your products, people, facilities, you name it—just make sure they're of interest to your customers.

- **Add videos to your page**—This is a great place (in addition to YouTube, of course) to post all the educational and informational you produce.

- **Add a discussion board to your page**—You can add tabs or subpages to your Facebook page; one very useful one is a discussion board page. This is where your customers can talk amongst themselves—with you joining in as necessary, of course.

- **Further customize your page**—Facebook offers a variety of tools you can use to customize both the appearance and content of your page; you can also link to content on other sites, including YouTube and Twitter. Use the tools at your disposal to make your Facebook page reflect your branding and a similar look and feel to your main website.

Figure 14.4   *A good example of a B2B Facebook page, from Salesforce.com. (Notice the links in the sidebar to Photos, YouTube, Twitter, Questions, and SlideShare.)*

- **Encourage customers to "like" your page**—In Facebook parlance, someone who "likes" your page (that is, who clicks the Like button on your page) becomes a subscriber to your content. Your status updates will show up in their news feeds, and they'll have access to all the content you post. You need to use other promotional media to encourage all your customers to go to Facebook and click that Like button. Make sure you include the URL for your page in all your promotional materials, and actively ask customers to "like" or follow you on Facebook.

- **Encourage customers to recommend your page to others**—This is part of the loyalty phase; encourage your existing customers to get their friends and colleagues interested in your page. The more noncustomers you have signed up, the more potential leads you have.

- **Post regularly**—You don't just want a static page on Facebook. You also want to regularly post interesting messages—what Facebook calls *status updates*. You should try to post somewhere between once a day and once a week; more frequently is better.

- **Post about topics of interest to your customers**—This goes without saying. Your posts have to be useful and interesting to your customers or they'll quit reading them—or even "unlike" you on Facebook. You can post about your company, your employees, your products and services, your customers, even industry issues. Just make sure each post is of value.

- **Ask questions**—Your posts can also include questions for your Facebook customers. Facebook is all about conversations; why not start the conversation yourself by posing a question or posting a survey? Ask your customers what they think about a particular development, industry trend, new product, or whatever. Not only do you get the conversation going, you also get free market research.

- **Encourage comments**—Your Facebook friends can post their own messages on your page. (If you've enabled said third-party posting, that is.) Encourage your customers to use your Facebook page to ask questions, comment on your products and services, and just generally get the conversation started. It's all about customer participation.

- **Monitor and respond**—It's not all about talking to your customers; it's also about listening to them. That means you can't just post your own content, you have to constantly monitor the comments that your customers make about your posts and to your Facebook page. Communicating on Facebook requires a lot of attention and the ability to respond quickly and intelligently. Make sure you assign the job to someone who is both technically proficient and PR savvy.

It's really a simple process. You create a Facebook page and keep it stocked with interesting content. You encourage your customers to "like" your page and recommend it to others. You post new content on a regular basis via status updates. Then you monitor your page to respond to comments and just generally join in the conversation.

Using Google+

The newest entrant into the social networking field is Google, with its Google+ service (plus.google.com). Google+ is a lot like Facebook, only more organized and with a cleaner interface. Within a few weeks of launch, it had attracted more than 20 million users, and experts believe it will hit 100 million users faster than any similar site.

One of the more interesting features of Google+ is how it ties together posts to the social network with Google's search engine. That's right, Google+ posts will not only show up in search results, but also influence other results. For example, mentions on Google+ should increase a company's search ranking. So, the more you get people talking about you on Google+, the higher your normal Google search ranking will be.

Although Google+ is still new and marketers are still figuring out its ins and outs, the basics of what you need to do with the site, at least from a marketing perspective, are already becoming apparent. Here is some basic advice for marketing on Google+:

- **Establish a Page for your business**—Google offers business Pages, similar to Facebook's business pages. You want to create such a Page for your business, and customize it (as much as Google allows) to reflect your company's brand.

- **Add content to your Page**—Like Facebook, Google+ lets you add photos and videos to your business Page; you should do so (see Figure 14.5). (And make sure you use your company logo as your profile picture!)

Figure 14.5 *SAP's Google+ Page.*

- **Invite your customers**—Naturally, you want to invite all your customers to become your friends on Google+. That's what it's all about.

- **Create segment-specific Circles**—One of the unique features of Google+ is the ability to group similar "friends" into Circles, and then direct your posts only to specific Circles. This is a great way to segment your customer list; you can create Circles by region, company size, industry, or whatever, and then segment your posts accordingly.

- **Post frequently**—As with Facebook, you need to keep your face in front of your customers. That means posting regularly, at least weekly and perhaps daily.

- **Post interesting and useful content**—Also as with Facebook, make sure your posts are interesting to and useful for your customer base. The more useful your posts, the more your customers will look forward to reading them.

- **Host video chats**—Google+'s Hangout feature lets you conduct video chats with up to 10 participants. That's an ideal way to host your own webinars or product demonstrations, free.

Using LinkedIn

Facebook and Google+ are consumer-oriented social networks that also happen to be used by businesses. LinkedIn (www.linkedin.com), on the other hand, is a social network designed specifically for business professionals—which makes it an essential part of your B2B digital marketing plan.

What LinkedIn lacks in raw usage numbers (it's only 100 million strong, compared to Facebook's 750 million users), it more than makes up for in other key factors. It has an older user base (big among the 35–54 group), a more affluent demographic, and high visibility among businesspeople of all stripes. In other words, LinkedIn is the go-to medium for reaching potential business decision makers in your industry.

> "LinkedIn is the go-to medium for reaching potential business decision makers in your industry."

How do you harness the power of LinkedIn for your B2B marketing? Here are some tips:

- **Create a company page**—Your company page on LinkedIn is your home base on the social network. It's more than just a profile of your company; it's also where your customers can read your posts and engage with you socially. You need to create one.

- **Customize your company page**—You can add tabs to your company page for various business-specific functions, such as a company overview, products and services, careers, and the like. You can also add photos and videos to your page, which is always good.

- **Add presentations to your company page**—LinkedIn provides a number of applications, such as SlideShare, that enable you to add PowerPoint presentations to your company page. If you have presentations to share with customers, this is a good way to do it.

- **Use polls to attract an audience**—Add the LinkedIn Poll application to your company page to ask questions of your current and potential customers—or of LinkedIn subscribers in general. It's a great way to engage your audience, and to attract new prospects.

- **Add Twitter and Blog feeds to your page**—LinkedIn offers several applications that let you add feeds from other sources—specifically your blog and Twitter account—to your company page. This lets you consolidate multiple information streams in a single place, which makes your LinkedIn page that much more valuable to your customers.

- **Create a LinkedIn Group**—LinkedIn Groups are mini-networks where like-minded professionals take part in discussions about a given topic (see Figure 14.6). Almost 18 million users take part in LinkedIn Groups every week, creating a vibrant community of businesspeople. Consider creating a group related to your industry, and then actively participate in it. You can help group members—your current and potential customers—share insights, learn best practices, and engage in industry debate.

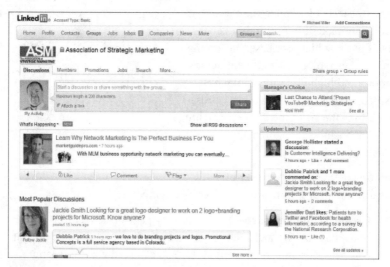

Figure 14.6 *The LinkedIn Group for the Association of Strategic Marketing.*

- **Promote your LinkedIn Group**—Use all the media at your disposal, digital and otherwise, to let your current and prospective customers know about your Group—and encourage them to join.

- **Participate in other LinkedIn Groups**—Your own Group is important, but so is your active participation in other Groups—specifically, Groups hosted or visited by your customer base. Social networking is a two-way street, and you need to participate as much as you host.

Even though LinkedIn has a smaller user base than Facebook or Twitter, you might find that you get better results from this social network for professionals. It's definitely worth your attention.

Using Twitter

Now we come to Twitter (www.twitter.com), which as you know really isn't a social network but rather something more akin to a blog, but with shorter messages. For many B2B businesses, Twitter is the first social media they add to their marketing plans.

Twitter is probably the easiest social medium to get started with and use on a regular basis (see Figure 14.7). You create an account for your company and then start tweeting. That's it.

Figure 14.7 *The Twitter feed for Cisco Systems.*

Of course, you do have to adjust your messaging to the medium. In Twitter's case, than means creating posts that have no more than 140 characters; that's the maximum you can include in a tweet. Past that, what you tweet about is up to you.

Here are some tips on how to best use Twitter in your B2B marketing plan:

- **Encourage followers**—Twitter works for B2B marketing only if you have lots of current and potential customers following you. To that end, use your other media to publicize your Twitter feed, and encourage customers to follow you there.

- **Tweet frequently**—Twitter followers expect a regular stream of tweets from the people and companies they follow. Tweeting once a week probably isn't going to be enough. Heck, once a day might not be enough. Many successful businesses tweet several times a day. It's all about maintaining a constant presence, and given the barrage of tweets out there, more is definitely better.

- **Keep it relevant**—What should you tweet about? Whatever your customers want to read, of course. You might post about new products, specials, industry news, whatever is of interest to your customer base. In short (and short is important on Twitter), you need to find some snippet of real news or information, and make that your tweet. In most B2B companies, that shouldn't be too much of a problem—there's always something new and interesting to tweet about. And if you can't find anything interesting to tweet about, maybe you shouldn't be tweeting.

- **Keep it short**—As previously mentioned, your tweets cannot exceed the 140-character limit. Because of this, tweets do not have to conform to proper grammar, spelling, and sentence structure—and, in fact, seldom do. It is common to abbreviate longer words, use familiar acronyms, substitute single letters and numbers for whole words, and refrain from all punctuation. You should also use a link-shortening service, such as bit.ly (www.bit.ly), when you want to include links in your tweets.

- **Break up long posts**—When you're posting to Twitter, think in terms of single-sentence communications—a single thought sent out into the Twitterverse. Instead of saving up all your thoughts for one long blog post, post them throughout the day in short, individual tweets.

- **Link to more information**—Sometimes you just can fit everything you want to say into 140 characters. In this instance, you can tweet a summary, something akin to a headline, and then link to a longer article on your blog or website. (Or, for that matter, to industry news on another website.)

- **Tweet about other media**—Use Twitter as a promotional vehicle for other marketing activities. If you have a new blog post, tweet about it; if you've posted new photos to your Facebook page, tweet about that, too. There's value to be gained by pointing from Twitter to other things you're doing in your company.

- **Use hashtags**—On Twitter, a *hashtag* is the equivalent of a keyword. You create a hashtag by putting the hash or pound character in front of a given word, like this: #hashtag. When you add a hash character before a specific word in a tweet, that word gets referenced by Twitter as a kind of keyword, and that word becomes clickable by anyone viewing the tweet; it also helps other users find relevant tweets when they search for that particular topic.

- **Monitor the Twitterverse**—It's likely that you'll have many customers who want to use Twitter as a means to contact you with questions and customer support issues, either as responses to your tweets or via private tweets. That's cool—it's nice to have another support channel. This means, however, that you have to answer these questions, and in a timely fashion. If you can't answer the questions directly, forward them to your customer support department. However you do it, make sure the customer is satisfied.

Twitter is a unique bird, as you'll soon discover. It's primarily a one-way communications vehicle, and a great way to get your messages—lots of them—in front of your most loyal customers.

> "Twitter is a unique bird, as you'll soon discover. It's primarily a one-way communications vehicle..."

The Bottom Line

Social media are becoming increasingly important for B2B marketers. Social networking, in particular, is an ideal way to build a closer relationship with your most loyal customers, as it affords the means for two-way communication. The most popular social networks for B2B companies are Facebook, Google+, and LinkedIn. In addition, Twitter lets you send short text messages to interested customers, which is a great way to keep in constant touch.

15

B2B Audio, Video, and Interactive Marketing

There's a lot of different digital media you can include in your B2B marketing strategy. We've already covered website marketing and search engine marketing, email marketing and blog marketing, even social media marketing; now it's time to look at the other media online—audio, video, and the interactive medium of web-based seminars.

As you might suspect, there are lots of ways to incorporate these into your digital marketing mix. How you do so depends to a degree on the media you choose as well as your company and the products and services you offer.

Using Podcasts for B2B Marketing

We'll start with the audio side of things, in the form of online podcasts. A podcast is like a radio show that's broadcast over the Internet. It's an ideal way to entice potential customers in the acquisition phase of the B2B buying continuum; it's also good for keeping customers interested during the retention phase.

Podcasts let you reach listeners at their computers or on the go; many people listen to podcasts on iPods and other mobile devices. And, because of the periodic nature of podcasts, you can develop a steady base of listeners who tune in week in and week out for whatever new you have to say.

Understanding Podcasts

A podcast is one of a series of episodic audio files, typically distributed over the Internet via RSS feed. Podcasts differ from other types of online audio in that they're downloadable files, rather than streaming audio, and thus can be downloaded for listening at any future time on just about any type of device that offers audio playback—MP3 players, smartphones, computers, you name it.

Podcasts are typically delivered via a central website or service, such as Apple's iTunes Store, although you can also host podcast files on your own website. Most podcasters deliver new episodes on a regular basis, often weekly. Most podcasts today are delivered primarily in the MP3 audio format.

You can think of podcasts as the online equivalent of radio shows, complete with host (or hosts) and various topics of discussion. In fact, some podcasts *are* radio shows—that is, terrestrial or Internet radio programs packaged in podcast format for streaming or downloading. But most podcasts are created specifically for the Internet, and are delivered as such.

You can find podcasts about every type of topic imaginable—including businesses and their products and services. These marketing-oriented podcasts are produced by companies to promote themselves or their products, and are distributed as part of their digital marketing strategy.

The most successful of these marketing podcasts are informational rather than blatantly promotional, offering a mix of news and information of interest to current and potential customers. Listeners get useful information, and the marketer establishes his company as a trusted authority on the topic in question.

It's soft-sell marketing, but it can be quite effective in the lead-acquisition process. The key is producing a podcast—or, more accurately, a series of podcast episodes—that current and potential customers want to listen to. That means producing a podcast that sounds professional, of course, but also one that provides value of some sort to your listeners.

You also need to find some way to let potential listeners know about your podcast, and make it easy for them to subscribe to receive future episodes. (You can use your existing digital and traditional marketing channels to do this, of course.) And, throughout the entire process, you have to ensure that you're imparting the desired promotional message—but in a subtle, barely-perceivable fashion. It's a different challenge from what you're probably used to.

Creating a Podcast: The Technical Details

Let's start with the technical stuff. What do you need to produce a podcast?

A podcast is, at its most basic, a radio show. That means you need to record one or more people speaking. You might also need to add some music (at least to bumper the spoken segments), and perhaps record remote guests who might be calling in via telephone. And, assuming that you're recording this for future distribution, you might want to utilize some form of audio editing software to mix together different segments and tighten up the loose ends, as well as save the finished product to a distributable audio file.

That might sound complicated, but it really isn't. Although you could rent or borrow a professional radio studio to do the work, that really isn't necessary. Instead you can get by with a few pieces of readily accessible and low-cost equipment, and record your podcast from any empty (and noise-free) office.

Here's what you need:

- **A computer**—Any computer will do.
- **A microphone**—Not the microphone built into your notebook PC; it isn't of high enough fidelity. Nor do you need to invest in a $1,000 professional mic; that would be overkill. Instead, look at one of the many USB mics designed specifically for recording podcasts, most of which are in the $100–$200 range.
- **Podcast recording/editing software**—This software not only records the input from your microphone, but it also lets you set the proper recording levels, save your program to an audio file, and even edit your audio files. (This latter feature is great for editing out mistakes and dead air, or splicing together different segments recorded at different times.) Some of the most popular such programs are free, such as Audacity (audacity.sourceforge.net) and PodProducer (www.podproducer.net). If you need more functionality, consider one of the following a low-cost podcast recording program such as Podcast Creator (www.industrialsoftware.com) or RecordForAll (www.recordforall.com).

That's about it in terms of equipment and software. When it comes to recording the podcast, it's a simple matter of connecting your microphone, setting your audio levels, and pressing the Record button on your audio recording program.

How long should your podcasts be? Most podcasts are in the 10–30 minute range. Anything less probably isn't worth listening to; on the other hand, if you go too long, you'll lose people's attention. Although hour-long podcasts certainly exist, you'll stand a better chance of success with a 15-minute or half-hour length.

When you're done recording, use the same program to edit your recording, if necessary, and then save the final product as an MP3 file. This is what you then distribute and syndicate over the Web.

Developing a Podcast Strategy

More important than the technical details, however, is your podcast strategy. Just what kind of podcast do you want to create, and what content should you feature?

Remember, a podcast isn't a commercial; you can't just hit the Record button and spend the next ten minutes talking about how great your products are. It's far, far better to provide valuable information about a related topic, and promote your product more obliquely.

For example, let's say your company sells medical supplies to hospitals and clinics. Instead of just talking about your latest meters and needles and such, you could instead talk about the state of medical care in general, the latest medical developments, or even about specific medical conditions. Interview doctors, industry experts, even patients. For that matter, you can interview key customers and talk about unique solutions you offer specific market segments.

That's the core content. You can then throw in references to your products, or toss in some self-produced commercials for said products. But mention of your company and products is secondary; the main focus of the podcast is on the healthcare industry in general.

You get the point. Your podcast has to offer unique value to listeners, and not just overtly promote your company and products. Your content must be useful, interesting, and unique; you can then use the podcast's content to establish your authority with potential customers.

> "Your podcast has to offer unique value to listeners, and not just overtly promote your company and products."

Note

How often should you podcast? Often enough to keep listeners from forget-
ting about you, but not so often as to be annoying. For most B2B companies, that means posting a new episode every week or two. Make it regular
so listeners will anticipate something new.

Distributing Your Podcast

How do you attract listeners to your podcast? You have to make the podcast readily available and "subscribeable." And you have to promote it to your customer
base.

First, you need to create a section of your website to host all your podcasts. Your
most recent podcast should be featured here, but past episodes should also be
available for downloading. A simple "click to download" arrangement works fine.

For most B2B companies, that's probably good enough; your customers will find
your podcasts on your website. But if you want to attract a larger audience, you can
make your podcasts available via Apple's iTunes Store, which is where the majority of listeners discover new podcasts. Know, however, that Apple doesn't host or
serve the podcast itself; it only links to the podcast's RSS feed. As such, you need to
submit the link for your RSS feed to iTunes, by clicking on the Submit a Podcast
link on the Podcasts page of the iTunes Store. It's easy enough to do, and gets you
listed.

Speaking of RSS feeds, you need one because a podcast isn't a podcast without it.
Having a feed for your podcast makes it easy for loyal customers to subscribe and
automatically receive notice when new episodes are available.

 Note

The easiest way to create a feed for your podcast is to use the Feedburner
service (feedburner.google.com). You can then post a button or link on your
podcast web page so that listeners can subscribe with a single click.

Using Video for B2B Marketing

Just as podcasts are the online equivalent of radio shows, web videos are the online equivalent of television programming—or, in some instances, television commercials.

Not that you can just upload an existing commercial to the Web and find success. In most cases, this sort of blatant self-promotion doesn't work at all. As with podcasts, the most successful online videos are those that deliver a more subtle message while providing viewers with something useful or entertaining.

Businesses use online videos to provide additional information to their customers, show them how to use their products or complete some sort of related project, relay the latest company or industry news, or just offer a bit of entertainment. It's a great way to feed the decision-making process during the customer acquisition stage of the B2B customer life cycle; it can also work to help retention, by showing customers how to use the products you sell.

To that end, I'm a big proponent of online video marketing. Although I think it's more effective for B2C businesses, it can also be a big help to B2B marketers. I certainly believe it's one of the most cost-effective forms of marketing available, period; you get a huge potential bang for a very small buck. In fact, if you do it right, you can start producing online videos with a minimal expenditure. What's not to like about that?

What Kinds of Videos Are Most Effective?

Success in video marketing, however, requires more than just getting the technical details right. It's all about what you put on the screen, producing videos that current and potential customers want to watch.

Some B2B videos are blatant commercials (including existing commercials repurposed for the Internet), some offer in-depth prepurchase information about a given product or service, some offer post-purchase information or support, and some use other approaches to gain viewers—and prospective customers. But which types of business videos deliver the eyeballs?

I find that successful business videos tend to fall into three major categories:

- **Informative videos**—This is a video that imparts information of some sort. An informative video can be the online equivalent of a newscast, where a "talking head" talks about industry issues and such. Alternately, an informative video might function as a video brochure, presenting in-depth information about your company or your products. What's key is that you present information that's relevant to the viewer, in the fashion of a television infomercial. It's a soft sell, not a hard one; it's the information you present that makes the video and attracts viewers.

- **Educational videos**—For education, think instruction—that is, a "how to" video, where you show the viewer how to do something useful, typically in step-by-step fashion. Ideally, you show or train customers how to use your products or services. Make sure you're demonstrating something truly useful, and then present the content in a step-by-step fashion, using multiple shots and camera angles.

- **Entertaining videos**—Informing and educating are important and will draw a fair number of viewers if you do it right. But everybody likes to be entertained—which is why pure entertainment videos typically show up at the top of the most viewed lists. As to what's entertaining, I wish I could tell you. Unfortunately, entertainment is in the eye of the beholder; what I laugh at might leave you cold. But here's what I do know about entertaining videos: When they work, they work really well. It's the entertaining video that is most likely to go viral.

In other words, for a video to attract business viewers, it must offer them something of value, hopefully in an engaging fashion. It must be something they want or even need to watch. If you can't provide unique value, no one will watch or share your videos.

When it comes to distributing your videos online, there's one primary site on which to focus: YouTube (www.youtube.com). YouTube is the number-one site for video viewing online, for both consumers and businesses, and the primary place for users of all types to upload their own videos. If you want to get your video viewed, no other site comes close in offering the number of eyeballs and ease of access.

 Note

Just as with social media, many companies do not allow their employees to access YouTube and other video-sharing sites. Survey your customers to see how many have video blocked at work, and adjust your marketing plans accordingly.

If you're not yet familiar with YouTube…well, where have you been the past five years? Anyone, individuals or businesses, can upload videos to the YouTube site. These can be home movies, video blogs, old television programs (as long as copyright isn't an issue), commercials, even independent films. Videos can be up to 15 minutes in length, although most are (much) shorter.

In addition, anyone can watch videos that have been uploaded, mostly at no cost. A video is viewed on its own video viewing page; users can leave comments and vote positively or negatively on any given video.

If a viewer likes a video, he can easily share it with others; this is how a video goes viral, by being passed around as a favorite. Viewers can post YouTube videos to Facebook or other social media, send links to videos via email, even embed videos in their blogs or web pages. All the sharing mechanisms are right there on the video viewing page, just below the video itself.

When you upload videos to YouTube, they're hosted on your own YouTube channel page (see Figure 15.1). This is your home page on the YouTube site, and all your videos are displayed there. Naturally, you can (and should) customize your channel page to reflect your company branding, and to include the specific content you want.

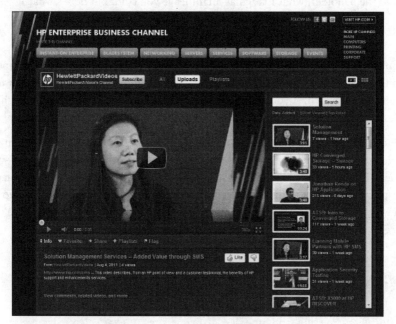

Figure 15.1 *HP's Enterprise Business channel on YouTube.*

YouTube represents an essentially free advertising channel. The site doesn't charge producers to store their videos or to serve up the bandwidth necessary to view them. It also doesn't charge viewers anything to watch those videos. (YouTube makes its money from advertising; it is part of the Google empire, after all, same as our old friend, AdWords.)

As such, you should always upload any videos you produce to the YouTube site; it won't cost you anything. You probably also want to host your videos on your own website; some customers will look for them there. One viable option is to let YouTube do the hosting and just embed your YouTube videos on your own site; this cuts down on your hosting and bandwidth costs, especially if your videos get a lot of views.

> ✉ Note
>
> You can also—and probably should—cross-post your videos to your own website, as well. Let YouTube do the hosting and then embed the videos on a special page on your site. That way, you reach existing customers who regularly visit your site as well as prospects who find you on YouTube.

Producing an Online Video

Just how do you create an online video? It doesn't have to be hard work or expensive. You do, however, have to get the technical details right.

The first choice you have to make is how professional you want to go. Obviously, big companies can go whole-hog on professional production, but it's not necessary; most online business videos are produced in-house using consumer-grade equipment.

If you go the professional production route, however, expect to spend some big bucks. It's not unusual to spend anywhere from $5,000 to $50,000 for a 2–3 minute video and to spend days if not weeks producing it. That's a lot of money and a lot of work for something that gets viewed on a little window on a computer screen.

If you decide to go the self-production route, you need to make an initial investment in equipment. Not a lot of equipment and not expensive equipment, fortunately, just a few things you can pick up at your local consumer electronics or photography store.

Here's the shopping list:

- **Camcorder**—I like a model with either hard drive or flash storage; that makes it easy to transfer files to your computer for editing. Get a model that records high definition (HD) video, and try to get one that has an input for an external microphone. Expect to spend between $300 and $500.
- **Tripod**—You need to shoot a rock-steady picture, which you can't do by holding the camcorder in your hands. Invest in a $30–$40 tripod so you don't have to worry about the shakes.

- **Lighting**—Normal room lighting isn't good enough for a professional-quality video. Invest $150–$200 on a lighting kit with two or three photofloods on stands. Position the lights in a V, with the subject at the center of the V and the lights facing the subject at 45-degree angles. It will make a very noticeable difference in picture quality.

- **Microphone**—To improve the audio quality—that is, to make what you're saying more understandable—replace the camcorder's built-in microphone with an external model. Go with a lavaliere mic that clips onto the subject's shirt; the sound quality will be impressive. A wired mic runs $40–$50, whereas a wireless model runs $150–$200.

- **Seamless background**—Don't position the subject in front of a cluttered background. Instead, buy a sheet of seamless background paper, cloth, or muslin. Go with a contrasting color—lighter if the subject is wearing a dark shirt, darker if the subject is wearing light clothing.

- **Video-editing software**—You'll want to import your video files from your camcorder to your computer. From there, you can edit together different takes, add transitions between scenes, and superimpose graphics and text onscreen. You do all this with a video-editing program, such as Windows Movie Maker or iMovie—included free with your Windows or Mac computer.

✉ *Note*

You probably won't find all this equipment at Best Buy. Instead, shop at your local camera store; this is the same equipment that still photographers use.

After you've assembled the equipment, you can start shooting. That's the easy part, really; it's also relatively easy to upload your videos to YouTube. The harder thing is determining what type of videos to shoot, and then writing your script and creating your storyboard. After you know what to shoot, however, the actual video production is surprisingly easy.

Tips for More Effective Online Videos

When it comes to producing effective online business videos, here are some tips to make your job easier:

- **Shoot in high definition**—Today's viewers expect HD videos, so you need to give them that. Fortunately, HD camcorders are relatively inexpensive these days.

- **Shoot for the smaller screen**—Even if you provide an HD video, most viewers will be watching your video in a small window in their web browsers. As such, you need to create a video that looks good at this small size, viewed on a typical computer screen. That means going big and bright; you can shoot an epic with a cast of thousands, but those thousands will look like little dots in a small browser window. The best online videos are visually simple, with a single main subject filling up most of the small video window. (That's your typical talking head video, folks.) Get up close and frame the subject so that he or it fills most of the screen.

- **Accentuate the contrast**—As noted previously, visual contrast is highly desirable with small-footprint videos. Put a pale or white-clad subject in front of a black background or a black-clad subject in front of a white one. And consider using brightly colored backgrounds, which really pop in the thumbnails on YouTube's search results pages; believe it or not, hot pink really grabs the attention of casual viewers!

- **Look professional**—or not—If you're representing a professional business, your videos need to look professional. Whether your video has a cast of one or of thousands, make sure that anyone on camera is well-dressed and well-groomed, that everyone is well lit and well-mic'd, and that the whole production has a professional sheen.

  Unless, that is, you want to give out a hip young vibe. In that instance, take off the suits and ties and emulate the personal look that's become ubiquitous on the YouTube site. In other words, make sure your video has a look and feel that matches your company's message.

  > "...make sure your video has a look and feel that matches your company's message."

- **Consider creating a slideshow**—If you don't need full-motion video or don't have access to a video camera, consider putting together a slideshow of still photographs. Just compile the photos into a slideshow, and then add background music or a voiceover. Likewise, some topics benefit from PowerPoint presentations, which can also be converted to video.

- **Provide unique value**—Beyond the technical details, you need to give viewers a reason to come back for future viewings and to share your video with others. People will watch your video if it's something they're interested in and if they can't find that information anyplace else. Your video must provide a unique value to viewers, something they want or need to know or do. That might be product information for prospects in the acquisition stage, or training videos for customers in the retention stage. It's all about the content, and don't forget that.

- **Be entertaining**—In addition to providing unique content, your video also needs to be entertaining—even if you're producing an informative or educational video. Produce a boring video, and no one will watch it. People like to be entertained, and you have to give the people what they want. Find a way to make your product, service, brand, or company entertaining. Not necessarily funny (although that helps), but approachable and enjoyable—at least enough to keep the viewer watching for the entire length of the video.

- **Keep it short**—YouTube lets you upload videos up to 15 minutes in length, but I don't recommend you go that full length. One way to kill your video's entertainment value is to make it too long. Viewers today—and especially ones online—have a very short attention span. It's imperative, then, that you keep your videos short enough so that viewers don't tune out mid-way. My recommendation is to keep your video no longer than two or three minutes—and the shorter, the better. Videos any longer than three minutes or so typically don't get big viewership.

✉ *Note*

If you have a message that takes more than a few minutes to present, consider chopping it up into multiple shorter videos. For example, if you want to post a ten-minute speech, edit it into four segments of two to three minutes apiece.

- **Keep it simple**—You don't have to spend a lot of money on a video for it to be effective. In fact, it's easy for a company to spend too much money on its videos; the result is typically an overproduced monstrosity that looks horrible online. In many cases, a single person talking directly to a camera is all you need. In fact, the YouTube community tends to reward simple and direct videos, and be turned off by overtly commercial productions; they prefer the immediacy of a low-budget video. Keeping it simple helps you connect directly with your viewers—which forges a tighter bond.

- **Stay focused**—Part of keeping it simple is focusing on a single message. Remember, you have only a few minutes at most to communicate to the online viewer. Don't spend that time trying to show your entire product line or even multiple features of a sophisticated product. Hone in on a single product and communicate its strongest feature or benefit. One video per product or feature should be your rule.

- **Avoid the hard sell**—Even though your message should be simple, you don't have to hit the viewer over the head with it. Online, the soft sell works better than the hard sell. That's why a how-to video showing your product in use typically works better than a straight-ahead product demonstration; the former is a soft sell that communicates a subtle message to the viewer—who will typically turn off a harder message.

- **Keep it fresh**—The video you create today will be forgotten a month or two from now. With tens of thousands of new videos being posted on YouTube every day, your video will quickly become yesterday's news. This requires you to constantly update your company's video library. Older videos need to be either refreshed or replaced by a new video; your company's channel will lose viewership otherwise.

- **Include your URL in the video**—The key to reaching new customers on YouTube is to lead viewers from your video on the YouTube site to your company's website—where you can then directly sell your products and services. Unfortunately, YouTube doesn't allow live links from a video to a third-party website. You can, however, include your website address or toll-free phone number in the body of the video, typically via a graphic overlay. You should also end the video with a similar blank screen with the URL or phone number highlighted. Make sure the URL is big and easily readable; high contrast colors, such as white text on a black background (or vice versa), provide the best results.

Note

You can also plug your site's URL by incorporating a subtle selling pitch in the script of your video. This is the same way that information "hosts" plug their products in their presentations.

- **Include your URL in the accompanying text**—As noted, you can't link to your website from within a YouTube video. You can, however, include your URL in the text description, just not as a live link. So, when you write the description for your video, make sure you include your URL or 800-number in the text.

- **Link from your channel page**—Although you can't include a live link in your video or accompanying text, you can include a direct link to your website in your YouTube channel page. Anyone clicking your username will see your channel page, with the link to your website prominently displayed. When viewers click the website link, they're taken directly to your site—where you can sell them more of what you have to offer.

- **Link to a landing page**—As with other digital marketing vehicles, don't link directly to your site's home page. Instead, create a special landing page that you link to from your YouTube videos or channel page. This landing page should have the same look and feel of your videos so that viewers sense the underlying connection. You can also include other videos on the landing page.

- **Customize your channel page**—As noted previously, your channel page is your home page on the YouTube site. Take the time to customize this page in terms of both design and content, to fit within your overall marketing strategy. You can then direct customers to this landing page, rather than to multiple individual video pages; it's a single gateway to all your online videos.

The key thing is to recognize that you're probably not going to reach new prospects via YouTube. You can, however, use your online videos to feed important information to prospects after they've found you. You can also use videos to service existing customers with useful post-purchase information. Just stay focused on providing that information, in video fashion, and don't obsess over big-time production stuff.

GOING VIRAL

The most successful online videos are those that go *viral*. A viral video is one that becomes hugely popular, with hundreds of thousands or even millions of views, via Internet-based sharing. That is, a viewer finds a video that he likes and then shares it with his friends, either on the YouTube site or via email or social media, such as Facebook and Twitter.

Viral videos are seldom the most practical ones. Instead, it's the entertaining or humorous videos that go big time. And by big time, I mean really big; the most viral of viral videos quickly move off YouTube and get picked up by traditional media. That's exposure with a capital E, and you can't buy it; it has to come organically.

Because of this potential for huge exposure, many companies aim for creating videos that go viral. Although having a video that garners millions of viewers might be good for the ego (and perhaps necessary to build a huge brand like Budweiser), that might not be the most appropriate goal for the B2B marketer. For most B2B companies, attracting a hundred targeted customers is both more profitable and more realistic than getting viewed by a million strangers with no intention of ever purchasing anything from you.

So, although striving for viral status might be appealing, it's probably not the best strategy for most B2B marketers. (It's also very difficult to do; the most embarrassing videos are those that strive to be virally entertaining and instead fall flat on their faces.) Instead of shooting for the moon with a video that might be entertaining to a broad demographic, focus on creating a video that appeals to your target audience. That's the way you achieve success in a low-key fashion.

Using Interactive Media for B2B Marketing

Our last bit of multimedia marketing is more interactive—in real time, no less. I'm talking about live web-based seminars, what some called *webinars*. These webinars might be able to replace physical seminars and conferences (including sales conferences) in your mix, and make it easy to engage both prospective and current customers in face-to-face social dialog—without anyone having to travel anywhere.

You can use webinars in both the acquisition and retention phases of the B2B buying continuum. During the acquisition phase, webinars help impart lots of useful information to prospective customers, get them familiar with your company and personnel, and thus generate viable sales leads. During the retention phase, webinars help cement the personal relationships created during the conversion phase, work toward training customer staff on how to use your products, and provide face-to-face forums for customer communication.

Understanding Interactive Media

A webinar, sometimes called a *webcast* or *web conference*, is essentially a live web-based video chat session. Most webinars involve broadcasting a presentation of some sort from the corporate mothership and receiving the presentation at multiple customer sites. Successful webinars often allow and encourage customer interaction, if not during the presentation then afterwards in a Q&A session.

Webinar presentations can be extremely simple or very complex. On the simple side, your presenter doesn't do much more than sit in front of a webcam and talk. On the complex side, the presentation is based on a series of PowerPoint slides and might include videos, background music, even links to live content on the Web, all narrated by the presenter. In such sophisticated webinars, the presenter can either narrate live or pre-record a voiceover track.

As I said, the best webinars encourage customer participation. This can take several forms—questions asked during the course of the webinar via text messaging or text chat; questions asked via webcam (video) or microphone (audio-only), typically at the end of presentation; or interactive participation, where each participant appears onscreen in a group chat to volley things back and forth.

In addition, you can adopt a basic form of interactive marketing by having your salespeople call on select clients via this type of video chat instead of in person. Again, it's a cost thing; for some smaller customers, you can build a good-enough personal relationship via web chat and save on the transportation bills.

One of the nice things about using this sort of interactive media is that it's relatively low priced. You don't need fancy equipment to get going—in most cases, a computer and a webcam will do the trick. And after you get it set up, it's a lot cheaper for both you and your attendees to just log on and get going; it's certainly a lot lower cost than purchasing plane tickets and hotel reservations to attend remote real-world conferences and such.

Do Webinars Make Sense for You?

Not every company is suited for this sort of interactive digital marketing. You might find that traditional conferences, seminars, and trade shows—let alone in-person sales calls—make more sense for the types of products you sell and customers you sell to.

Adding interactive webinars to your marketing mix makes sense in the following situations:

- Your audience is geographically dispersed—that is, it's tough to reach them all in a single trip.
- You lack a critical mass of customers in specific local markets—that is, there aren't enough customers in any given market to warrant a physical appearance.
- Your audience is tech savvy so that they're comfortable doing the webinar thing on their computers.
- You want to create a series of events on a small budget.
- You have a way to maintain the relationships you build after the event—whether that's in person, or via phone or email.

Tips for More Effective Interactive Marketing

To create a successful webinar, you have to keep in mind why businesspeople "attend" these sorts of web events. Some honestly want to learn something that will help them do their job, or learn more about a given industry trend. Some buyers want to obtain more information about a given product. Some want to confirm their decision to purchase either from your or from a competitor.

In all cases, you want to present content in your webinars that is informative, useful, relevant, and unique. The webinar itself doesn't have to be an overly polished presentation; the topic you address and the content you present is more important than embracing professional production values. The webinars are hosted from a regular office, using standard computer equipment; you don't have to go all pro on it.

With these basics in mind, here are some specific tips you can employ to create more effective web seminars:

- **Clearly define your target audience**—Who you're trying to reach will determine what kind of webinar you produce. If you're looking for new prospects, your webinar should be chock full of pre-purchase product information. If you're looking to retain existing customers, the webinar should be more interactive and suitable for relationship building. Know who you're targeting before you put it all together.

- **Clearly define your goals**—Likewise, your target audience will define your goals for a webinar. If it's a prepurchase crowd, you want to obtain solid leads. If it's a post-purchase crowed, your goals may be more nebulous.

- **Price it right**—If you're trying to attract new leads, your webinar should be free or low cost. If you're using webinars to train existing customers, it might be okay to charge for them; it's also common to provide this sort of post-purchase training at no cost, at least to active customers. If you want to maintain relationships with decision makers at key accounts, offering free admission is also a good idea. However, if you're providing skills-based information to nonpurchasing personnel, you can charge for it—and you might discover that webinars of this sort can be a real money maker for you.

- **Use the right webinar software or service**—There are lots of services and software you can use to conduct webinars and web chat sessions. Some of the most popular include Adobe Connect (www.adobe.com/products/adobeconnect.html), Cisco's WebEx (www.webex.com), GoToWebinar (www.gotomeeting.com/webinar/), and ON24 (www.on24.com); each has its pros and cons. Check out the features and pricing of each before you commit.

- **Promote your webinars**—What if you put on an ass-kicking webinar and nobody came? That could be a problem if you don't promote your webinars. You need to get the word out, which you can do via email, blog postings, social media posts, and so forth.

- **Practice in advance**—Don't assume everything will go smoothly, especially your first time at bat. Do a thorough run-through of your presentation a week or so in advance, and make sure you have a tech support person handy on the day of the event, just in case.

- **Engage attendees**—Presentations can be boring, especially if all you do is sit back and listen to someone else talk. To that end, it pays to make your webinars as interactive as possible. Instead of forcing attendees to sit through 30 minutes of slides, ask questions throughout the presentation, either informally or as formal surveys or polls.

- **Include a call to action**—This should go without saying, but I'll say it anyway. Whatever your goal is with your webinar, make sure you let your attendees know what the next steps are. Say something like "if you liked what you saw here, here's how you can engage with us going forward." Then provide a phone number or URL or email address, and maybe even some sort of discount or deal or other special offer just for attendees. Make them feel special, and make it clear how to proceed from here.

- **Offer your webinars on demand after the fact**—Make sure you record the webinars you give, and then make those recordings available afterwards, either for attendees who want to revisit the experience or other customers who couldn't make it for the live version.

- **Create takeaways**—If you're giving a PowerPoint-type presentation in a webinar, have a copy of that presentation (in PowerPoint format) available for participants to download and print out; it's best to do this *before* the presentation so that attendees can follow along as its given. For that matter, you might want to create a fancy set of handouts, maybe even in book format, to send to attendees afterwards. Having something in their hands is always good.

- **Put follow-up questions on your website**—It's likely there might be more questions asked during the webinar than you have time to answer; it's also possible some attendees will ask questions after the fact. Both are good reasons to create a section of your website or online message forum where these questions can be posted and answered after the webinar.

- **Follow up**—If you're using your webinar for customer acquisition, have a salesperson follow up with all attendees within 48 hours. For that matter, follow up with those who planned to attend and didn't, for whatever reason. Don't let the leads cool; strike while they're hot.

As you might suspect, webinars can be quite useful for both customer acquisition and retention. In either instance, you need to present a topic that is of vital interest and then keep your attendees interested, from beginning to end—and even after the webinar ends. Be useful and informative, not boring, and make sure to follow through. That's the road to interactive media success.

The Bottom Line

Audio, video, and interactive media can be important for both the acquisition and retention phases of the B2B customer life cycle. Audio marketing typically consists of podcasts; video marketing consists of online videos, commonly distributed via YouTube; and interactive marketing means real-time webinars with current or prospective customers. Use all these media to impart necessary pre- and post-purchase information—in an interesting fashion.

16

B2B Public Relations

Public relations has always been an interesting component of the B2B marketing mix. It's not like advertising because you don't pay for placement or performance. And it's not like direct mail because you can't directly track results. What you have is a marketing method that can't guarantee placement and doesn't produce measureable results. Marvelous!

That all changes on the Internet, however. Not the bit about guaranteeing placement; you still have to influence other media to take up your story. But public relations activities on the Web can be tracked, and you can measure direct results—the number of leads that are generated from a given PR effort.

In addition, there's a lot more you can do online with your public relations efforts. There are new people to talk to (bloggers and social influencers) and different methods to employ (email, instant messaging, social media). Like I said, it all changes on the Internet.

What Is Online PR—and How Does It Differ from Traditional PR?

Like traditional public relations, online PR is all about influencing people. It's not about buying placement; it's about generating word-of-mouth attention that hopefully will generate some solid leads.

But who do you influence online—and how? That's where online PR differs from the traditional model.

Who You Influence

When we're talking online PR, we're talking about influencing a different group of people than you do with traditional PR. Old-school PR is about influence of traditional media—industry newspapers and magazines, maybe even radio and television.

Online PR deals with another group of influencers. These are people who've become trend setters to their online followers; a mention or endorsement from one of these folks is as good as gold.

Who are these online influencers? It's a diverse group, including the following:

- Professional writers, columnists, and reviewers for various websites
- Bloggers, both personal and professional
- Twitterers with large and loyal followings
- Facebookers with similarly large and loyal followings

Of these influencers, only the first group—writers, columnists, and reviewers—is similar to your traditional media targets. After all, a paid reviewer for an online publication isn't that much different from a reviewer for a print magazine or newspaper.

But the other influencers on this list are much, much different from the people you're used to dealing with. First, most of them aren't paid professionals. That is, they're not paid (although a few might generate some PPC ad revenue from their blogs), and they're surely not trained professionals. In fact, most of the influencers online are civilians, people who do what they do merely because they like to, not because it's a job. That makes for a bit of a different push, as you might imagine.

In addition, your online PR efforts often get seen directly by potential customers. That is, your press releases go out into the ether and end up reproduced on this website or that message forum exactly as you wrote them. Now, this sometimes happens in the print world, but those kinds of placements are traditionally in low-value publications. Online, a reprinted (or reposted) press release can get a huge number of views, and lead traffic directly back to your website. Which means, of course, that you need to take the prospective customer in mind when you're writing your online press releases; you can't rely on the target media to do any filtering for you.

Your press releases are also likely to end up in the search results of buyers searching for the topic mentioned. So, someone querying Google for "widgets" will see your press release for your new widget line in his search results. That's added exposure, friends, which is a very good thing.

So, when you're putting together your online PR plans, your goal is to get placement in a number of important online channels (in addition to the online arms of traditional media, of course):

- Industry websites
- Topic-related websites
- Media-sharing websites (YouTube, Flickr, and so on)
- Industry message forums
- Topic-related message forums
- Topic-related blogs
- Topic-related Twitter feeds
- Topic-related Facebook pages
- Social media bookmarking sites (Digg, Delicious, and so on)

What kind of placement are you looking for? It could be anything, including straight-up press release reproductions, brief mentions, official endorsements, news stories, interviews, reviews, you name it. The important thing is to get the word out—and then hope prospective customers get the word.

How You Influence Them

Online PR differs from traditional PR not only in who you try to influence, but also in how you do that. It mainly concerns the methods of contact available.

Obviously, you can still contact people in new media using old media, but why would you want to? I'm not sure a blogger would appreciate getting an old-fashioned press kit in the (postal) mail. It's kind of incongruous.

> "Online PR differs from traditional PR not only in who you try to influence, but also in how you do that."

Instead, you want to use the new media at your disposal to connect and interact with your new media contacts. It only makes sense that bloggers and Twitterers and the like will respond more positively to an outreach via the Internet than they would via a phone call or letter.

To that end, how do you reach your online contacts? Here's the list:

- **Email**—A bit passé among the younger crowd, email is still the best way to reach most online professionals.

- **Instant messaging**—Maybe not the best approach for an initial contact, instead a great way to work a continuing conversation with a busy online writer.

- **Blog comments**—If you're trying to reach an influential blogger, what better place than his blog? You can leave a public comment on an existing blog post, of course, but it might be better to get the blogger's email address and contact him that way.

- **Twitter**—Twitter allows private tweets, so why not use them? If you want to reach a prominent Twitterer, tweet your initial contact.

- **Facebook**—You can send private messages to fellow Facebook members, or you can just go to a person's profile page and write on his wall.

- **LinkedIn**—Many online professionals are members of the LinkedIn social network; sometimes this is the only contact information you can find for people. Use this to your advantage to make professional contact via LinkedIn's private messages.

As to what you send these folks, it all depends. An initial outreach may consist of nothing more than a short email or IM, or perhaps even a private message on Facebook or Twitter. More extensive information can include an online press release or digital press kit, or a link to a "media room" on your website where you provide digital photos, backgrounders, and the like.

Using the New Technology

The Internet makes available a lot of a great deal of new technology that can benefit PR professionals. Although some tools are relatively recent, some have been around quite a long time.

Online PR Databases

The earliest digital tools for PR professionals were and are online PR databases, such as Dow Jones Factiva (www.factiva.com), Cision (www.cision.com), and, to a lesser degree, LexisNexis (corporate.lexisnexis.com). These databases are the digital equivalents of old-school clipping services, where you can find both articles and contact information. It's what you use to find out who to contact and how, as well as to discover whether your previous efforts have borne fruit.

 Note

Cision is the new name for Bacon's, which previously acquired the competing MediaMap database and publications.

What do you find in these databases? Here's a short list:

- Contact information for both old and new media publications and journalists
- Print articles in which your company or product is mentioned
- Where your product or company is mentioned online—websites, blogs, even social media
- Tools for monitoring and analyzing the impact of your PR activities
- Early warning of new trends and issues

You can use these services to plan your PR campaigns, identify target publications and people, and, in some instances, place your online press releases. Equally important, you can track the placements you receive, both online and in traditional media. (For that matter, you can track the placements your competitors receive.)

These online databases, however, can be expensive—especially when you realize that much of the data they house can be had for free elsewhere online. Although these databases remain popular with large PR companies, and they are admittedly tailored for PR use, you can find similar information by searching Google, Bing, or any other free general search engine. Now, you might have to search harder, and the results might not be as easy to use as what you get from the paid services, but what you get from Google is free.

Social Media Search

These online PR databases do a great job of tracking mentions in traditional media and on major news-related websites. They do less well in tracking mentions in social media, such as Twitter, Facebook, blogs, and social bookmarking sites. For this, you might want to invest in software or services that search the social media for mentions of your company or products or any other terms you specify.

The following are some of the top tools for tracking mentions in social media:

- Alterian SM2 (socialmedia.alterian.com)
- CoTweet (www.cotweet.com)
- Hootsuite (www.hootsuite.com)
- IceRocket (www.icerocket.com)
- Radian6 (www.radian6.com)
- Scout Labs (www.scoutlabs.com)
- SocialMention (www.socialmention.com)
- Trackur (www.trackur.com)

Press Release Distribution

How do you distribute your digital press releases? Naturally, you should send press releases directly to the online media you've targeted. But you can also get general distribution for your press releases by using an online press release distribution service.

These distribution services post press releases from a variety of sources across a large number of industries; they also automatically feed content into the news sections of the major search engines. By posting releases on their sites, they make the press releases searchable by Google and other search engines. That's a good thing.

Most distribution services also distribute your press releases directly to appropriate online and offline media outlets. They'll also send your releases to other outlets you specify.

In addition, some of these services will work with you to make your press releases more effective, particularly in the area of SEO. Some will even host photos and other accompanying media, if you need that.

The major online press release distribution services include the following:

- Business Wire (www.businesswire.com)
- CisionWire (www.cision.com)
- Free Press Release (www.free-press-release.com)
- i-Newswire (www.i-newswire.com)
- Marketwire (www.marketwire.com)
- Online PR News (www.onlineprnews.com)
- PR Leap (www.prleap.com)
- PR Log (www.prlog.org)
- PR Newswire (www.prnewswire.com)

- PR.com (www.pr.com)
- PRWeb (www.prweb.com)
- SEO Press Releases (www.seopressreleases.com)
- Wired PR News (www.wiredprnews.com)

These are all good sources, but the big dogs here are Business Wire and PR Newswire, along with Business Web, CisionWire, Marketwire, and PRWeb. Although many of the other services are free, these are not—but then again, they have a broader reach.

As to pricing, they're all over the place. As one example, PRWeb charges anywhere from $80 to $360 per press release, depending on how widely you want it distributed, whether you want to work it over for search engine optimization and such, and whether it includes multimedia attachments. Do your homework before you sign up.

The Benefits of Online PR

Your goals with online PR should be similar to what you've always tried to achieve with traditional PR. In fact, many of the activities are the same—you write press releases, establish relationships with key contacts, and follow through to see if your efforts bore fruit.

Online public relations comes into the mix primarily during the reach phase of the B2B buying continuum. By getting other sites to write about you and your products, you're creating valuable word-of-mouth advertising that gets your name in front of potential customers and hopefully entices them to connect with you to get more information. And we all know where that can lead...

> "Your goals with online PR should be similar to what you've always tried to achieve with traditional PR."

In this aspect, traditional and digital PR is very similar. But there are differences between the two, chief of which is the interactive conversations that develop online. Whereas traditional PR is pretty much a one-way effort, in that you put the press release out there and that's that, online PR is a two-way street. That's because a significant portion of your online PR efforts are targeted at potential customers, encouraging them to contact your company directly.

✉ *Note*

One way to encourage readers to respond to a press release is to offer something of interest or value in the release itself. This is called *response PR.*

What you end up with is a two-way conversation that provides some of the primary benefits of online PR. A successful online PR effort results in more than just a placement in a prominent publication; it drives measurable traffic and sales to your website.

Note the word *measurable* in the previous paragraph. That's something new with online PR. Traditionally, you couldn't really measure the effects of your PR efforts; all you could track were articles that mentioned your company or product.

Online, you can go beyond tracking placement to measuring how effective each placement is. It's a simple matter to track clicks back to your site and where those clicks came from. You can measure, with relative ease, which of your PR efforts produced the most concrete results.

This trackability has several benefits of its own. Obviously, you can now determine which PR efforts are working and which aren't, and fine-tune your activities accordingly. But you can also hold your PR people accountable for results. This might be the first time in their careers that PR people have fiscal responsibility, and; it could be a bit of a shocker for them.

There's another big difference with online PR: There are a lot more places where you can get mentioned. Online media don't necessarily displace traditional media; (most) newspapers and magazines and television outlets continue to exist, even with new online competition. But there are a lot of new media outlets, from websites to blogs to Twitter feeds, and they're all ripe for news about your company and products.

Reaching all these sources means a lot more work for your PR person or department. It's fair to say that because of the increased number of influencers online, PR has never been more important than it is today. You have to put forth the effort to reach all these folks—and that's what public relations is all about.

Developing New Online Sources

Let's start with the new sources you need to develop for your online PR efforts. The Internet has created a large number of new outlets for the dissemination of news and information, and you need to learn how to take advantage of them.

Targeting Websites and Online Publications

The online outlets most like traditional media outlets are websites and online publications. In some instances, websites are actually offshoots of traditional media; in other instances, they're unique entities. But in most cases, news-oriented websites and online publications operate a lot like their old media counterparts.

What this means is that you have to target a mix of editors, staff reporters and reviewers, and freelance writers. If anything, there are probably more freelance writers online than there are with traditional media, but that's purely a subjective assessment; you still have to deal with the mix.

You'll find a familiar chain of command at the larger websites and publications. When the site's big enough and the staff's large enough, you're likely to find separate editors and writers and reviewers to pitch your stories to. Just go to the website and look for an About or Contact Us link to see who's responsible for what. Email is probably the best way to contact these folks.

Smaller websites and publications, however, are likely to have much smaller staffs. In fact, some sites have one-person staffs—it's all run by a single guy or gal, with most if not all the writing outsourced. If nothing else, this makes it easier to figure out whom to contact; there's no big bureaucracy to slow things down.

Targeting Online Writers and Reviewers

You can also pitch your wares at to individual writers and reviewers—those folks who provide content to all those websites and online publications and blogs. Most of these people write for multiple sites, so you can often get a good bang for your efforts by pitching across multiple segments.

How do you contact these writers? By email, of course, but finding a good email address might take a bit of work. Start by seeking out articles across the Web that fit into your target profile, and then find out who's writing them. If you're lucky, the articles you like will be bylined and have the writer's email address attached. You can always Google a given writer if no email address is handy. And there's nothing stopping you from contacting the hosting site or publication and asking to contact the writer of an article you like. Work hard enough and you'll get to the person in question.

I've found freelance writers to be particularly receptive to PR efforts. They're often struggling to find the next article to sell, and you can provide a nice angle for a given site or publication, which gives the writer a nice leg up. That's sure to be appreciated.

Targeting Bloggers

Blogs are a great place to plug your wares. There are lots of B2B bloggers out there, and they have lots of posts to write. Convince the bloggers who speak directly to your target audience to talk about your company or product, and you'll gain a certain legitimacy among the followers of those blogs.

After you identify a particular blog as reaching the audience you want to reach, you now have to establish a relationship with the person or persons who write that blog. This is old-school PR, updated for the Internet age. You can make your presence known by posting some comments to posts on that blog, and then follow up from there by emailing the blogger directly. The key is to treat the blogger like a real human being (which he probably is, to some degree) and get to know him on a personal level. Find out what he likes and what he doesn't, what he thinks is important, what makes him laugh. Get him to like you and to trust you. Then, and only then, can you pitch him for a story or product placement.

It's the same way you used to (and still might) get to know important contacts in traditional media. The big difference is that for many bloggers, it's not a 9-to-5 job. In fact, many bloggers have another day job, and do the blog thing after work and on weekends. Don't assume that you can IM or call a blogger in the middle of the afternoon and get an immediate response.

Another big difference is that (most) bloggers, B2B or otherwise, are not trained journalists, and as such don't follow the same rules and practices as do folks in the traditional media. If you play things by the book, this shouldn't make much of a difference. But do know that some bloggers can be easily influenced, or even purchased outright. Not that you'd ever think of doing so, but I'm just saying.

When it comes to pitching a blogger, keep these points in mind:

- **Personalize the pitch**—Don't send out blind emails to bloggers. Get to know the bloggers first, and then contact them with personal messages.
- **Be relevant**—A generic pitch won't cut it. Make sure you tailor your pitch to the particular blog, to the point of suggesting specific blog posts the blogger might make.
- **Make it easy**—Provide everything the blogger needs to create a post. That probably means posting your press release or landing page online and providing bloggers with the URLs to link to this info. Also provide links to photos (sized appropriately for blog use, of course), as well as your email address and IM they can use if they have questions or need more information.

You also need to be persistent. As with traditional media contacts, not every blogger will respond to the first pitch you make. If at first you don't succeed, keep trying—and keep fine-tuning your pitch as time goes by. And when a blogger does mention your product or company, make sure you follow up with a thank-you email—and another pitch, if you have one.

Targeting Online Message Forums

Online message forums are ripe for PR attention. But who do you contact?

The answer is, no one—and everyone. PR on a B2B message forum is more about interacting socially than it is about sending out press releases and pitching contacts. It's a matter of monitoring the appropriate forums for threads that best suit your interest, and then participating in those threads.

That's right, I said *participating*. Message board PR is a form of social media marketing, which means you have to monitor and participate in the community conversations. If that's not your cup of tea, tough; it has to be done. Either learn how to be social or hire someone to do it for you.

 Note

Participating in online forums and social networks should be natural, not blatantly promotional. Don't fall into the practice that some call *astroturfing*, where you leave favorable messages about your products without disclosing your official affiliation—or honestly engaging the rest of the community.

Targeting Social Media

It's the same thing with other social media—Facebook, Google+, Twitter, and the like. You really can't post a press release on Facebook and expect a positive response; nor can you condense a press release to a 140-character tweet and broadcast it to your legion of followers.

You can, however, translate the key information in a press release to a format that should work on Facebook and Twitter. You can even include a link in tweet or status update to the complete press release posted elsewhere online. But you can't just tweet "New press release posted"; you have to convey the message in the press release as information of interest to your Twitter followers and Facebook fans.

So, for example, if you issue a press release announcing your new fall product line, you don't want to post "New office supply products announced." That's boring, and offers no real benefit to readers. Instead, you might want to tweet something along the lines of "More offices are switching from inkjet to laserjet printers," or

"What's the right copy paper for your needs?" It's like writing an ad headline; you have to entice readers to click for more information.

Not sure how this fits into your PR efforts? Maybe it doesn't. Maybe you create a dedicated social marketing department and let it handle this sort of thing. But for many companies, social media is going to fall under the purview of the PR department, so you better get used to it.

Creating an Online Press Room

Back in Chapter 9, "B2B Website Marketing," we discussed all the different parts of an ideal B2B website. As you recall one of my recommendations is to create an online press room, where the members of the press media can visit to find things they can use to spice up their press release coverage—images, videos, corporate bios, and, of course, press releases.

Instead of waiting for a journalist to request a particular photo and then snail-mailing or emailing that particular item, you can place all your available media for the press in a dedicated section of your website—an online press room, as it were. This makes it easier for print and online journalists to find key company information and all the picture and media files they need.

Why Do You Need a Press Room on Your Website?

An online press room is a section of your website for the press. It contains all your press releases (archived by date, typically), product photos, brochures and catalogs, and how-to videos, that you make available to members of the press. In fact, it can be used by both traditional print media and today's online media; it's a virtual storehouse of digital media of all sorts.

 Note

An online press room is sometimes called a *media room* or *press page*.

As such, an online press room (see Figure 16.1) is a very important part of your website, and critical to your traditional and online PR efforts. The pages within your online press room, if you don't hide them behind some sort of password-protected firewall, also help your site show up in the search results for Google and competing search sites; someone searching for product information, for example, is likely to find links to that product's spec sheet, press release, and digital photograph in the search results.

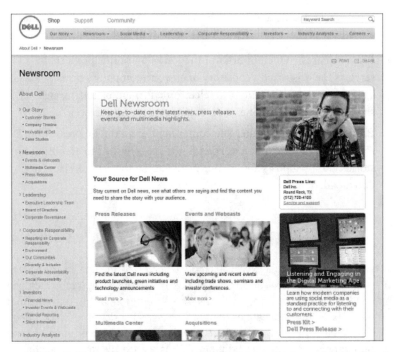

Figure 16.1 *Dell's online press room—digital media and information for everybody.*

A well-done online press room can be one of the most highly trafficked areas of your website. It can turn B2B journalists who were just browsing into interested writers about your company and products. It can also, of course, make life a whole lot easier for journalists on a deadline; they can download what they need when they need it, without the traditional approval and shipping delays.

Your press room is likely to be used by a broad segment of the media. It might see use by websites and blogs looking for photographs and artwork to accompany articles and posts; journalists (traditional and online) and bloggers looking for story ideas or details for a story in progress; print publications looking for photographs and artwork to accompany articles in progress; investors or potential investors looking for company information; and even potential customers looking for product information to fuel their own decision-making process.

Keep all this in mind when you design and stock your online press room. It's for the press, of course, but also for investors and customers.

Stocking Your Online Press Room

What sort of things should you include in your online press room? Just about anything the press might need to write or produce a story, of course. That includes photos, press releases, detailed spec sheets, even management bios and headshots. Let's take a look at the major items you'll want to include:

- **Press releases**—One important function of an online press room is to serve as the organized depository of all your company's press releases. The press releases have to be in electronic format, of course, and should be viewable online or downloadable for offline use.

- **Product photos**—Another key component of an online press room is a section of product photos. The photos are intended to accompany stories and blog posts about your products, so they should be easily downloaded.

FORMATTING PHOTOS

A few words about what types of product photos to include in your online press room. First, know that these photos will be used by both traditional and online publications, so you'll have to size and format the photos appropriately. For online publications, that means a smaller, lower-resolution photo in JPG format. For print publications, you need a much larger, much higher-resolution photo, suitable for printing. TIFF is a good file format for print, as is EPS, although high-res JPG files also work. In any case, you need to provide both low-resolution and high-resolution files, and make the choice simple.

Catering fully to the needs of the media, you might want to supply several different photos for each of your products. I'm talking about shooting the product from different angles, as well as supplying photos of various product details. For example, if you sell consumer electronics products, include photos of the product's front panel, back panel, and remote control. Think of any particular need the press might have, and provide photos that fill those needs.

- **Videos**—With both the Web and traditional broadcast media in mind, you should also consider adding to your online press room any online videos you've created. These might be introductory product videos, how-to videos, even videos talking about your company or its management team. If there's a possibility that some online outlet might use the video and provide you with additional exposure, it's worth including.

- **Product spec sheets**—It's not just images that the press need. They also need information. To that end, include detailed product spec sheets in your online press room. These might duplicate items already present on individual product pages on your site, but that's okay; the press is more likely to find these documents from the press room gateway than by browsing or searching your main website. PDF is always a good format for these.

- **Brochures**—A similar situation exists for product or product line brochures. You might offer them on the consumer site of your website, but provide them to the press in your online press room, as well. As with spec sheets, PDF is the format of choice for these items.

- **Logos**—Don't forget to include images of your company, brand, and product logos. Include logo files in various sizes, colors, and configurations, for a variety of print and online uses.

- **Company background**—Members of the press and potential customers both come to your online press room to find out more about the company. To that end, include a detailed company backgrounder as part of your offerings. Include anything you might think the press and investors might be interested in, including a company timeline. PDF is a good format for this information.

- **Management bios**—As part of the company background information you provide, you should also include brief bios of key company management. That includes your president, CEO, and other top-level people. The bio doesn't have to be long, but it should include the basics.

- **Management photos**—Naturally, you should include downloadable photographs of each person highlighted in your management bios. This should be your typical headshot; if you don't have any yet, just get some. As with product photos, offer both a low- and high-resolution version of each headshot.

- **Other company photos**—What else might the press be interested in using to accompany an article about your company, brands, or products? How about pictures of your corporate offices, factories, or warehouse? What about a picture of how your product is made? What about pictures of your product in use? What about pictures of customers using your products? Get a little creative here, and think about what sort of eye candy might be interesting to accompany various types of articles. As with all images, make them available in both low- and high-resolution formats.

- **Press kits**—Your job (or one of your jobs) is to make life easier for the press. The easier you make it for them, the more likely it is they'll cover you. That probably means gathering various examples of the items we've previously discussed into online press kits. You might create kits around specific product lines, product releases, promotions, or whatever. Include all relevant information and media—press releases, spec sheets, product photos, logos, and the like.

- **Upcoming events**—Let the media know that your company is a busy one. Include a list of and links to all upcoming conferences, trade shows, webinars, and other events that your company is attending or participating in. This enhances your corporate credibility and your image as an industry leader.

- **Media coverage**—Here's a good one. Be sure to include copies of or links to favorable media coverage your company and products have received. Include mentions and reviews in traditional media, as well as reviews and mentions in blogs and online news sites. Filter the list, of course, so that you don't draw attention to negative reviews and mentions. Show journalists and potential customers all the good things.

- **Contact information**—Finally, include a link that visitors can use to contact you for more information. Make this a personal contact—a link to a specific person in your PR department. Definitely include an email address; unless you're averse to direct communication (and if so, why are you in the marketing business to begin with?), you should probably include a direct-dial phone number, too. Heck, include your IM info if you're online doing instant messaging most days. Make it easy for reporters and reviewers to get in touch with you—and make sure you return said emails and phone calls in a timely fashion!

OPEN OR CLOSED ACCESS?

Many, if not most, companies make their online press centers freely available to all comers—traditional journalists, nontraditional bloggers and their ilk, and the general public. Other companies, however, consider their press materials somehow proprietary and not suitable for use by the general public. How a product photo or specification, which ultimately is used in public media read by the general public, isn't fit for public consumption escapes me. But this is the way some companies think (especially those ruled by a heavy-handed legal department worried about copyrights and the like), and why they make their press rooms private.

There are multiple drawbacks to having a closed online press room, not the least of which is the issue of controlling access. Who decides who gets in and who doesn't? How does an interested journalist gain access? (Typically by emailing the contact and getting a password in return—but how do you know who to contact in the first place?) How fast can a journalist get access to the site? Issues abound.

In addition, if your press room is closed to the public, potential customers can't see what's there. Not that a press room is optimized for customer use, but it can be another gateway for buyers to find out more about your company and what you sell. Keep it private, and you lose that advantage.

My advice is to keep your online press room open and don't hide anything from anybody. Hey, if an interested consumer wants to view a spec sheet or download a product photo, what's the harm? And who's to say who's a customer and who's a journalist, anyway? If a so-called personal blogger wants to talk about your product and include a photo, all the better!

In my eyes, there's nothing to be gained by controlling access to your press materials, either by password protection or requiring users to register before being granted access. You want your products to gain the widest possible exposure, don't you? Then let anyone who wants to access and download your photos, press releases, and the like. The more placements you get, the better.

The Bottom Line

Public relations for B2B companies is moving online. Your PR department needs to target sources for online exposure, from blogs to websites and beyond, and use a variety of digital tools to reach these web-based influencers. You should also put together an online press room where interested parties can go to find press releases, images, and other items of use when they're writing about you.

17

B2B Mobile Marketing

It's a fact. More and more people—especially people in businesses—are using mobile phones and other devices to connect to the Internet, instead of their computers. You need to adapt your digital marketing tactics to compensate for this shift to mobile access, and to take advantage of it.

That is what is meant by mobile marketing—marketing to users of mobile devices.

Why Mobile Is Important

Mobile marketing is relatively easy to define and just as easy to understand. Put simply, it's marketing on or with a mobile device, such as a mobile phone or tablet PC. And it's becoming increasingly important.

Mobile Marketing in the B2B World

For all practical purposes, B2B mobile marketing today takes place on mobile phones and tablet devices. Not just any mobile phone, of course, but rather today's generation of so-called smartphones. These are mobile phones with built-in Internet access, web browsing, email, and the like. I'm talking Apple's iPhone, of course, but also Android phones, Windows phones, and Blackberries. These devices are near-ambiguous in the corporate world, in addition to being widely adopted by regular consumers.

Mobile B2B marketing, then, targets those activities you engage in that reach business buyers over the mobile web. These activities include

- **Mobile website**—That is, the mobile version of your company website, important for those customers accessing your site from their mobile phones.

- **Mobile search**—This is similar to traditional web-based search marketing, but fine-tuned for users searching from their mobile phones. (The fine-tuning has a lot to do with location because mobile searchers tend to search for local businesses while they're on the go; it's less a factor for B2B marketing than it is for the B2C world.)

- **Mobile email**—Naturally, smartphone users can receive email on their devices; mobile marketers are learning to take advantage of this opportunity.

- **Mobile advertising**—These are ads you purchase on mobile websites—ads specially formatted for the mobile screen and targeted to mobile customers. Most mobile advertising, as with most web advertising, is of the PPC nature.

- **Mobile applications**—Many smartphone users can install small applications on their devices. B2C businesses are increasingly creating mobile apps to serve their customers and promote their brands; it's less a factor for B2B marketers.

- **Mobile social networking**—More and more Facebook and Twitter users are accessing their social networks from their mobile phones. Again, savvy mobile marketers are exploiting this new usage model.

There are probably more types of mobile marketing being experimented with than I mentioned here. That's okay; mobile marketing is a relatively new medium for marketers, and we're all feeling our way.

Mobile Marketing: Big and Getting Bigger

So, why all this attention on mobile marketing? It's because mobile web use is fast gaining on traditional computer-based web use. If web marketing is your thing, you have to reach prospective and existing consumers no matter which types of devices they use to access the Web—but then take advantage of the unique features of each device.

Let's start with some statistics. At the beginning of 2010, there were more than 4.7 billion subscribers to cellular telephone services worldwide, with 285 million of these people in the U.S;[1] fully 91% of all Americans had a cellphone subscription (as of year end 2008). It gets even more interesting when you drill down to look at mobile Internet usage—it's estimated that mobile web usage will surpass PC-based access by 2013.[2]

More important to B2B marketers, the business world has enthusiastically embraced mobile computing. Research finds that 72% of the U.S. workforce works at least part-time on a mobile basis.[3] And 64% of B2B decision makers use smartphones and other mobile devices to read email and browse the Internet.[4]

It should come as no surprise, then, that mobile marketing is projected to become one of the fastest-growing types of digital marketing, second only to social media marketing. Forrester Research predicts that spending on B2B mobile marketing will quadruple from its 2009 levels, rising to $106 million in 2014.[5]

It's more than just the numbers, however. Unlike connecting to the Web via computer, which can only be done while a customer is setting in front of his or her PC, a customer can connect to the Web via mobile phone anytime and anywhere. People always have their phones with them; this gives you nonstop connectivity to your customers.

---

1. Plunkett Research, Ltd.

2. Gartner, Inc., "Gartner's Top Predictions for IT Organizations and Users, 2010 and Beyond: A New Balance," 2010

3. IDC, "Worldwide Mobile Worker Population 2009-2013 Forecast," 2010

4. MarketingSherpa, "2011 B2B Marketing Report," 2010

5. Forrester Research, "U.S. Interactive Marketing Forecast, 2009 to 2014," 2009

This is especially important in the business environment. Although target buyers are often tethered to their office PCs during work hours, they don't do all their research at work. It's quite common for businesspeople to fill their downtime, either at home or while traveling, by doing product research on their mobile phones or iPads. For that matter, there are many times where a business buyer is away from his office (at the airport, sitting in a boring meeting, or even waiting for an appointment) and mobile is the only way to access the Internet. With mobile access in mind, you have to make your content easily accessible by those using mobile devices—business buyers expect it.

How Mobile B2B Marketing Differs from Traditional B2B Marketing

What makes mobile B2B marketing different from traditional B2B marketing? It's all about the size of the presentation—and where customers receive your message.

Marketing for a Smaller Screen

Let's talk size first. When it comes to mobile marketing, bigger is not better. In fact, small is all—as in, adapting your marketing to the small size of the mobile phone screen.

Most web-based marketing is designed with traditional web browsers and the computer screen in mind. Web pages keep getting wider and wider to fill the space on widescreen monitors; we employ banner ads and full-screen graphics and fill every inch of screen space available.

That is not the tack to take with mobile marketing. What works on the big computer screen is totally useless on the small screen of a typical mobile phone. You don't have much width, you don't even have much depth if you want to avoid scrolling. Your visual message needs to be simplified and smallerized, pure and simple.

> "When it comes to mobile marketing, bigger is not better. In fact, small is all—as in, adapting your marketing to the small size of the mobile phone screen."

You also have to make sure your images and text are visible on the small screen. You might be surprised how small and downright unreadable some of the items you currently employ are when viewed on a mobile device. It might look fine on a 19" monitor running at 1280 × 768 pixel resolution, but appear ant-like on a mobile device with a 3.5" screen running at 240 × 320 resolution.

Then there's screen orientation. You're used to computer displays that are wider than they're tall (landscape orientation). Most cell phones displays are in a portrait orientation, taller than they're wide.

All this requires a rethinking of your visual presentation. You need to present less information on a smaller screen. It's a challenge.

Targeted Marketing

The information you present needs to be tailored to the mobile market. Mobile business users, although they have their phones with them all the time, aren't constantly connected as are users connected from their offices; they connect to the Internet on an as-needed basis. Your ability to communicate with them, then, depends more on them reaching out to you than the other way around.

This isn't necessarily a bad thing. When you think mobile marketing, think targeted marketing, not mass marketing—which is ideal for the B2B environment. When you're marketing via mobile, you can send out a very targeted message to those few mobile customers who are interested in what you're offering at this moment.

✉ *Note*

The mobile web also lets you use access location-based information about your customers. That's a nice demographic touch, being able to target customers based on location. More important, many buyers will use your mobile site to locate your offices when they're traveling to you, so make sure you include a map or other means to locate you physically on your mobile site.

Even though mobile marketing is especially suited for local consumer businesses, who can target promotions at people near a specific location, you can still reach out via mobile to B2B customers with products and services of interest to companies in specific locations. For example, if you sell maintenance services, you can promote furnace cleaning to customers in Minnesota and air conditioner maintenance to those in Florida. Targeted marketing is the key.

Adapting Your Website for Mobile

With more and more businesspeople accessing the web from mobile devices, instead of computers, having a version of your website that works with these devices is fast becoming imperative in the B2B world. You can't just assume that your current website will look good on a mobile phone; most sites simply aren't designed for small cellphone screens.

Take a test. Grab the nearest web-enabled mobile phone, fire up the web browser, and browse to your normal website. How's it look? Not too good, probably (like what you see in Figure 17.1); the home page is probably too wide and the elements too small to view comfortably. What fits comfortably on a big computer screen is overkill on a mobile screen. (And if your boss questions why you need to spend the money on a mobile site, hand him your cell phone to perform this same test.)

Figure 17.1   *An example of a B2B company not doing mobile right. Sysco's site has not been optimized for mobile use; you see the same site on an iPhone you do on a computer screen.*

It's not just about looks, either. Website functionality needs to be different—simplified, actually—for mobile users. That's because it's more difficult to navigate a website on a mobile phone than it is on a computer; you don't have a mouse to move around with. For that reason, a mobile website has to be navigable with fewer clicks than a traditional site.

Speaking of functionality, know that some mobile web browsers do not display some technologies well or at all. As a prominent example, Apple's Safari browser, used on the popular iPhone, is not compatible with Flash media. If you have any Flash elements on your page, they simply won't display on an iPhone. That's a big ouch.

If you want to play on the mobile web, then, you have to have a website that works with cell phones and other mobile devices. As a marketer, you should be somewhat indifferent as to how customers access your web content—but you do have to make sure your content works with all devices that can access it.

The good news is that it's relatively easy to create a mobile-friendly version of your website. Your IT guys should have the tools, or be able to readily obtain the tools, to do the job.

What do you need to do to create a great-looking and fully functional mobile website? Here are some of the elements to keep in mind:

- **Orientation matters**—Pages on the traditional Web have a landscape orientation with horizontal menu bars, as users typically have widescreen computer monitors. Cell phone screens, however, are more portrait or vertically oriented. This means you need to reorient your web pages to fit the format of the mobile screen.

  Take, for example, Accenture's traditional home page (see Figure 17.2). It has a lot of different elements, and the elements are organized to fit on a widescreen computer monitor; it's definitely a landscape orientation. Compare that to the company's mobile page (see Figure 17.3). In addition to reducing the number of elements presented, those items are presented in a vertical list, to match the vertical nature of the mobile phone screen.

Figure 17.2 *Accenture's traditional home page—horizontal content for widescreen viewing.*

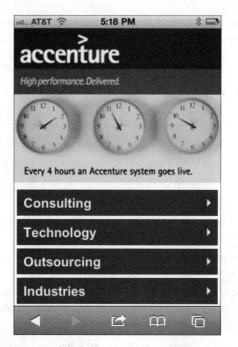

Figure 17.3   *Accenture's mobile home page—fewer elements, arranged vertically.*

- **Reduce the number of elements**—Designing a mobile website is all about simplifying. The typical cell phone screen is only so large; you can only fit a limited number of items on the screen and have them big enough to be visible. To this end, you need to reduce the number of elements that appear on the screen at one time. Instead of displaying a dozen different elements, opt for a half dozen or fewer. It's a matter of what can fit in the limited space, and choosing those elements that are most important.

✉ Note

When you're reducing the number of elements you present on your mobile site, make sure you prioritize those elements that remain. Browsing through pages on a mobile site can be quite time-consuming; make sure users see the most important content at the top of the first page.

- **Add a search box**—When you limit the content you present on your mobile page, you reduce the number of navigational avenues into your site. Because there are fewer navigational options, it's important to provide a way for users to find specific content. That argues for a site search box, placed prominently on the home page. You have to give customers a way to find what they're looking for, no matter what.

✉ *Note*

If you don't have the IT staff or budget to code a search engine for your mobile site, you can use Google's free Custom Search for Mobile instead.

- **Minimize the images**—Here's something else about really good mobile websites—they don't use a lot of graphics. Space is at a premium, and you can't waste it with superfluous images. In most instances, you can present content more efficiently in text than in pictures; let that drive your mobile page design.

> "...don't make visitors suffer through an interminable download just to look at a pretty picture."

✉ *Note*

Using text instead of images also affects the download time for your mobile pages. Mobile web access is typically slower than you get on a computer-based connection; everything takes longer on the mobile Web. Keep this in mind and reduce the number of large elements that take a long time to download—don't make visitors suffer through an interminable download just to look at a pretty picture.

- **Keep it small**—With cellular data network speeds in mind (and knowing that even 3G networks aren't always speedy), you need to work hard on keeping the file size for the entire page as small as possible. You want to aim for a maximum page file size of 20KB. Smaller is better.

- **Embrace white space**—When designing for the mobile screen, it's tempting to try to cram as many elements as possible into the smaller space. Resist the temptation. White space is an important element of any page design, and even more so for small screens. Too much stuff in a small space is both visually unappealing and difficult to navigate. The admonition to keep it simple applies to design as well as content.

- **Don't do tables**—If you use tables on your main website, ditch them for your mobile site. Tables simply don't display well on mobile devices; if a table is too wide (which it probably is), it throws off the entire page.

- **Consider color contrast**—Getting into the design side of things, know that not all mobile devices have great screens. (The iPhone shines here, but not every phone is an iPhone.) Some devices simply don't reproduce color well; some devices don't even have color screens. To that end, pay attention to the contrast on your page, and make sure the text color is in sharp contrast to the background color. And when in doubt, remember that good old black text on a white background works best.

- **Minimize text entry**—If you require a lot of customer interaction on your site, rethink how you get visitor input. Put simply, it's difficult to enter text on a mobile phone; you have to click here and press there and then tap an onscreen keyboard multiple times just to record a single letter. Consider accepting input via simple radio buttons or lists that visitors can select from. Require as few input keystrokes as possible.

My final word of advice for designing an effective mobile website is one you've heard throughout this book. When it comes to determining what you put on a mobile page, you need to *think like the customer*. The goal is to know what your B2B customers are looking for on your mobile site, and then present that content in an easy-to-find fashion.

This is important for any website, of course, but more so for a mobile site, where you don't have a lot of screen real estate to work with. You can't present multiple tunnels into your content; you have to determine the one best way and present it front and center. That means knowing, not guessing, what the mobile customer deems important. If it's not there on that first small page, the customer won't stick around to hunt for it.

In addition, know that the mobile business surfer is more time constrained than the buyer sitting in front of a computer screen in his office. Mobile users are, most often, mobile—that is, they're accessing the Web while they're on the go. They need to get their information quickly so that they can get on with whatever else it is they're doing. (Like driving their cars or catching their flights....) They're surfing in a very directed fashion. Don't make them work for that information; give them what they need as quickly as possible.

WHY A SINGLE SITE WON'T WORK

I know that there are some readers out there questioning why they need to design and host both normal and mobile versions of their website. After all, why couldn't you design a single site for both computer and mobile viewing? If you went this route, you'd certainly expend a lot less effort (and money) in designing the sites.

However, there are tons of issues with what I'll call the lazy marketer's approach, chief of which is that trying to serve two audiences with a single site does both of them an injustice. That is, there's no way to make a site that's ideal for all types of viewing devices.

If you make a full-featured site for traditional computer viewing, it simply won't look good on a mobile device. The orientation will be wrong, it'll be too busy, the elements will be way too small, and you'll undoubtedly use some elements that just won't work on some cell phones.

If, on the other hand, you design a site that plays well with mobile devices, you'll be leaving a lot of content on the table for computer users. Why limit yourself to what content and technology you can use just to appease the mobile segment of your audience? Your traditional site will be at a disadvantage to those competitors who optimize individual sites for both computer and mobile viewing.

Going with different sites for different types of access, then, is the right approach. I'm shocked, however, to see the number of big-name sites (such as Sysco's) that don't yet have mobile versions available. That's a big problem, but also an opening for more savvy competitors. If you're smart, you'll invest in a separate mobile version of your site and optimize it for viewing on the most popular mobile devices. Yes, it's more work, but as more and more business buyers access the web from their iPhones and Androids and Blackberries, it's work that will pay dividends.

Adapting Email Marketing for Mobile

Mobile email is an interesting topic, especially when you examine just how businesspeople use their mobile devices in this regard. In many cases, businesspeople don't actually read their email on their phones—or at least, they don't read *all* their messages. Instead, they use their phones to do a bit of email triage, deleting unimportant messages then and there, answering time-sensitive messages on the spot, and then saving what's left over to deal with when they're back in the office.

Knowing this, if you send out an email message that isn't that critical, chances are it will either be deleted immediately or saved for some theoretical future response—which means it probably gets deleted once the recipient is back in the office and dealing with a very full inbox. In other words, it's very, very easy for email marketing messages to fail completely in the mobile world.

That said, you can and still should use mobile email as part of your digital marketing strategy. It may be the only way to reach many on-the-go executives.

At the very least, knowing that at least some of your emails will be read on mobile phones, you need to design your emails with mobile in mind. Each and every email message has to be mobile-friendly, in terms of look and feel, length, and content. Keep these points in mind:

- **Use short subject lines**—The full subject needs to be readable on most mobile devices; if not, recipients are more likely to delete without reading.

- **Use a narrow width**—For nontext emails, keep the width at 640 pixels or less; 320 pixels is actually safest. Recipients don't want to have to scroll sideways or unduly zoom in to read. Because most smartphones have screens between 320 and 480 pixels wide when held vertically, keep this in mind.

- **Keep it small**—Speaking of small, keep the file size of your messages under 20KB. Anything larger might take too long to download.

- **Avoid images**—Images take up too much screen space and file capacity. Use a text-only or HTML-lite design for better mobile acceptance.

▶ *Caution*

Even though you need to adapt your emails for mobile, you shouldn't trim the content itself; that minimizes the email experience and effectiveness.

- **Consider using a preheader and hosted email**—This way you can include a "view on mobile" link in the preheader, which then links to a text or HTML-lite version of the message.

- **Think fat fingers**—For anything the recipient might need to click, such as text links or buttons, remember that all the clicking or pushing will be done by fingers, and the typical adult finger covers 45 pixels onscreen. For this reason, you'll want to increase both the size and padding of links and buttons to accommodate.

- **Think ergonomics**—Here's an interesting little factoid. Mobile usability experts tell us that most people, even lefties, handle their phones with their right hands. Keep this in mind when placing icons and links in your mobile emails.

- **Create mobile-friendly landing pages**—You also need to consider mobile when designing the landing pages that mobile email recipients may click to. Make sure your landing pages are optimized for mobile use, in terms of both look and feel and usability. (And, for iPhone users everywhere, avoid Flash on your landing pages.)

Adapting Other Digital Media for Mobile

You need to examine your entire digital marketing arsenal with mobile use in mind. Anything you expect customers to access via the Internet has to be rethought in terms of mobile access, as well.

We've already addressed website design (which should also apply for your blog design) and email marketing for mobile. Let's take a quick look at the other key digital marketing vehicles and see how mobile affects what you're doing—and how.

Mobile Search Engine Marketing

Mobile search, of course, is traditional web searching conducted on mobile phones. The big difference between mobile and traditional search for B2B marketers is the importance of high search result rankings. Google and other search engines typically display 10 results on a web search results page; you can appear anywhere in the top 10 and still get a decent click-through rate. Mobile search results pages aren't that long, however; on some devices, you might only see three or four results on a screen.

That makes it much more important to rank at the very top in terms of search results. Lower rankings will get relegated to a subsidiary screen, with the resultant decrease in visibility and click-throughs. For this reason, you need to ramp up your SEO efforts to make sure that mobile users will find you online—before they find your competitors.

> "...you need to ramp up your SEO efforts to make sure that mobile users will find you online—before they find your competitors."

✉ *Note*

> Another difference in mobile search engine marketing concerns the emphasis on generating local search results. This is much more important for B2C businesses than it is in the B2B world.

Mobile Advertising

Another key component of your mobile marketing strategy is that old standby, advertising. Mobile advertising is a bit different than traditional web advertising, however, because you have size considerations as well as audience considerations to take into account.

The mobile web features both text-only and image ads. In most cases, both text and image ads use the PPC model.

Text-only ads look a lot like normal PPC text ads but with less copy—just 24 to 36 characters of text, followed by your destination URL.

Mobile image ads, on the other hand, look more like traditional banner ads, but with a banner that fits easily on the mobile screen. The banner is clickable.

Speaking of clickable, you have the option of what you want a click to do. By default, clicking a mobile ad takes the consumer to a landing page on the advertiser's website—one designed for mobile viewing, ideally. But you can also opt to include a "click to call" link in your ad; clicking this link initiates a phone call to a number you specify. This is a great option for B2B marketers because it lets you connect directly with prospects or customers on the go.

Mobile Social Marketing

More and more people are accessing their favorite social media from their mobile phones. As such, you need to exploit this new usage model.

Twitter seems predesigned with mobile in mind; after all, a tweet is very much like a mobile text message. For the other social networks, you need to think of content that plays well in the mobile space. Consider creating mobile-friendly polls and surveys, keep your posts short, and go light on the images and videos. Use Twitter as your model here; the closer your posts resemble text messages, the better.

Mobile Audio/Video Marketing

Podcasts are perfect mobile marketing vehicles from the start because most people listen to them on their iPods and other portable music players; it's a short and easy step to then listen to podcasts on an iPhone or other smart phone, most of which have built-in music player apps. There's probably nothing you need to do special here, just realize that the more mobile your audience base, the more likely they'll be to become podcast listeners.

As to mobile video marketing, all you have to do is focus on YouTube. There are YouTube apps for all major smart phone platforms, so if your videos are uploaded to YouTube, anyone with a mobile phone can view them there with minimal technical issues.

You should, however, consider the very small screen of most mobile devices (iPads excepted, of course); make sure your videos view well on small screens. That means a big subject against a high-contrast background. Talking head videos work best in this environment; detailed how-to videos with lots of small details, not so much.

Mobile Interactive Marketing

Don't rule out mobile when you're planning your company's webinars. Although most webinar participants will join in via traditional desktop or notebook computers, mobile phones and tablets can also be used in this regard. With this in mind, avoid filling the screen with all sorts of subsidiary details (they'll be too small for mobile users to view), and make sure your presentations use lots of large bullets while eschewing fine print.

Using SMS Marketing

There's one more mobile marketing variation that deserves mentioning, and it has nothing to do with the Internet. It's a unique feature to mobile phones, and one used by a vast majority of phone users. I'm talking text messaging, otherwise known as SMS (short message service).

SMS messages can be powerful vehicles for your marketing program. Most users check an incoming text message within three to five seconds of arrival; few marketing media demand this sort of instant attention.

Of course, your messages must be both relevant and important to your recipients. A text message that isn't useful gets deleted immediately. (And chances are future message from you will be summarily ignored.)

For that reason, you should focus on texting information that is either time- or location-centric. Here are some tips on what works best:

- **Send "insider" information**—Offer to notify your top prospects and customers first, via SMS, about special events, new product launches, conferences and webinars, even trade show parties—whatever they're really interested in.

- **Send information that can't (or shouldn't be) ignored**—This time-sensitive information can include order cutoff deadlines, the ending of an important promotion or sale, reminders about recurring mainte-nance, registration for special events, and the like—things that custom-ers might miss out on if they don't act quickly.

- **Send location-centric info**—If you're at a trade show, text informa-tion about your booth, party, or other events. If you're at a conference, remind attendees of classes, seminars, dinners, and such. Even if you're not at an event, use SMS to notify accounts of events happening in their area.

- **Don't abuse the medium**—Text message are intrusive, which means you don't want to get carried away. Send too many texts and even the important ones will get ignored. Recognize that subscribers sign up for your SMS alerts for a specific purpose; abuse this trust and they'll unsubscribe.

Of course, before you can start texting you have to build a subscriber list for your SMS alerts. This is similar to building an email mailing list; you have to ask for per-mission to send certain types of alerts. You can let subscribers manage their SMS alerts in the same preference center used to manage email subscriptions.

The Bottom Line

It is essential that you adapt your digital marketing for mobile users; an increasing number of buyers and influencers are using mobile devices to research their busi-ness purchases. This means making your website and email mobile-friendly, and taking advantage of mobile possibilities for other digital marketing vehicles. You can also consider adding SMS text messaging to your marketing mix, when you have timely and relevant messages to impart to your customer base.

18

Quantifying Results

You can spend a lot of time and effort building your B2B digital marketing program. But how do you know when it's working? More importantly, how do you know which components are working?

Analyzing the performance of your efforts is part and parcel of any successful marketing program. Fortunately, digital marketing is inherently more measurable than just about any type of traditional marketing you've used in the past.

Analyzing Digital Media Performance

The performance of most digital marketing media can be quantified rather objectively. Either the numbers are good or they're not.

> ✉ *Note*
>
> Some digital media—social media in particular—are more fuzzy in their impact. We'll examine how to measure this sort of non-numeric success in Chapter 19, "Qualifying Results."

Let's look at each digital marketing medium individually, along with the key metrics you'll want to measure.

Analyzing Website Performance

If you want to see how well your website is performing, you need to know a few things. It helps to know how many customers are visiting your site, of course. It's also nice to know how many pages are viewed, as well as which are your top-performing pages.

That's just the tip of the iceberg. There's a lot more you can discover about the current and potential customers visiting your site—information that provides important insight into the kinds of visitors your site is attracting and how they're finding your site. Given all you can track, however, here's a list of what I feel are the most important metrics for B2B sites, the ones that truly measure your digital marketing performance:

- **Visitors**—The first metric that most people involved with a website want to know is how many *visitors* there were to the site. The more visitors you have, the busier your site is. You can track both "raw" visitors and *unique* visitors; the unique number is more relevant because the raw visitor data can count the same visitors more than once. When you track unique visitors, you're tracking individual people, even if they make multiple visits to your site within a 24-hour period.

- **Visits**—When a visitor views your site, that counts as a *visit*. Obviously, you can have more visits than you have visitors because people can visit more than once a day. That said, it's nice to know how often your site is being accessed, so the visits number is good for that.

- **Page views**—Most of us want visitors to view more than just one page on our sites. To that end, you should look at the *page views* metric. A page view is just as the name describes: a view of a single page by a site visitor. A visitor can view more than one page per visit, of course; in most instances, the more page views, the better.

- **Session duration**—Do you want visitors to get their information quickly and then leave? Or do you want them to stick around a bit and see all that you have to offer? In either instance, you're interested in the *session duration* metric. Session duration measures the average amount of time that visitors spend on your website per visit. A shorter session duration might indicate that visitors don't like what they see and thus leave prematurely; a longer session duration could indicate that visitors are having trouble finding what they want—or that they really like what they find and stick around to read more.

- **Bounce rate**—The shortest visits are those where someone lands on your site and then clicks away to another site, without ever viewing a second page. This single-page exit is measured by the *bounce rate* metric, which calculates the percentage of visits where the visitor enters and exits on the same page, without visiting any other pages in-between. Obviously, a high bounce rate is a bad thing.

✉ *Note*

You can measure bounce rate for your entire site and for individual pages. This last approach is recommended if you've created multiple landing pages on your site, for use with PPC advertisements and the like. Identify those pages with a high bounce rate and then try to discover the reason for it and fix the issue.

- **Percent exit**—Related to bounce rate is the *percent exit* metric, which measures the percentage of visitors who exist from a given web page. This metric is interesting in that a high percent exit could indicate people getting frustrated with a given page. (It can also indicate a natural exit point from your site, of course, such as the conclusion page of your checkout process.)

- **Top exit pages**—It's also interesting to learn which pages visitors leave from—that is, the top *exit pages* on your site. Ideally, these are pages created to be exit pages, such as your "thank you for contacting us" pages. You have some investigating to do if you find people are exiting from pages that should be leading them to other pages instead; you typically want visitors to follow one or more specified paths through your site, and any page that isn't propelling visitors further down that path need to be examined.

- **Top pages**—Okay, so you know that you're getting visitors to your site; what pages are they looking at while they're there? You can learn which of your site's pages are most popular by looking at the *top pages* metric. This is simply a list of the pages with the most page views, in descending order. You might be surprised; for many sites, the top page is not the home page.

- **Top landing pages**—This leads us to a discussion of your site's *top landing pages*. A landing page is the first page that a visitor lands on. Some visitors land on your home page, of course, but many don't. A visitor can land on a page buried deep in your site if that page is linked to from another site, or if that page pops up in Google's search results. In any case, the top landing pages are arguably the most important pages on your site; they're certainly the first pages that most visitors see. Know what they are and pay attention to them.

> "...the top landing pages are arguably the most important pages on your site; they're certainly the first pages that most visitors see."

- **Traffic sources**—How are people finding your site? That information is typically available in some sort of *traffic sources* analysis. A traffic source is the site visited just before a visitor hits your site; presumably, something about that site led them to yours. Traffic sources can include search engines, referring sites (sites that link to yours), advertisements, or direct traffic (where a visitor manually enters your site's URL). What percentage of visitors you get from each type of traffic source tells you what part of your digital marketing plan is most effective. It also provides guidance into where you should direct future activities.

- **Keywords**—For most sites, you'll find that your top traffic source is a search engine. Now it's time to drill down a little deeper and find out what people are searching for that's led them to your site. To that end, you want to look at the *keywords* metric in your web analytics. These are the top terms searched for by visitors who came to your site from a search engine. Knowing what people are searching for helps you determine what keywords to use in your site's SEO, as well as what keywords to purchase in your PPC advertising.

Track these metrics to learn more about how people are finding your site and what they're doing once they get there.

CHOOSING A WEB ANALYTICS TOOL

To gather data about your website's performance, you use a *web analytics* tool. Web analytics is the collection and analysis of data relating to website visitors. It's a way to measure the traffic to your website, and then find out what visitors are doing during their visits.

Which are the most popular web analytics tools? Here's the list I'd choose from:

- ClickTale (www.clicktale.com)

- Google Analytics (www.google.com/analytics/)

- Logaholic (www.logaholic.com)

- MetaTraffic (www.metasun.com)

- Mint (www.haveamint.com)

- Omniture (www.omnigure.com)

- Piwik (www.piwik.org)

- Unica (www.unica.com)

- VisiStat (www.visistat.com)

- WebTrends (www.webtrends.com)

- Woopra (www.woopra.com)

- Yahoo! Web Analytics (web.analytics.yahoo.com)

Interestingly, the most popular of these tools, such as Google Analytics, are free. Others are available on a paid subscription basis. But know that most of these tools track the same key metrics, so you might as well look around for the lowest-cost solution available.

Analyzing Search Engine Marketing Performance

As previously noted, most of the new traffic to your site will come from search engine results. As you're also aware, you can improve your search rankings by performing search engine optimization (SEO) on your site.

There are lots of ways to track the effectiveness of your SEO efforts, from monitoring site visitors to looking at your ranking at Google, Yahoo!, and Bing. Here are the ones I view as most important:

- **Visitors**—Our first key metric is one with which you should be quite familiar—the number of visitors, either on a site-wide or page-specific basis. To measure ongoing SEO success, you want to look at the number of visitors over time, not just those on a specific date. If you see that the number of visitors per day is increasing over time, you know you're doing something right.

- **Page views**—Page views matter to SEO for two reasons. First, you can see how the popularity of a page increases over time; an increasing number of page views means that you're doing something to attract more traffic to the page. Second, you can determine the relative popularity of pages on your site—that is, which are your site's most popular pages, as determined by their respective number of page views.

- **Landing pages**—Look at the most popular landing pages on your site, and try to determine why these pages attract so many visitors. Is it because they're searched for or because they're linked to? (You can use two of the other metrics—queries and inbound links, which we discuss in short order—to help answer this question.)

- **Referring sites**—Now let's turn our attention to how visitors get to your site—from search sites, referring sites, direct links, or other method. Next, take a look at which specific sites are driving the most traffic to your site. Chances are, Google, Yahoo!, and Bing will be among the top traffic drivers. Display this data in descending order, and make a note to pay special attention to the top-referring sites; it's also a good idea to find out why a lot of traffic is coming from a given site.

✉ Note

If your site shows a low percentage of traffic coming from search engines, don't assume that search engines aren't important. It's just as likely that your site is ranking low with the major search engines, and you need to further beef up your SEO efforts.

- **Keywords/queries**—For the portion of traffic coming from the search engines, you want to determine which keywords are generating the most traffic. Take a look at the list of queries or keywords generated by your analytical tool; this will tell you the most important keywords for your site. If this list matches your own internal keyword list, great. If not, you might want to either rethink which keywords are most important (based on the ranking of actual keyword queries) or rework your site's SEO to better emphasize your desired keywords.

- **Search engine ranking**—There's one more metric you want to analyze to determine the effectiveness of your SEO activities—raw search engine ranking. It makes sense, really; if you're optimizing your site to rank higher with the search engines, you need to find out whether your ranking actually is improving. A high ranking means more people will see and click through to your site; a low ranking means fewer visitors. It's really that simple.

DETERMINING YOUR RANK

That said, determining your site's search rank is anything but simple. That's because there isn't a single "search rank" metric. You need to determine where your site ranks when someone searches for each of the keywords you've deemed to be important. You end up with multiple ranking—one for each keyword you target.

To determine your search ranking at Google, Yahoo!, or Bing, you have to query the search site for the keyword in question, and then see where your site ranks. You really do have to manually query each search engine for each keyword you select—or use a tool that does the querying for you. That's a lot of work.

Analyzing Advertising Performance

After you start advertising online, it's time to start tracking your campaign's performance. That means looking at different types of raw data and then analyzing that data in various ways. You can learn from both your successes and your failures and use this information to create better-performing campaigns in the future.

When you're tracking the performance of your online ad campaign, what data should you be looking at? Here's a list of what I feel are the most important metrics for both PPC and display advertisers:

- **Impressions**—How many times was your ad displayed? That's the *impressions* metric, which is especially key for CPM display advertising; the more impressions, the more people who were exposed to your ad.

Note

Impressions are also important for PPC advertising. You need your ad to be displayed before it can be clicked; the more impressions you get for your ads, the more clicks you'll theoretically generate.

- **Clicks**—How many times was your ad clicked? That's the *clicks* metric, key to PPC advertising; the more clicks, the more traffic you have to your landing page. Of course, you can't get a lot of clicks if you don't start with a lot of impressions, so that's always job one. But a large number of impressions doesn't always result in a large number of clicks; if your ad isn't interesting or compelling, people won't be inspired to click it.

> " ...high CTR indicates that your ad is doing its job; a low CTR indicates that you need to retool your ad copy."

- **Click-through rate**—Raw clicks are important, but not necessarily the best measurement of an ad's effectiveness. A better measurement of ad effectiveness is the *click-through rate* (CTR). This metric measures the number of clicks as a percentage of the number of impressions. A high CTR indicates that your ad is doing its job; a low CTR indicates that you need to retool your ad copy.

 Note

CTR is totally independent of the number of impressions your ad receives. This enables advertisers on a budget to compare the effectiveness of their ads against big-budget competitors. If your ad has a high CTR, increasing your budget is sure to result in more absolute clicks—and more customer conversions.

- **Percent of clicks served**—When looking at the performance of individual ads within an online ad campaign, take a gander at the *percent of clicks served* metric. This data point tells you which ads in an ad group are getting the most displays; it divides the number of impressions for a given ad by the total number of impressions for all the ads in an ad group. Naturally, an ad with a higher percent of clicks served number is outperforming the other ads in the campaign; an ad with a lower number is underperforming the other ads.

- **Average position**—In what position was your ad displayed on a search engine's results pages? That's the *average position* for an ad; the higher an ad's position, the more clicks the ad will get and the more traffic that ad will drive to your landing page.
- **Cost**—How much have you paid in total for a given keyword, ad, or campaign? That's the *cost* metric—as in, this item costs you this much money over a specific time frame.

Note

Remember, your cost for an ad campaign will never exceed your specified budget. In fact, it most often will come in under your budget because you won't always be the high bidder on all the keywords you choose. Consider your daily budget as a max spend amount; your actual spending is reflected in the cost metric.

- **Conversions**—In web analytics, a *conversion* occurs when someone clicks your ad and then proceeds to do what you want them to do— make an inquiry, leave their contact information, or even make a purchase.

Note

Do not confuse the website conversion metric with the B2B notion of conversions, which has to do with turning a lead into a paying customer. You can register a conversion on your website (by getting the customers' contact info, for example) without necessarily having that visitor make a purchase.

- **Conversion rate**—This is the number of conversions divided by the number of clicks.
- **Cost per conversion**—This is how much each conversion cost you.

Analyzing Email Performance

Tracking the performance of an email marketing campaign is similar to tracking a traditional direct mail campaign, except more so. That is, when you're dealing with email, there are more metrics that you can directly track—which is a good thing.

With traditional email, about the only metrics you can track are leads generated or (if you're soliciting sales) revenues generated. Well, you can track both these metrics with email campaigns, too, along with a lot of other important data points. These email metrics include the following:

- **Delivery rate**—The *delivery rate* metric tells you precisely how many people received your emails. Because emails sometimes get sent to the wrong address, get bounced from full inboxes, or end up in spam filters, you need to know how many of them actually got to recipients as planned. Unfortunately, this metric is not easy to track; it's more estimated than measured.

✉ *Note*

Here's how to estimate delivery rate, based on the notion that most email experts believe that 20% or so of legitimate (non-spam) emails mistakenly get blocked as spam. So, calculate your bounce rate from a given mailing, add 20% to the number, and subtract the total from 100%. This gives you your approximate delivery rate for that mailing.

- **Open rate**—Next, you want to see how many recipients actually open your emails, versus how many ignore them or delete them without reading. The percent of messages opened is your *open rate*. To track this, you must insert a snippet of HTML code into your email message that tracks when an image in your email shows up in someone's inbox. The image doesn't get downloaded (from your website) and displayed (in the email message) until the recipient actually opens the email message. When the message is opened, the image is displayed, and your server tracks that action.

✉ *Note*

Because open rate tracks the display of an image, it doesn't track any text-only emails you send; it only works with HTML messages. It also doesn't track emails that are opened in email programs configured not to display HTML images.

- **Clicks**—*Clicks* (on links in your emails) are the easiest part of the process to track. You can track either total clicks or unique clicks. Unique clicks tell you how many recipients clicked on a link in the email; total clicks help you determine whether recipients click on multiple links, or respond more than once. As such, unique clicks are probably more useful to measure.

- **Click-through-rate**—After you know the number of clicks you receive, you can calculate the *click-through rate* (CTR). You can calculate CTR as clicks versus emails sent, clicks versus emails successfully delivered, or clicks versus emails opened. You can also calculate CTR using either unique or total clicks. Most marketers calculate unique clicks versus emails delivered, so if you're looking at benchmarks, use this approach.

- **Conversions**—Again, this is the web analytics type of *conversion*, not the typical B2B measurement of success. When it comes to email marketing, a conversion occurs when a recipient actually does something when he or she clicks through from the email to your website.

- **Conversion rate**—You calculate the *conversion rate* by dividing total conversions by the number of emails successfully delivered.

- **Cost per lead and cost per sale**—These metrics help you analyze how much money you're spending for each individual result, whether you're tracking leads generated or actual sales made.

- **Return on investment**—If you're emailing to generate purchases, you should calculate the *return on investment* (ROI) of your email campaign. You know how to calculate ROI—divide the profits generated by the money spent.

- **Unsubscribe rate**—There's one final email metric you probably want to track, and that's your total *unsubscribe rate*—the percentage of people who are removing their names from your list. If you have too high an unsubscribe rate, or a rate that's increasing, you have a problem somewhere that you need to address. Maybe you're sending out too many mailings, or maybe the mailings aren't targeted enough. Whatever the cause, let the unsubscribe rate alert you to potential problems.

Analyzing Blog Performance

Blog marketing is an important component of your online marketing plan. But how do you measure its effectiveness? After all, you have to measure both the performance of your company blog and the performance of your PR efforts toward other bloggers. That's a lot to track.

What you have to do is split your blog marketing into these two key areas, blogging and what is essentially online public relations. You can then measure the first component (your blog) using standard website analytics, and the second component (your influence on other bloggers) using analytics common to your other PC efforts.

Let's start by looking at how you track the performance of your company or product blog. Look at these traditional website metrics:

- **Page views**—Track this one over time to see whether your traffic is increasing or decreasing.
- **Unique visitors**—Same as with page views; helps you track traffic over time.
- **Session duration**—This tells you whether visitors are fully reading an article or getting turned off before they get to the end.
- **Traffic sources**—Use this metric to determine where your blog traffic is coming from—search engines (and if so, for which keywords), links from other blogs, and so forth.

What's slightly different about blog analytics, as compared to general web analytics, is that you want to track these metrics for each individual post on your blog, as well as for the blog itself. You then want to develop a matrix to compare these metrics between all the posts, so you can determine which posts are drawing the most traffic, keeping readers engaged, and the like.

The goal here is to determine which types of posts are getting the most reads—and then to write more of them. Identify which posts aren't getting read, and post fewer of them. Figure out what's working and why, and use that to fine-tune your blog content going forward.

Beyond basic web analytics, you also want to measure how engaged the readers of your blog are. This means finding out how many readers subscribe to your blog's feed, how many click through to links on your main website, and how many bother to leave comments on your articles. You're also interested in the comments, themselves, of course, which is a bit more subjective analysis.

All of this means you need to be looking at the following new metrics:

- **Feed subscriptions**—This is a simple and important number to track, and an important one. Readers who subscribe to your blog's feed obviously find it important enough to them to do so. The more subscribers you have, the more you're doing something right—something that's essential to those subscribers.
- **Inbound links**—You know you're doing something right when other blogs start linking to your posts. A post with a large number of

inbound links has a perceived level of authority that a less lined-to post does not. For this reason, you want to track inbound links—and do so for each of your posts individually.

- **Comments**—When you want to increase the interaction with your customer base, the best way to measure this is via the comments left on your blog posts. A post that has a large number of comments has obviously touched a nerve (positively or negatively) with your customers. They read the article and were involved enough to spend the time to leave their comments. That's a good thing. So, you should definitely measure the number of comments for each blog post—but don't stop there. These comments are an invaluable source of feedback from your most-interested comments, which means you need to read them and digest what your customers are saying. Ignore comments at your peril; they can help you not only fine-tune your blog posting, but also improve your business.

- **Click-throughs**—It's important to remember that your blog is a means to an end, and that end involves driving customers to your main website to make a purchase, request more information, or whatever. To that end, you need to track the number of click-throughs from the blog itself and from each blog post back to a page on your website. Track the sheer number of click-throughs, as well as which pages are clicked to. Which blog posts are driving the most business to your site—and which, although perhaps interesting, aren't helping your business that much? These are the questions you want to answer.

> "The point with these blog-specific metrics is to determine which posts are best engaging your readers, and thus driving the most traffic back to your main web pages."

The point with these blog-specific metrics is to determine which posts are best engaging your readers, and thus driving the most traffic back to your main web pages. That means comparing these metrics for each post on your blog, to determine which posts are working the best.

Then there's the matter of tracking how effective you are in getting other blogs to write about your company and your products. This is online PR tracking, and it will tell you not only how effective you are in gaining publicity, but also how effective other blogs and websites are in driving traffic back to your website. Look to the "Analyzing Online PR Performance" section, later in this chapter, to learn more.

Analyzing Social Media Performance

Social media is all about conversation, but how do you measure conversation? Obviously, there are subjective evaluations that can be made, which are discussed in the next chapter. But there are also some tried-and-true hard metrics that can at least measure how many conversations you're engaging in online—and, to some degree, the quality of those conversations.

What metrics are we talking about? Here's what to look for:

- **Page views and unique visitors coming from specific social media sites**—Okay, this is a bit of a combined metric. Most web analytics tools track page views and unique visitors, as well as traffic sources. What you need to do is correlate the data so that you know how much traffic to your website is being driven by each of the major social media—Facebook, Twitter, LinkedIn, and so on.

- **Subscribers, fans, and followers**—These are metrics that come directly from the individual social media sites. You can track how many subscribers you have to your Twitter feed, how many fans you have of your Facebook page, and so forth.

- **Shares and bookmarks**—If you're doing social bookmark marketing, with services such as Digg and StumbleUpon, you need to track how many "likes" you receive, how many times your site is bookmarked, and how often your content is shared.

> ✉ *Note*
>
> Many of these social marketing metrics are site-specific. That is, you measure how many fans or likes you get on Facebook, how many times you're bookmarked on Delicious, and so forth. You can then compare and contrast the eyeballs you're receiving from each of these social media and determine which are performing best for you.

Analyzing Podcast Performance

Tracking the performance of your company podcasts is a two-fold process. You should track the individual downloads of each podcast episode, as well as the overall number of subscriptions you get for the podcast feed. Here's what to look for:

- **Subscriptions**—Not only do you want to track the total number of subscribers, you also want to track *where* they're subscribing—on your site, on iTunes, or wherever. This will tell you which sites were the best sources for new subscribers.

- **Downloads**—You should also track the performance of individual podcast episodes. Episodes downloaded from your website can be easily tracked as part of your normal web analytics efforts.

- **Call to action**—Assuming that your podcast includes some sort of *call to action*—the mention of your company website or toll-free phone number, a link to a product page, or the like—you can and should track that call to action. That means trying to track traffic to your website, or to a particular page on your site, generated from the podcast.

Analyzing Online Video Performance

What makes for a successful online video? There's a lot you can track, including the following:

- **Views**—This is literally how many times your video was viewed. More is obviously better—although it doesn't tell you whether viewers stayed to watch the whole thing.

Note

In my mind, raw views is a false measurement. Just because your video has a lot of viewers doesn't mean it has accomplished the goals you set out to achieve. A video with 100,000 views is nice, but it means nothing if you wanted to capture some solid business leads and it didn't do that. Entertaining YouTube viewers is one thing; generating leads or establishing brand image is quite another.

- **Discovery**—This is a YouTube-specific metric that tells you how viewers found your video—linked from other videos, searched for on the YouTube site (and with what keywords), external links, and the like.

- **Audience Retention**—This is another YouTube-specific metric, which analyzes how popular your video is over the course of the video—that is, at what point(s) viewers lose interest while watching.

- **Conversions**—How many viewers linked from your video to your website (or called your 800 number) and then did whatever it was you asked them to do? This is important in all forms of digital marketing, videos included.

Analyzing Interactive Marketing Performance

When we say *interactive marketing*, we really talking webinars and other web-based conferences. There's not a lot to track here, but it's all important:

- **Attendees**—Naturally, you should track how many people attended your webinar "live." (If you charged for admission, you can also track that.) Equally important, track the quality of the attendees—what position they hold, what company they represent, and so on. A smaller number of high-quality prospects is probably better than a larger number of low-quality attendees.

- **Downloads**—If you offer your webinars for later download, track the number of downloads.

- **Conversions**—If you want attendees to do something after the webinar, track that.

Analyzing Online PR Performance

One of the more useful aspects of online PR, as compared to the traditional type, is that you actually measure the success of your efforts. I'm not just talking about seeing how many blogs you pop up on, although that is an important measurement. Online, you can track how many people thought enough of your placement to click through to your website and get more information or buy something.

What metrics should you use to judge the success of your online PR efforts? Here's the list:

- **Placements**—This is an old school measurement, tracking how many outlets picked up your press release and mentioned your company or product.

✉ *Note*

How do you know how many placements you've received online? Although some traditional clipping services purport to measure online placements, I don't really trust their results. You're better off searching Google, Yahoo!, and Bing for mentions of your company or product, perhaps keying off a keyword or phrase in a particular press release. If you want to get fancy, set up a Google alert for a particular search phrase, so you'll be notified when a new placement appears online.

- **Rankings with the major search engines**—Your press releases, if well written and well optimized, should pop up in the search results when someone queries the relevant topic. The higher you appear in the results, the more visible—and more effective—the press release.

- **Page views and unique visitors**—What you're really interested here is traffic from referring websites and blogs. That should include traffic coming from your archived press release, hosted either on your site or with a service such as PRWeb, back to your main site. An effective press release will generate more traffic. It's as simple as that.

✉ *Note*

Smart marketers put tracking links in their press releases that link to unique landing pages on their site. That way there's no confusion over someone stumbling over that page by accident; visitors to that page are a result of your PR efforts only.

- **Time on site**—Generating more traffic is great, but not so if people quickly lose interest and vamoose. An effective placement directs visitors to a targeted landing page and keeps them there long enough to register an impression—or generate an action.

- **Conversions**—Speaking of actions, just what is it you want these visitors to do—get more information, leave their contact info, buy something, or what? Whatever it is, you need to track it. Find out how many conversions are coming from the referring sites where you've placed your press release or received a sympathetic mention. That's the true measure of your PR campaign's effectiveness.

Analyzing Mobile Marketing Performance

Tracking the performance of your mobile marketing efforts means paying attention to many of the same metrics as you use for the rest of your digital marketing plan, with a few new metrics thrown in for good measure.

When it comes to tracking the performance of your mobile website, you want to track all the expected website metrics—unique visitors, page views, time on site, and the like. You can also track location (if you're interested in where your site visitors are, geographically) as well as the mobile carriers and devices used by visitors. That last metric can help you fine-tune your site for the most popular mobile devices used by your customers.

Analyzing Performance by Buying Stage

So, now you know the technical analytics you can measure for each digital market-ing vehicle. But how do you judge how successful each vehicle is in regards to the goals you have for each stage of the B2B buying continuum?

Analyzing Reach

How do you know when you've reached a new prospect? It's all a matter of *impres-sions*—how many instances or how much face time you get in front of potential customers.

 Note

When measuring reach, you want to try to isolate your exposure only to potential customers. Reaching a broader audience (a consumer audience, for example) doesn't really matter if they won't ever become a customer for your business.

To that end, you want to pay attention to the following marketing vehicles and metrics:

- **Website**—Unique visitors and page views. You'll also want to track referring sites, so you know how customers are finding your site.
- **Search engines**—Search engine ranking. You'll also want to track which keywords are generating the most traffic back to your site, so you know what potential customers are searching for.
- **Advertising**—Impressions, clicks, and click-through rate.
- **Email**—Delivery rate, open rate, clicks, and click-through rate.
- **Blog**—Unique visitors and page views.
- **Social media**—Page views and unique visitors coming to your site from specific social media.
- **Podcasts**—Downloads.
- **Videos**—Views.
- **Webinars**—Attendees.
- **Online PR**—Placements, page views, and unique visitors (resulting from placements).

Remember, reach isn't really about anyone doing anything, just the amount of exposure you generate for your company, products, and services to potential customers. You can achieve all the reach and the world and not generate a single sale; but you can't generate any leads or sales if you don't have any reach.

Analyzing Acquisition

Customer acquisition is all about convincing someone who sees your ad or search engine listing or whatever to contact you for more information. That is, you want to generate a solid *lead* that you can then follow up with, in whatever fashion.

The easiest way to measure acquisition is to simply count the leads you generate. You can then, in many cases, associate a given lead with the vehicle(s) that lead to that contact. This can be done by physically asking that question, or by automatically tracking the number of prospects who enter their contact information on your website. This will tell you how successful each marketing vehicle was in generating leads.

DEFINING A LEAD

Believe it or not, but not every B2B company defines a lead in the same way. How do you know when you've really acquired a potential customer?

One common definition of a lead is that it's a prospect that has the interest and authority to make a purchase from you. That's different from just a contact, which is nothing more than a person's name or email address. Without more qualifying information, you have no idea whether that contact has the interest or authority to make a purchase. In other words, whereas all leads have contact information, not all contacts are actually leads.

Technically, then, just having a visitor to your website fill in their contact information doesn't necessarily count as acquiring a lead. You'll need to either ask for additional information (company, position, purchasing authority, and so forth) or follow up personally to qualify the lead.

In other words, just because an individual inquires about your products or services doesn't make him a solid lead. That makes measuring acquisition a little more difficult—or you can just assume that all inquiries lead to leads.

Analyzing Conversion

Conversion is the easiest metric to track; it's sales, pure and simple. In this instance, however, you're tracking initial sales from first-time customers.

Now, there are several ways to track conversion. You can track:

- Number of new companies who become customers
- Number of individual locations within companies that become new customers
- Number of individual items ordered, or orders generated, by new customers
- Dollar value of new orders from new customers

You probably already know how you track conversions in your company. You can then tie these conversions to specific marketing vehicles that drive specific initial purchases.

Analyzing Retention

Retention is a lot more difficult to measure. How active does an existing customer have to be to count as being retained? Is a customer that merely receives your mailings and emails a retained customer, or does that customer have to order something within a set period of time to count?

Again, it's likely that your company already has its own metrics in place to measure customer retention. To those, however, you can add a number of new metrics that measure customer interaction—the presumption being that a customer who interacts with you online has been retained.

What metrics should you use? Here's my list:

- **Email**—Subscriptions, clicks, and click-through-rate. You should also track your unsubscribe rate; a customer who unsubscribes from your emails may be lost.
- **Blog**—Feed subscriptions and comments. It's a matter of seeing how many customers follow your blog on a regular basis, as well as how many offer their own comments.
- **Social media**—Subscribers/fans, shares/bookmarks, and comments. Again, you want to measure both the number of followers you have and how much they interact with you.
- **Podcasts**—Subscriptions.
- **Webcasts**—Attendees (from within your customer base).

Analyzing Loyalty

For our purposes, a loyal customer is one who recommends your company to someone else—who can then become a potential lead or customer. Unfortunately, loyalty is difficult to measure.

One approach is to try to track this the old-fashioned way, by asking new leads or customers where they first heard of you; if the source is another company or person, that's a measure of loyalty. But you can also look for customers using social media who "like" or recommend your page or feed; that's a form of recommendation. For that matter, you can look at new subscribers and see if you and they have any mutual friends; that's a sign that the other party recommended you.

The Bottom Line

When it comes to measuring the success of your digital marketing efforts, there are a lot of things you can track. Website, SEO, and blog performance can be tracked by looking at unique visitors and page views; ad performance can be tracked by measuring impressions and clicks; email performance can be tracked by measuring delivery rate, open rate, and clicks; social media performance can be tracked by measuring subscribers and followers, as well as website traffic generated from social media; podcast performance can be measured by counting subscriptions and downloads; video performance can be measured by tracking views; webinar performance can be measured by counting attendees; and PR performance can be tracked through placements and website traffic generated. These are all quantitative metrics that can be compared to each other, to past performance, and to industry standards.

19

Qualifying Results

Not all digital marketing activities can be quantitatively analyzed. Some activities, especially those in the social media realm, yield more qualitative results. With these activities, numbers (if indeed numbers do exist) do not tell the whole story; it's more about how the marketing activity enhances customer relationships.

How can one qualitatively judge the performance of these select digital marketing activities? It's all about evaluating customer engagement.

Analyzing Social Media

In the previous chapter, we learned how to quantitatively measure the performance of your digital marketing activities. There's a lot of things you can count, and they all count.

Social media, however, is a bit of a different beast. Yes, it's fair to examine numerical metrics, such as how many Twitter followers and Facebook fans you have; you need to count the number of customer you engage with.

That said, measuring how many people you engage with via social media is just part of the equation. You also need to measure the *quality* of that engagement.

Here's the thing. Not all followers of your Twitter feed are going to read every tweet. Not all visitors who "like" your Facebook page are going to actively engage in conversations. Not all conversations are going to result in new leads or repeat sales.

This is why social media is somewhat difficult for numbers-oriented marketers and management to get their heads around. Because of the way social media works, you might determine that a site that registers fewer fans is actually more important to you, and that may be difficult to explain.

What matters with social media is the quality of your interaction with customers. That's not something you can measure with numbers. It's engagement over eyeballs, pure and simple.

That said, you need to come up with some way to track this customer engagement, even if it's purely subjective. This is your opportunity to get a little creative; you have to find some way to describe and measure a positive interaction as opposed to a negative one. It can be done, as long as you're comfortable with the wiggly nature of soft metrics.

> "That said, you need to come up with some way to track this customer engagement, even if it's purely subjective...it can be done, as long as you're comfortable with the wiggly nature of soft metrics.

That's just the way it is with social media; like social marketing itself, performance is open to discussion. Although the big bosses might not like this immeasurable facet of your marketing program, it's something you have to get used to. There really is no hard and fast way to measure the quality of a conversation, after all. It's a form of word-of-mouth marketing, and that is inherently immeasurable.

✉ *Note*

Some forms of social media—in particular, social bookmarks and shares—don't necessarily result in strong engagement with visitors. When someone bookmarks or shares your site with others, people checking out that bookmark (by clicking to your site) don't necessarily know what to expect. You're going to get a lot of "lookers," more than you would normally get, which results in lower time onsite numbers and a higher bounce rate. Yes, your traffic will go up, but these aren't necessarily qualified visitors. Some of them will turn into qualified leads, but certainly not all.

MEASURING ENGAGEMENT—BY THE NUMBERS

This chapter is all about qualitative analysis, but numbers still enter into it. After all, you can't have quality conversations unless you have some conversations with your customers. Quality has to be built on quantity.

For this reason, the first means of measuring social engagement is to simply count eyeballs—which we do by monitoring the number of unique visitors and page views on your website that come from specific social media. This at least tells you whether people who read your tweets or your Facebook page are inspired to follow through by visiting your website.

Next, look at the time onsite and page views per visit metrics. The longer a potential customer spends on your site, the more engaged he is—and the deeper the relationship you're building.

Bounce rates are also important, for just the opposite reason. People who leave your site quickly are most definitely *not* engaged—which means there's something about your site that doesn't build on what people first experienced on your Facebook page or Twitter feed. There's something wrong somewhere.

Analyzing Engagement

Social media is all about customer engagement. It's this engagement that helps to retain a customer, and to encourage the type of loyalty that results in referrals and recommendations.

The problem is, how do you measure this customer engagement—especially in the B2B environment, with its long sales cycles? It's a somewhat subjective analysis—although some objective metrics exist.

Forrester Research has proposed that customer engagement be defined as the level of involvement, interaction, intimacy, and influence that an individual or company has with a brand over time.[1] If we accept this definition, we have four components that we can analyze:

- **Involvement**, or customer presence at various "touch points." This is the most numeric metric here; you're measuring things such as page views, number of comments, and the like.

- **Interaction**, which measures discrete actions performed by the customer. This can include "liking" your Facebook page, rating a product, and the like.

- **Intimacy**, which has more to do with the content posted by a customer—positive versus negative blogs posts or reviews, and such. This metric is often tied into *sentiment analysis*, which we'll discuss in a moment.

- **Influence**, which is the likelihood of a customer to advocate on your behalf. This metric is the closest we have to measuring loyalty, or the intent to recommend or refer.

The goal here is to analyze each of these components to determine your customers' real feelings about your company and brand. It moves from the broadest possible numeric measurement down to the most subjective or qualitative measurement of what a customer is really thinking.

Table 19.1 details the four components, and what you want to track for each.

Table 19.1 Tracking the Four Components of Engagement

Involvement	Interaction	Intimacy	Influence
Page views	Comments on blog posts	What customers are saying on third-party sites	Product/service satisfaction ratings
Time on site	Contributions to forum discussions	What customers are saying in social media	Brand affinity
Pages viewed	Product reviews		Content shared with friends/colleagues
Search keywords		Opinions expressed in customer service calls	Original posts on third-party blogs
Navigation paths			Net Promoter score

---

1. Forrester Research, "What Engagement Means for Media Companies," 2009

NET PROMOTER SCORE

The Net Promoter Score (NPS) is a tool used to gauge the loyalty of customer relationships. It divides customers into three categories, based on a 10-point scale:

- **Promoters** (score 9–10). These are your most loyal and enthusiastic customers, most likely to refer others.

- **Passives** (score 7–8). These are satisfied but unenthusiastic customers. Not only do they not actively recommend your company, they're especially vulnerable to competitive offers.

- **Detractors** (score 0–6). These are generally unhappy customers. If they make their opinion known (more likely for those with the lowest scores), they can damage your brand via negative word of mouth.

The NPS is defined by asking the question, "How likely is it that you would recommend our company to a friend or colleague?" It was introduced by business strategist Fred Reichbeld in a 2003 article in the *Harvard Business Review*, and since widely adopted by marketers. Learn more at www.netpromoter.com.

Analyzing Comments

Social media can be a good indicator of engagement. Start by looking at how many comments you receive on the posts you make. Measure the number of comments you receive on each Facebook status update and Twitter tweet; measure the posts to your LinkedIn group and comments on your blog posts; for that matter, count the number of comments left on your YouTube videos. Obviously, the more comments you receive, the more you're engaging your audience.

Conversely, those posts or tweets that don't inspire a lot of comments aren't that engaging; posts that result in tons of comments are a better draw. By measuring comments on a per-post basis, you can determine which topics are more interesting to your customer base, and fine-tune your posting going forward.

"Not all posts with lots of comments are good for you...if the negative comments outweigh the positive ones, you've done yourself more harm than good.

Note

Not all posts with lots of comments are good for you. Some controversial posts will generate a lot of responses, but if the negative comments outweigh the positive ones, you've done yourself more harm than good.

Analyzing comments, however, is more than a simple numbers game; social media, by definition, is somewhat subjective. Questions abound: How can you measure the effectiveness of one conversation versus another? How can you value a tweet versus a Digg? Is a Facebook comment more or less valuable than one on Google+?

The best conversations draw customers closer to your company and your products. You get the feeling that these people have a vested interest in what you're doing, and that they want to share in your success. These are in-depth conversations about your products and services, their features and functions, how they work, what people use them for, and what people would like to see in the future.

Less useful are conversations that amount to online bitch sessions, customers just complaining about this or that thing or another. That's not the same as customers asking for help or advice; those conversations can actually prove useful, especially when you provide helpful solutions. No, I'm talking about people who use your online forums to vent about how much they hate your company and your products. That's not a quality conversation.

Also of lesser quality are those conversations that are nothing but gossip. What's the CEO up to this week? Who's sleeping with whom? Do you think the stock price will go or down next quarter? Gossip isn't a positive conversation; it's wasted time.

Another type of negative conversation is the one that goes unanswered. A customer asks a question, publicly, and you don't reply. That's not a conversation, that's a wasted opportunity. Don't let that happen too often.

Instead, use each and every comment as an opportunity to more fully engage both the customer who started the conversation and others who might be reading—or waiting to add their two cents' worth. A company skilled in social marketing can turn any comment into a quality engagement with the customer base. It just takes a little imagination—and the willingness to engage.

Take, for example, a typical comment along the lines of "We love your new product." Okay, not a very meaningful comment, but still something you can work with. Instead of not replying at all, or posting something like "Thanks," turn this into a learning experience. Reply with a question, like "Thank you. What is it you like best?" or "How does it help you get your job done?" or some such. Don't let the customer get away too fast; pull him into what could become a far-reaching conversation.

Likewise with negative comments. When you get a comment along the lines of "This thing is horrible," try to respond in a way that elicits more information, addresses the customer's issue, and hopefully turns around a bad situation. Instead of ignoring the complaint, respond with "I understand your dissatisfaction. What specific problems are you having?" More often than not, you can actually solve the problem (which probably isn't a real problem, just a misunderstanding or misoperation) and make lemonade out of the proverbial lemons. Don't let negative comments lie; respond to them and try to turn the negative into a positive.

The key is to use social conversations to more fully engage your existing and potential customers. To this end, expanding your reach to new audiences is paramount. Now, this probably won't happen directly on a Facebook page or in a Twitter feed, but can happen when your followers share their comments with their friends and colleagues. It's this sharing nature of social media that exposes your company and products to new faces. When one of your customers shares your post or tweet with a dozen or so of his online friends, that's a dozen new impressions you're making, and a dozen new potential leads.

MAKING ENGAGING POSTS

To foster customer engagement in social media, you have to start things rolling by making your posts engaging. That is, at least some of your posts should be of a general enough nature that your online followers will want to share them. Posting about the detailed construction of your latest widget probably won't do it, even though hard-core followers might get all drooly about it. Instead, you need some posts that reach out in a more general fashion that readers who are not yet customers might find interesting.

When you make these general posts, make sure you include some sort of call to action, even if it's just a link back to a product page on your website. Saying "Isn't this new product really neat?" doesn't go far enough; you have to say "Go to our website to learn more" or "Tell us what you think." The former approach is a call to action that drives new visitors to your site; the latter encourages conversation on the social network.

Analyzing Sentiment

Engagement goes beyond what customers are saying in a literal sense to what they actually feel. To this end, the third component of customer engagement, intimacy, attempts to analyze what exactly customers mean in the content they post. It doesn't measure how many comments are made or reiterate the comments themselves, but rather analyzes the sentiment behind the comments.

This brings us to a relatively new metric, dubbed *sentiment analysis*. This involves parsing and analyzing the comments that customers and others post online, typically via social media. It's not just reading the comments verbatim; the emphasis is on the context, tone, emotion, and objectivity of the comments.

Although sentiment analysis is still in its infancy, the thinking behind the technique is sound. You want to measure not just what people are saying, but how and why they're saying it.

ANALYZING THE ENTIRE PROCESS

Social media should not be analyzed in a vacuum. In most instances, it's a combination of media that leads to the ultimate sale—not just one medium alone.

Rather than measuring social media in isolation, a better practice is to follow the path a new customer takes from initial contact to lead qualification to the first purchase, looking at all the touches that occurred along the road to the sale. If you are recording the touches as best you can (knowing that not everything can or will be measured), you will see the blend of media and their sequence—as well as their relative importance in the process.

The Bottom Line

Customer engagement is difficult to measure; it's qualitative, not quantitative, and rather subjective. That said, there is some quantitative analysis to be made, primarily by measuring the number of customers who "like" or comment on your social media. More qualitative analysis focuses on the content of those comments, which can indicate just how strong a bond customers have with your company and brand.

20

Looking Forward

If you've read this far in the book, you've learned all about the various components of B2B digital marketing, how to implement them for various results, and how to measure those results—as well as you can, in any case. But your job isn't done yet.

Results in hand, you need to judge how successful you've been, and decide what elements of your plan may need to be modified. You also need to look forward to other changes that may be on the horizon, and adjust your plan accordingly.

The work never stops, does it?

Evaluating—and Modifying—Your B2B Digital Marketing Strategy

Successful marketing is all about learning and adjusting. You learn what works and what doesn't, and then adjust what you're doing accordingly. You never, ever proceed on a course of action just because that's what you'd said you'd do; you need to shift course when necessary.

Evaluating Results

In the previous two chapters, we talked about ways to quantitatively and qualitative analyze the performance of various digital marketing initiatives. It's imperative that you examine this performance quickly and frequently; you need to know, as soon as you can, what's working and what's not, so that you can readjust your plans accordingly. Is your email marketing campaign paying off? Are you getting the results you want from your company blog? Are you generating a sufficient number of quality leads from your online advertising? And how many customers are you engaging on Twitter and Facebook?

It gets even more complex. You need to track not only the raw results of individual activities, you have to track results against expectations and results against expenditures. You need to know what activities are giving you the most bang for the buck.

In addition to tracking results individually, you need to compare the results of all your activities against one another. That is, you need to develop a sense of which activities are both most important and most effective. Is social marketing more or less important to you than email marketing? Does online advertising generate more leads than search engine marketing? Understanding the relative importance of each activity will help you adjust your marketing mix going forward.

For that matter, you need to examine specific combinations of tactics. You might find, for example, that telemarketing followed by email contact is the best approach to generate leads, or that PPC advertising followed by phone calls works best for you. You need to have a sense of the flow of the process.

You also need to balance short-term versus long-term results. As much as management might like to think, marketing is not all about short-term results; you need to invest in the future of your digital marketing program. There no doubt will be some newer activities that aren't paying off big just yet, but hold immense promise for the future. You have to plant the seeds of your future success, and that means nurturing those seeds that have yet to fully bloom. When it comes to embracing new technologies and activities, you need to be patient and persevere—and give the new kids a bit of a break, budget-wise.

Adjusting Your Budget

Evaluating the various components of your marketing plan also affects your budgeting. To that end, I recommend viewing your digital marketing budget in a somewhat holistic manner.

You see, in the old days, you had a handful of different line items and you managed them separately. That's not the case anymore; because everything you do online (and off) is interconnected, so must be the items in your marketing budget.

And there are a lot of items. Digital B2B marketing has more components than does traditional B2B marketing; it's not just advertising, telemarketing, direct mail, and trade shows anymore. You now have budget items for PPC advertising, online display advertising, SEO, email marketing, blog marketing, social media marketing (and perhaps several line items under this one, for Facebook, Twitter, and so forth), video marketing, podcasts, mobile marketing, and, of course, online PR. That's a lot to keep track of.

What's even more challenging is that each of these items relates to each other item. You can't segregate the items in your digital marketing budget; one line item affects another. Hence the holistic thinking.

In addition, you need to view your digital marketing budget as somewhat fluid. As you move throughout the budget period, you might find that social media is becoming more important and email less so, or maybe that your online advertising isn't working as well as your blog marketing. You need to be able to quickly shift marketing dollars from one activity to another so that you can rapidly react to new opportunities. You just can't focus myopically on the individual line items in your budget; the lines have to blur and shift.

✉ *Note*

In addition to budgeting money, you also need to budget your time. Some digital marketing activities are relatively low cost but time intensive. You simply may not have the time to do everything you'd like to do, so make sure your analysis takes into account both financial and time constraints.

This creates a bit of a management challenge, of course—especially in managing your managers, or at least those who monitor your budget. It might be difficult to convince the bean counters why it's not that important to hold the email marketing line to its assigned numbers when there's more opportunity in social marketing, for example, but it's something you have to do. You have to force management to focus on the big number, not on all the little ones.

Adjusting Your Plan

This last point brings us to the topic of change, of which there is a lot in digital marketing. What was hot just three years ago is cooling down today; what seems cutting-edge today might be old hat three years from now.

> "You have to force management to focus on the big number, not on all the little ones."

Consider the world of digital marketing five years ago. Nobody was talking about video marketing or social marketing; the staples of most marketing plans were search engine marketing and PPC advertising, and email marketing was the big new thing.

Today, we still have PPC advertising and SEO, and email marketing has become a tried and true tool. But the latest big things are Facebook, Twitter, and YouTube, with mobile marketing rising large on the horizon. It's a totally different mix, even if most of the old components remain.

What this means in terms of marketing management is that you need to keep on top of all developments, no matter how unimportant they might seem at the time. Unless you want your competition to get the jump on you (or your customers to abandon you), you need to be first out of the block in experimenting with new media and channels. You need to be fast and first, and not shy about experimenting—and sometimes failing.

To do this, you personally need to be engaged with and immersed in developing online communities and technologies. You don't want to read about something new in the trade papers (or trade websites); you want to experience it firsthand. You have to be part of it to know what it's all about.

This argues, of course, for that fluidity we discussed in regard to budget management. Not only do you need to be able to shift your budget around to exploit new technologies and channels, you probably need to set aside a portion of your budget just for this eventuality. Carving out a piece of your budget (10% or so) for "new activities" just makes sense.

It's all about change, and managing change. The world around you is constantly changing, and you can't ignore that fact; the better you can react to and exploit that change, the more successful you and your company will be.

CHASING TRENDS

Digital marketing is important and getting more so, but it isn't the entire world. There's no aspect of digital marketing that exists in and onto itself; it's all there to serve your company and your customer. "I market, therefore I am" should not be part of your marketing philosophy.

To that end, you should never let yourself be taken in by the hype. (And in digital marketing, there's a lot of hype.) It's easy, I know, to be seduced by the latest technology or approach or whatever; you won't be the first marketer to get all hot and bothered by what's hot this week in digital marketing, whether that's social media or YouTube or whatever, and convince yourself that it's something you need to do now—and in a big way.

If you let yourself be guided by these impulses, you'll end up doing a lot of stupid things you'll regret later, and (even worse) scattering your efforts across too many fronts. Instead, you need to remain calm, cool, and collected, and relatively unswayed by the allure of the new. Keep focused on your overall plan, while still addressing new developments. Don't let yourself be diverted by all the shiny new things; experiment judiciously, not foolheartedly.

What you don't want to do is have a digital marketing strategy du jour. Yes, it's important to remain flexible and embrace important new developments, but your overall goals and strategy should remain relatively constant. Fit the new developments into your existing strategy; don't warp your strategy to embrace everything new that comes along. Consistency, a big picture viewpoint, and long-term thinking are key. With a steady hand at the oar, small course corrections are easy to make when market changes warrant.

Looking to the Future

Speaking of change, it's no secret that the Internet in general and digital marketing in particular are constantly evolving, and new ways to communicate and promote are always emerging. It's not enough to get good at the B2B promotional opportunities available today; you also have to keep on top of those opportunities that will develop in the future.

What's next, then, for B2B marketing? Let's look at some of the more important trends.

Email Is Fading

This is a tough one to accept, especially when so many B2B companies depend so much on email marketing. But the signs are clear: email is a fading medium.

When I'm trying to stay on top of technological trends, I just watch what the young folks are doing. Watch college students, watch high-schoolers, and observe what technologies they're using (and how), as well as those they're not. Within a few years, you'll see their behavior migrating into the general population.

College students, after all, were the first to embrace social networking; Facebook was created as a community for students, not for the general public or businesses. The same thing is true of email and instant messaging and with the public Internet in general. The kids do it first, and then the rest of us follow.

That said, I definitely notice how my own step kids are using the Internet. And what I see today is that they're not communicating online in the same way that we're used to. Specifically, they're not using email. They're instant messaging and (on their phones) text messaging, they're tweeting and Facebooking, but today's youth seldom bother to check their email inboxes. It's not something they use on a regular basis.

Why is this? I think it's the immediacy, or lack of. Kids have gotten used to immediate gratification, and I really mean immediate. Instant messaging and text messaging are done in real time; email isn't. The (slightly) older generation might think that email is fast, at least when compared to postal mail, but youngsters think it takes way, way too long. They don't have the time or the patience to wait for a response, so they quit using it.

There's also the long-form nature of email. Again, older users might consider email to be a condensed version of traditional paper letters, but you're still talking sentences and paragraphs. To today's youth, a sentence is about as long as they can handle; writing or reading a paragraph is simply out of the question. It might be the attention span thing again, or maybe writing and reading skills have dramatically declined. Whatever the case, kids today don't like to read much, and they certainly don't like to write anything that's too involved.

> "This decreasing importance of email as a means of communication means that email marketing is likely to be less important going forward than it is today."

This decreasing importance of email as a means of communication means that email marketing is likely to be less important going forward than it is today. Now, it's going to take a while, especially in the business environment where email is the primary means of both internal and external communication. But progress is inexorable; youth will have its way, and their usage patterns will infiltrate even the largest organizations. I'm not saying you should dump your email marketing program this instant, but you should be evaluating other ways to contact the younger buyers on your customer list.

Blogs Are Fading

When you're evaluating that whole long-form versus short-form thing, you have to consider what this means for the future of blogging. Back in the day (meaning two or three years ago), everybody and their brother had a personal blog. Not so today. Most people found that they didn't have the dedication to write regular blog posts, so they just dropped it. There are a lot of abandoned blogs out there now.

That doesn't mean that people aren't posting their innermost thoughts online anymore. They are. They're just doing it in shorter tweets and Facebook status updates. Let's face it; social networks have made it much easier for folks to share their personal diaries online. There's a lot less effort involved to make a post to Facebook than there is to create and maintain a blog. If nothing else, you don't have to write as much—and people definitely don't like to write as much as they used to.

We're seeing a similar trend in the universe of company blogs. Not necessarily that these blogs are going away, but that they're being supplemented—if not totally supplanted—by social media. Certainly, a blog affords the luxury of relatively long and informative posts, but users today don't necessarily seek out or embrace such content. Shifting your efforts, however slightly, from your blog to Facebook or Twitter may be in order.

Social Networking Is Taking Over

To that last point, social media is hot and getting hotter, even in the business environment. I know, most B2B companies have been a little reluctant to jump into the social media waters, but that's where things are going.

Social media are the darling of B2C marketers today, and for good reason; it's where their customers are. More and more people of all ages and income levels are using Facebook, Google+, Twitter, and the like; the phenomenon that started with younger users has migrated into the general population and shows no sign of abating.

> "Social media are the darling of B2C marketers today, and for good reason; it's where their customers are."

History shows that where B2C goes, B2B follows—eventually. Certainly, more and more individuals within companies are using social media to network with others and find useful information. This is spilling into purchasing decisions; social media are, more and more, influencing the influencers within companies.

Ignore social media at your peril. Although all growth slows, I don't expect a major slowdown anytime soon in the social media world. This means a continuing opportunity for B2B marketers.

It also means more competition as more and more B2B marketers jump on the social networking bandwagon. If you were on Facebook in the early days, you might have had your category pretty much to yourself. That won't be the case going forward. You have to prepare for increased competition for buyer eyeballs across all major social media, which argues for more aggressive and creative marketing. The social media business base will continue to grow, but it's going to be more difficult to make your presence known.

Mobility Matters

The migration to the mobile Internet has been a subtext throughout this book. As I've mentioned several times previously, more and more people are using their mobile phones to connect to the Internet and do web-related tasks—and we have to adapt to that reality.

The move to mobile connectivity offers two-fold opportunities. The first, and the most obvious, is the simple displacement of existing activities from the computer to the mobile phone. That is, instead of checking email or surfing the Web on a desktop or laptop computer, your customers are doing these things on their phones, instead. This argues for making your website and blog and all other web-related activities mobile-friendly—and for optimizing your site and blog for mobile search.

The second opportunity concerns those activities that are new and unique to mobile browsing. The important question is, in what different ways are people using their mobile phones than they did their computers? Answer this question, and you'll discover new promotional opportunities.

One such new opportunity concerns timing, or rather availability. Even if a buyer uses a mobile phone to do nothing more than what she did on a computer, she has her phone with her all the time. You never lose her; you have nonstop connectivity to this person, wherever and whenever she goes. That's a 24/7 opportunity to exploit.

There's also the localized opportunity, if that's important to your business. Because you can target your mobile marketing by the user's location, you can provide more contextually relevant information. That should help you better target your marketing activities and achieve better results for doing so.

Bottom line, the B2B market is becoming more mobile; this is a large and growing trend. You need to adapt your digital marketing strategy accordingly.

The Bottom Line

Here's the ultimate bottom line, for this chapter and for the entire book: Everything changes. Traditional media didn't always used to be traditional; at one point in time, newspapers were the big thing, radio was brand-spanking new, and television was something only dreamed of. Today, all those media are old, and what's new is happening on the Internet.

But the Internet itself is constantly changing. What was hot five or ten years ago is much cooler today; today's big things will also cool as even newer ways of doing things evolve. As a B2B marketing professional, you need to keep on top of everything that's changing, not necessarily to jump wholeheartedly on an unproven bandwagon, but to become aware of those developments that might change the way you reach your customers—and the way they reach you.

So, whether it's the move from email and blogging to social networking, or the move from desktop computing to the mobile Internet, you need to be on top of it, constantly analyzing how it may affect your business. That doesn't mean abandoning everything that's more than a few years old, or letting your traditional marketing skills wither and die. It simply means that you need to keep on top of developing trends, keep your skillset fresh, and be prepared to adapt your plans as necessary.

What's key is that you follow your customer base as it moves to new media. You don't necessarily want to get too far ahead of what your customers are using—there's no point broadcasting to a nonexistent audience, after all—but you do need to be there when customers shift the way they gather information. If your B2B customers are embracing social media, you need to embrace social media; if they're going mobile, you need to go mobile, too. You need to stay on top of the trends so that you can walk hand-in-hand with your customer base into the new frontier.

It's an ever-changing world out there, and you're part of it. Get used to it, and learn to embrace change. That's how you'll stay successful in this B2B marketing business—and in life, in general.

Index

que®

Biz-Tech Series

Straightforward Strategies and Tactics for Business Today

The **Que Biz-Tech series** is designed for the legions of executives and marketers out there trying to come to grips with emerging technologies that can make or break their business. These books help the reader know what's important, what isn't, and provide deep inside know-how for entering the brave new world of business technology, covering topics such as mobile marketing, microblogging, and iPhone and iPad app marketing.

- Straightforward strategies and tactics for companies who are either using or will be using a new technology/product or way of thinking/ doing business

- Written by well-known industry experts in their respective fields— and designed to be an open platform for the author to teach a topic in the way he or she believes the audience will learn best

- Covers new technologies that companies must embrace to remain competitive in the marketplace and shows them how to maximize those technologies for profit

- Written with the marketing and business user in mind—these books meld solid technical know-how with corporate-savvy advice for improving the bottom line

 Visit **quepublishing.com/biztech** to learn more about the **Que Biz-Tech series**

B2B DIGITAL MARKETING

Using the Web to Market Directly to Businesses

Technical/Business GUARANTEED
By John M. Cox

MICHAEL MILLER

Safari
Books Online

FREE
Online Edition

Your purchase of *B2B Digital Marketing* includes access to a free online edition for 45 days through the **Safari Books Online** subscription service. Nearly every Que book is available online through **Safari Books Online**, along with thousands of books and videos from publishers such as Addison-Wesley Professional, Cisco Press, Exam Cram, IBM Press, O'Reilly Media, Prentice Hall, Sams, and VMware Press.

Safari Books Online is a digital library providing searchable, on-demand access to thousands of technology, digital media, and professional development books and videos from leading publishers. With one monthly or yearly subscription price, you get unlimited access to learning tools and information on topics including mobile app and software development, tips and tricks on using your favorite gadgets, networking, project management, graphic design, and much more.

Activate your FREE Online Edition at
informit.com/safarifree

STEP 1:   Enter the coupon code: JXLFHFH.

STEP 2:   New Safari users, complete the brief registration form.
            Safari subscribers, just log in.

If you have difficulty registering on Safari or accessing the online edition,
please e-mail customer-service@safaribooksonline.com